# Spirituality According to Paul

## Imitating the Apostle of Christ

## RODNEY REEVES

**IVP** Academic

An imprint of InterVarsity Press
Downers Grove, Illinois

InterVarsity Press
P.O. Box 1400, Downers Grove, IL 60515-1426
World Wide Web: www.ivpress.com
E-mail: email@ivpress.com

InterVarsity Press® is the book-publishing division of InterVarsity Christian Fellowship/USA®, a movement of
students and faculty active on campus at hundreds of universities, colleges and schools of nursing in the United States
of America, and a member movement of the International Fellowship of Evangelical Students. For information
about local and regional activities, write Public Relations Dept., InterVarsity Christian Fellowship/USA, 6400
Schroeder Rd., P.O. Box 7895, Madison, WI 53707-7895, or visit the IVCF website at <www.intervarsity.org>.

Scripture quotations, unless otherwise noted, are from the New Revised Standard Version of the Bible, copyright
1989 by the Division of Christian Education of the National Council of the Churches of Christ in the USA. Used by
permission. All rights reserved.

While all stories in this book are true, some names and identifying information in this book have been changed to
protect the privacy of the individuals involved.

Design: Cindy Kiple

Images: St. Paul, one of a set of paintings of the Apostles, by Adam Elsheimer at Petworth House, Petworth, Sussex,
    Great Britain. National Trust Photo Library/Art Resource, NY.

ISBN 978-0-8308-3946-9

Printed in the United States of America ∞

 InterVarsity Press is committed to protecting the environment and to the responsible use of natural
resources. As a member of Green Press Initiative we use recycled paper whenever possible. To learn
more about the Green Press Initiative, visit <www.greenpressinitiative.org>.

**Library of Congress Cataloging-in-Publication Data**

Reeves, Rodney, 1957-
   Spirituality according to Paul: imitating the apostle of Christ/
Rodney Reeves.
      p.cm.
   Includes bibliographical references and index.
   ISBN 978-0-8308-3946-9 (pbk.: alk. paper)
   1. Christian life. 2. Spirituality. 3. Paul, the Apostle, Saint.
4. Bible. N.T. Epistles of Paul—Theology. 5. Bible. N.T. Epistles
of Paul—Criticism, interpretation, etc. 6. Jesus Christ—Example.
I. Title.
   BV4501.3.R436 2011
   248—dc23

2011023155

| P | 19 | 18 | 17 | 16 | 15 | 14 | 13 | 12 | 11 | 10 | 9 | 8 | 7 | 6 | 5 | 4 | 3 | 2 | 1 |
|---|----|----|----|----|----|----|----|----|----|----|---|---|---|---|---|---|---|---|---|
| Y | 27 | 26 | 25 | 24 | 23 | 22 | 21 | 20 | 19 | 18 | 17 | 16 | 15 | 14 | 13 | 12 | 11 | | | |

To my parents,
Clarence and Carole Reeves,
who taught me to cherish the Scriptures

# Contents

# Preface

"SO WHAT?" THAT'S THE QUESTION I seem to get more often than any other, whether in church meetings or college classes. Having finished a talk on Paul's eschatology for church folks or wrapped up a university lecture on the socioeconomic level of Paul's converts, the response is the same. Even though I spend the better part of an hour trying to explain the complexities of a particular subject in Pauline studies—stuff I really like to talk about—the deafening silence of my listeners' nonverbal response screams, "Who cares?" Despite attempts at making the talk more appealing with all of the bells and whistles of technology—Google Earth takes us to the very place Paul visited ("See? The apostle probably stood right here and saw the same amphi-theatre!")—I'm left with the unmistakable impression that I'm losing my audience. Yawns and catatonic stares nearly compel me to do a song and dance to make the subject come alive. And yet, as soon as a student asks the perennial question "What difference does it make today?" everyone seems to perk up and lean in.

At first, I'm offended by their fleeting interest. I remind them that scholars have spent years investigating these important issues in Pauline studies, digging out vital historical information to help us understand the apostle's letters. "Pauline scholars are the CSI investigators of the New Testament," I say enthusiastically with a knowing look. The wry smiles on their faces make it apparent that I'm trying too hard. When I finally get around to their question—"So what?"—my answer seems to provoke more interest, more questions. "Should we take the same approach as Paul?" "Would Paul's advice work today?" "Do you think Paul was right?"

I realize, of course, by the nature of their questions that they have been listening. It's because they understand very clearly that Paul's world is different from our world, that Paul faced different challenges than we do today, that Paul's assumptions do not translate directly into our context, they must ask "So what?" They want to take Paul's advice *seriously*. It's not enough for them to understand the historical meaning of Paul's letters. They want to know—they must know!—if Paul's gospel still matters today, especially since the apostle dealt with some of the same issues we face: gender battles, social contests, racial prejudice, marital struggles, sexual vices. Indeed, Paul didn't hide behind vague theological ideas when he wrote his letters to the churches of the first century. He deals with the messy details of daily life for Christ believers. Do we eat this or that? Should I have sex with her or not? Do we have to believe everything you do? Should I get married? Should we help the poor who refuse to work? Because Paul's instructions are so specific, based on his experiences and ideas about what the gospel should look like in his time, we can't help but wonder: is Paul's timely advice timeless?

Trying to answer the "So what?" question has brought Paul's gospel into better focus for us—not just his theological ideas, but his personal experience of the gospel of Jesus Christ, his spirituality. Typically, Paul's letters have been used as resources for his theology. We've grown accustomed to studying Paul for his theological insights, siphoning from his letters what he believed, distilling the contents for "hard doctrine." Yet, for Paul, the gospel was not merely what he taught, but how he lived. He wanted his converts not only to believe what he had "received"; he expected them to follow "his ways" in Christ (1 Cor 4:17). What I hope to do in this book is uncover Paul's ways, that is, the unfolding story of his spirituality, how he lived the gospel. Paul's letters provide invaluable insights into this story. Scholars have seen for quite some time the dynamic interplay between the problems Paul addressed in his letters and the appropriation of his gospel. My aim is to help readers identify with the problems of Paul's churches, see how Paul tackled these issues when he applied his gospel (his life) to real-life difficulties, and then trace Paul's influence on spiritual formation for today. In this way, Paul not only becomes our teacher (reading his letters as if they were written to our churches); he becomes our mentor, a life worth imitating.

I have many persons to thank for their help in this study of Paul's spirituality. First, I'm grateful to all my students over the years, especially those who weren't satisfied until we considered the implications of Paul's gospel for today. The open-endedness of the answers we explored helped me realize even more how the Word of God is timeless. I'm thankful to God for the love and support of my family: my wife, Sheri, and our children, Andrew, Emma and Grace. Every day they reveal to me what it means to imitate Christ. I also appreciate family members and friends who read part of the manuscript, giving good advice and much-needed encouragement: Sheri, Andrew, Emma and Denny Reeves, Darryl Schafer, Mallory Roth, Steven Purcell, Don Denton, Lauren Cawein. I very much appreciate the sage advice and reliable support of Dan Reid. His careful eye and gentle nudging inspired me to navigate unchartered territory in writing—both style and content. I'm told sailors have uncommon interest in getting the details right and great imagination when pursuing desired destinations. It was great encouragement knowing I had an experienced Pauline scholar looking over my shoulder throughout the trip. I also want to thank David Capes and Randy Richards for their friendship and their exemplary model of generous scholarship. I've learned so much from them; to me they imitate Paul better than anyone.

# Introduction

HOW ARE CHRIST BELIEVERS supposed to follow a man we've never met?

"Imitate me." If someone in our churches were to present themselves as the model Christian, making the claim that following them would be the same as following Jesus, most of us would dismiss them as ridiculous. Can you imagine? "Okay, everyone, listen to me. Do you want to know how to live the Christian life? Want to know what it takes to follow Jesus? Looking for a model of discipleship? Here I am. Imitate me." I can hear the catcalls now: "Ah, sit down and shut up. Who do you think you are? Do you honestly believe that we need to imitate you or anyone else?" But the truth of the matter is believers *will* imitate someone, whether they are good models for discipleship or not. Students quote professors. Churches take on the personality of their minister. Children pray like their parents. We are all looking for someone to show us how to live what we believe. So what are we to do? Where can we find an exemplary life to imitate?

When I read the Gospels, I often envy the twelve disciples. Following Jesus required no guesswork. If he went to Capernaum, then they followed him to the seaside town. If he sent them to surrounding villages to preach the gospel, then they did what they were told. To be a disciple of Jesus, to live the gospel of Jesus, was as simple as imitating him—doing what he did, saying what he said. Even when he left them after the ascension, they still knew what to do. Jesus promised his disciples that they would remember what he taught them because he would send his Spirit, the Holy Spirit, to empower them—not only to be his disciples but also to "make disciples of all nations" (Mt 28:19). The twelve disciples *knew* Jesus. So preaching his gospel was personal. They didn't write it down right away. Instead, they knew they needed to get the message out as soon as possible: Jesus is the Messiah and he's coming back soon. By the time they eventually got around to writing their Gospels, another man (Paul!) had taken their message to the ends of the earth. And what's so amazing is that this man had previously been their enemy; and even more astonishing is that Paul probably never met the historical Jesus.

How could this be? How could Paul preach the gospel according to Jesus when he didn't follow him? We might assume he read about him; Paul got his gospel from Matthew, Mark, Luke and John. But that wasn't the case, either; the Gospels were not written until shortly after Paul died. Indeed, we have an advantage over Paul. Want to know what the gospel is? Want to live like Jesus? Simply read the stories; follow the example of Jesus and become like one of the twelve disciples. But Paul didn't have that option; he couldn't read Gospels that hadn't been written yet. So what is even more puzzling to me is: How did *Paul* follow Jesus, a man he neither met nor read about? But Paul didn't act like that was a problem for him or his converts. He claimed he got his gospel from God; Christ had revealed it to him (Gal 1:12). And Paul expected his converts to imitate him because he claimed he imitated Christ (1 Cor 11:1; 1 Thess 1:6). Even to the average person that sounds a little presumptuous. Wouldn't it seem natural for Paul's converts to question him about the fact that he preached the gospel of a man he didn't follow while that man was alive? And, even more obvious, wouldn't Paul's opponents have every right to question his apostleship since he wasn't a member of the Twelve? (Didn't they draw straws to replace Judas?) Couldn't they say, "Sorry, Paul. You got here too late. We've already found Judas's replacement"? Yet Paul had no doubts about his apostleship; he insisted he was one of their number—a man audacious enough to get in Peter's face and argue with him about what Jesus meant by the gospel (Gal 2:11-14). In that debate, whom would you side with: the man who walked on water with Jesus or the one-time Pharisee who persecuted the church of God?

Paul expected his converts to side with him because he was the apostle to the Gentiles. He defined what the gospel was supposed to look like. That's because, to him, the gospel of Jesus Christ was more than a message to preach; it was a way of life. Paul wanted all his converts to learn "his ways" in Christ Jesus, to follow him, to imitate him because he was the gospel message for every Gentile Christ believer (1 Cor 4:16-17). They had heard the gospel from him; they were supposed to see the gospel in him. He was their gospel source. To be sure, Paul had heard things about Jesus. Paul learned some of the stories about him, knew some of Jesus' teaching. For example, Paul recounts what happened to Jesus the last night of his life, how he was betrayed and established a memorial meal for his followers to observe (1 Cor 11:23-26). But Paul rarely quotes Jesus' teaching and barely refers to the earthly ministry of Christ other than his death, burial and resurrection. In fact, to Paul, that was the essence of the gospel of Jesus: that Christ died for our sins, that he was buried, and that he was raised on the third day and appeared to the apostles (1 Cor 15:3-8). And since the gospel was more than a set of beliefs—it was a way of life— Paul believed his life revealed the gospel of Jesus Christ: he was crucified with Christ, he was buried with Christ and he was raised with Christ. Participation in the death, burial and resurrection of Christ was the template of Paul's spirituality.

That's why Paul believed he was the gospel source for his converts. Paul saw every event in his life, every relationship he had, as opportunities to experience the death, burial and resurrection of Christ Jesus. Essentially Paul was saying to his converts: "Want to know what the gospel looks like? You're looking at it. My life displays the crucifixion of Christ. I am buried with Christ through baptism. I am raised with Christ to walk in this new life. Old things have passed away in my life; everything is becoming new because the Spirit of Jesus is in me. If you follow me, you'll follow Jesus—the man you've never met but see in me." So when Paul said, "Imitate me," he wasn't being presumptuous, or controlling, or pretentious, or arrogant. Rather, Paul was stating the

obvious: he was the only way his converts would know the gospel. They
didn't have the Gospels in written form. They never heard stories about
the historical Jesus. And, as Gentiles, they could barely make sense of
the Hebrew Scriptures. They needed someone to mentor them, to teach
them, to help them live the gospel they believed. Paul was the man. If
they would simply imitate Paul, then his converts would be imitating
Christ.

But imitating Paul wasn't easy; living like their apostle didn't mean
doing everything he did. For example, Paul went to synagogue; should
his converts try to join the synagogue? Paul was circumcised; should his
converts submit to circumcision? Paul kept Jewish law; should his converts keep the law? Paul traveled all over the Mediterranean world to
preach the gospel; should all of his converts leave home and become
itinerant preachers? Paul wasn't married; should his converts remain
single? If the gospel is a way of life—and Paul's ways were supposed to
be their ways—then it would have been natural for his Gentile converts
to assume that they must do *everything* Paul did in order to participate
in the death, burial and resurrection of Christ. Probably much to their
surprise, Paul didn't think that Gentile Christ believers should imitate
him in every way. For example, he got angry when he found out the
Galatians wanted to get circumcised. Other apostles had visited Paul's
churches, and some of them (we don't know their identities) didn't see
anything wrong with Gentile Christ believers wanting to get circumcised. In fact, it soon became apparent to several of Paul's churches that
the gospel ways of their apostle were different from other apostles.
Whom were they supposed to imitate?

That's why Paul wrote letters. He had to sort out for his converts
when they were supposed to imitate him and when they weren't. Rep-
licating the gospel wasn't a matter of blindly following Paul, doing exactly what he did. Rather, Paul believed the gospel was a Spirit-filled
life that empowered Christ believers to sacrifice themselves (death), to
rely on each other (burial) and to live as heavenly people (resurrection).
In other words, imitating Paul didn't mean following him. It meant
imitating him by yielding to the same power—the Holy Spirit/the
Spirit of Christ—who would transform their lives into the same gospel

story.[1] This is why Paul continually emphasized that his converts were "in Christ" (Rom 8:2; 2 Cor 5:17), and that Christ is "in you" (Rom 8:10; Col 1:27). Their spirituality would be defined by their union with Christ—what scholars refer to as "participation with Christ" or "being in Christ." In other words, Paul wasn't simply holding up Christ as a moral example to follow: "If I try harder I can be like Jesus and live by his teachings."[2] Rather, Paul believed Christian spirituality depended upon a relationship with God through Christ. The exemplary life of Christ would only be empowered by the Spirit of Christ: "When I yield to the Holy Spirit I am imitating Paul." By submitting to the same Lord, their life together would look like the sacrifice of Christ (the crucified life). Filled by the same Spirit, their life together would look like the body of Christ (buried through baptism). Embodying the same faith, their life together would look like the end of the age (resurrection hope). Indeed, the story of the death, burial and resurrection of Christ would be their gospel paradigm for holy living. Paul saw this story played out in his life, in the lives of his friends and he expected to see it in the lives of his converts. This is why Paul says, "Imitate me." But, what about us? When Paul said, "Imitate me," was he speaking only to his converts, or should we take him at his word? Are we supposed to imitate Paul?

How can Christ believers follow a man we've never met? Maybe Paul can show us how. We tend to reduce Paul's gospel to "four spiritual laws" or a "Romans Road" for unbelievers. Or even when we read the Gospels according to Matthew, Mark, Luke and John we act like we're reading someone else's story, a narrative of events that happened long ago. Besides, Jesus was the Son of God. Who could ever live up to the impossible standard of trying to imitate a perfect man? Yet Paul knew he wasn't perfect; in fact, he was quite prepared to admit he was the worst sinner of all (1 Tim 1:15). Nevertheless, he believed he imitated Christ. That's because he was convinced that the gospel is the story of Christ—death, burial and resurrection—that *will be* the narrative of spirituality for all time. And he believed that he was the one to show us how to live that story because he walked in the power of Christ's Spirit. Maybe he was right. Perhaps Paul could be the one to teach us how to follow Jesus, to live what we believe, to show the world what the gospel is supposed to look like. When he wrote, "Imitate me," maybe he was talking to us too.

PART ONE

*Crucified with Christ*

# 1

## Foolish Death

### *Suffering the Loss of All Things*

❧

"**WHO LIVES THERE?**" That's the question our daughter asked when we drove by a cemetery several years ago. Emma was only six years old at the time. We had passed by that graveyard many times before. Had never talked about it. Never pointed it out. It's one of the older cemeteries in Jonesboro, Arkansas, the kind that have the large monuments, statues of angels and crosses. I really don't know why she assumed such a place had anything to do with people. But she did. "That's where dead people live," I said rather callously, enjoying the paradox. My wife, Sheri, was taken aback by my blunt response, giving me the "that-was-insensitive look" I have come to recognize so well. "What do you mean?" Emma asked with her usual matter-of-fact tone. "Well, when we die, in the meantime our souls go to be with Jesus in heaven, but our bodies stay here—so they have to put them somewhere until they are raised at the end of time." Sheri interrupted my indelicate, theological answer with a more careful explanation: "Most of the time the body is placed in a box called a 'casket.' Then, family and friends go to the cemetery to have the funeral, and the casket is placed underground." No response. Emma seemed satisfied with the little tutorial about death, caskets, dead bodies and cemeteries. Then, several minutes later, after the conversation had thankfully turned to another subject, Emma interrupted. "Then why does our church have a cross on it? Dead people don't live there too, do they?"

Indeed, a cross is supposed to show where you can find a dead man. When we hang them around our necks or mount them on top of our church buildings, we're actually declaring to the world: "Dead people live here."

The cross meant the same thing in Paul's day: death. But it wasn't a Christian symbol like it is today. Back then people didn't look at a cross and think of Jesus. Instead, Paul hoped that people would see the cross of Christ in his *life*—that converts and pagans should recognize the Crucified One in the living death of Paul the apostle. What should that look like? Think of what the cross meant to first-century subjects of the Roman Empire: shame, humiliation, weakness, loss, death. Paul believed his life would reflect all of these things because he was "always carrying in the body the death of Jesus" (2 Cor 4:10). Paul believed he was united with Christ in his death. But why? Why did Paul believe that his life must reflect the cross of Jesus? Why did he embrace weakness and shame and humiliation as the only way to live? Did it have to be this way for him? Does it have to be that way for us? Why choose to suffer the loss of all things—living a crucified life—when the gospel is supposed to help us, save us, make life better for us? Indeed, when I think about how good my life is, how God has blessed me with so many good things, I cannot help but wonder: Why did *Paul* suffer the loss of all things after he met Jesus on the Damascus road? And what about me?

Everyone agrees that everything changed for Paul when he met Christ on the road to Damascus. The book of Acts emphasizes the story; Paul confirms the same: the Christophany is where it all began. It must have been quite a shock. Up to that point, Paul was convinced that he was in the center of God's will, doing exactly what God wanted him to do—arresting fellow Jews who belonged to "the Way." As persecutor of the church, Paul considered himself "blameless" in the ways of righteousness (Phil 3:6). He was doing God's work, zealous for God's law. Imagine his surprise when he found out he was doing the exact *opposite* of what God wanted. Sight one moment, blind the next; Paul lost it all that day—the day he was knocked to the ground and blinded by a heavenly light. He knew what this experience meant. He had been wrong—wrong about Jesus, wrong about the law, wrong about the Christians, wrong about the cross. And he knew what this experience would mean. Nothing would stay the same: in an instant, old things passed away and everything became new. It was an unbelievable reversal—the rumor spread quickly: "The one who formerly was persecuting us is now proclaiming the faith he once tried to destroy" (Gal 1:23). Embracing the cross of Jesus meant turning his back on his previous life. But did it have to be that way? Why did Paul automatically assume that he had to give up his "earlier life in Judaism"—that he couldn't be a Pharisee and preach the gospel of Jesus Christ at the same time (Gal 1:13-16)?

Some think Paul was tired of trying to please God by obeying all the rules, that trusting in Christ came as a welcome relief to this frustrated, obedient Jew. But that doesn't square with the way Paul characterized his life in Judaism before he met Christ. For him, the law was the means to life—a gift from God. Paul was zealous for the law; it was holy and good (see Rom 7:10-12). And he was keeping it better than anyone (Gal 1:14). He *liked* the way things were before Damascus. So why did he give it all up?

Some scholars point to what Paul *heard* on that fateful day in order to account for the dramatic change.[1] When Christ commissioned him to preach the gospel to Gentiles, Paul immediately recognized his days as a Pharisee were over. The Pharisees directed their attention to other Jews; their goal was to get their kinsmen to join them in their quest for holiness. In other words, "Pharisaism" was a Jewish campaign, an intramural effort within the walls of Judaism. When Paul heard that he was supposed to preach the gospel to Gentiles, he knew his campaign would be toward those "outside the law." He interpreted the charge to go to the Gentiles and preach the gospel as a prophetic call. Like Jeremiah, he was called to be the apostle to the Gentiles before he was born (Jer 1:5; Gal 1:15). Like Isaiah's servant, Paul was commissioned to take the good news to the nations in order to bring Israel back to God (Is 49:5-6; Rom 11:12-14). The prophets of old predicted the world would come to an end when Gentiles turned to God. This was why God called Paul to preach the gospel.[2] Some scholars even think that, because of the Christophany, Paul believed that Christ had empowered him to bring about the end of the world by taking the gospel to the ends of the world (Is 52:15; Rom 15:18-21).[3] As the commissioned apostle to the Gentiles, Paul saw himself as the servant of the Lord, the slave of Christ (Is 53:1; Rom 10:16).

Other scholars say it's not what Paul heard on the Damascus road but what he *saw* that brought about such a radical change in his life.[4] When Paul saw the resurrected Christ it was the end of the world. Seeing the Messiah in all his glory meant that the kingdom of God had already begun. That's what Paul had been told all of his life: if you see a glorified Messiah, it's all over. It's a constant idea throughout the Old Testament. When a person saw God (or even an angel), they thought they were dead—the end of their world!—because no one looks upon the face of the Lord and lives to tell about it. Likewise, many Jews believed that when Messiah appeared in all his glory it would signal the end of this age, this time, this world. That's what happened to Paul the day Christ appeared to him. His world was over. His life had come to an end. Traditions (preserving the old) became irrelevant because the new had come. Old ways died. The new age had begun. Nothing would be the same again.

Indeed, Paul used end-of-the-world language when he described the Christophany. He claimed the gospel of Jesus was "apocalypsed" (meaning "revealed") in him (Gal 1:16). And what happened to him on the road to Damascus was in fact an apocalyptic, end-of-the-world event.[5] The Christophany didn't just happen to him, but exploded within him. From that day forward, Paul's life would no longer be defined by the law, by ethnicity, by nationality, by traditions—everything that had given him an identity was gone. From the time he hobbled into Damascus as a blind man until the day he was executed, his life would look like the Crucified One. Paul lost it all that day: status, family, ethnic pride. Everything that defined who he was—how he saw himself and the world—was gone. Before, he saw all things through the lens of the law—a binary world of men/women, Jew/Gentile, blessed/cursed, holy/unclean. But now, after Damascus, he sees neither Jew nor Gentile, male nor female, slave nor free. Can you imagine how difficult it must have been? Keeping the law didn't define who he was anymore, so now he could hang out with Gentiles and eat pork chops. (In Paul's day of honor and shame, "kosher" table company was important as "kosher" food.) Before, only Jewish men could read from the Torah, but now women could handle the Scriptures. The orderly world, the comfortable world, the world as he knew it—that life was no more. When Paul gained Christ, he lost everything.

I'm still trying to figure out what I lost when I gained Christ. I know I lost the weight of my unforgiven sin. I know I lost the doubt of what would happen to me when I died. (Whew! No more sleepless nights worrying about hell!) But did I lose what Paul lost? Those of us who are Americans, living the comfortable life, pursuing the American dream—what did we lose when we gained Christ? "Wait a minute," someone might say. "Who said we had to lose? Can't we simply 'add' Christ to what we already have? Can't we gain Christ without losing anything?" That's the way many of us would see our "conversion" experience. We simply added faith in Christ to our collection of beliefs. The only thing that changed—that is, converted—was the way we saw sin. What used to be fun is now a destructive habit. That which consumed our lives—addiction?—is now a passing thought: "Do I really want to do *that* again?" No, on this side of the cross we are grateful to have given up what was destroying us. Good riddance.

But Paul's not talking about that—giving up sin. He's talking about something else. Accepting Christ meant rejecting something else. Having faith in Christ led to denying other things; it is the way of the cross! If we're going to imitate Paul, perhaps he will help us figure out what we lost when we gained Christ.

## Bragging Rights

After Damascus, Paul found there were certain things he couldn't "boast" about anymore. In Paul's day boasting was a necessary social function—"this is who I am." Bragging revealed importance—"this is why I matter." Paul used to boast about his pedigree, his religion, his passion for "the cause," how he was always right. After Damascus the only thing he could boast about was the cross of Christ—a constant reminder of his own weaknesses, his own inadequacies, how *wrong* he could be. He used to persecute the church of God (1 Cor 15:9; Gal 1:13). He used to pray for the wrong thing (2 Cor 12:8). He used to count on his own righteousness (Phil 3:9). He used to think Christ was a cursed man (Gal 3:13; 2 Cor 5:16). He didn't deserve to be called an apostle (1 Cor 15:9). Essentially he claimed that he was the worst sinner who ever lived (1 Tim 1:15). That's quite an admission from someone who used to think of himself as "blameless." Indeed, as long as Paul preached "Christ and him crucified," as long as he boasted in the cross of Christ, longing to know the fellowship of his sufferings, "becoming like him in his death" (Phil 3:10), Paul lost the right to claim he was right by his own standards.

"How come nobody is singing 'God Bless America' like we did after 9/11?" That's the question my eighteen-year-old son asked me after the hurricane Katrina destroyed New Orleans. Of course Andrew wasn't expecting an answer. He was making a point. America's response to the disaster seemed to bring out the worst in all of us. Katrina never became a rallying cry for justice like 9/11. No war songs, no patriotic displays during baseball games, no clasping of hands and welding of hearts—no one to blame but ourselves. (What? Were we going to sing songs to rally support against a divine foe, defiantly overcoming the devastation caused by an "act of God"?) Experts tried to sort out the mess: why the poor were ignored, why racial hatred rose to the surface so quickly, why euthanasia became the default mode in hospitals, why our government failed so miserably to help its own people. We were all looking for someone to blame. The mayor blamed the governor, while the Democrats blamed the Republicans. This was political payback. Television preachers blamed the people of New Orleans, the residents of "sin city." God was collecting on New Orleans's debt of immorality. (By the way, one of the best arguments I heard defending God's honor after the hurricane came from an atheist. Essentially, he said it was foolish to blame God for the disaster. Instead, we should blame the hubris of American ingenuity to build a coastal city several feet below sea level. We were asking for it.) Some even suggested Katrina was divine retribution for the war in Iraq. It's no wonder none of us thought to sing "Amazing Grace" or "God Bless America." We were all convinced Katrina was God's curse, and New Orleans was our scapegoat.

I wish Christians could hear this once and for all: the cross should make us all reticent to declare who is cursed by God. It is astonishing to me how quickly we offer our judgments about the misery of others. Infallible opinions reveal the arrogance of our assertions. Whether we admit it or not most of us look callously upon the suffering of the masses because we think "they're getting what they deserve." God's judgment always seems to fall on others, never on us. We simply add up the equation of cause and effect, figuring that someone must have done something very wrong to get such a bad result. But this equation is where Christians are very inconsistent. We don't say that about Jesus. "He was innocent," we say. "He didn't deserve the cruelty of the cross," we insist. In what must sound like a twist of fate, we will speak of the death of Christ as God's *love* for us. Indeed, because of the cross, Christians hold to the preposterous idea that curses should be embraced as blessings, that the unjust death of Jesus is where we find justification, that blame is irrelevant to the purposes of God and that dark days are a sign of divine favor. Good Friday should stand as an eternal marker to all pious judges that none of us get what we deserve.

After his Damascus road experience, Paul offered no more confident assertions based on his own righteousness: "I'm right because I'm a Jewish man," or, "I'm right because I follow the law," or, "I'm right because I'm an expert." His zeal for the law was gone. Rather, because of the Crucified One, Paul would point to a curse and claim a blessing, he would expose weakness and call it strength, he would extol humility as a virtue, he would talk about failure as if it were success (2 Cor 11:23-33). That's why the cross was the only thing worth boasting about (Gal 6:14). The cross of Christ not only explained a broken world; but it also made a broken world right.

## Identity

The cross made Paul reconsider his Jewish identity. Everything that had defined who he was became "garbage."

Circumcised the eighth day, a member of the people of Israel, of the tribe of Benjamin, a Hebrew born of Hebrews; as to the law, a Pharisee; as to zeal, a persecutor of the church; as to righteousness under the law, blameless.

Yet whatever gains I had, these I have come to regard as loss because of . . . the surpassing value of knowing Christ . . . and I regard them as *rubbish*, in order that I may gain Christ. (Phil 3:5-8)

Actually, the word Paul uses here is more indelicate than "rubbish" or "garbage." After Damascus, Paul considered his old identity, his old ways, as "dung." And yet to Paul these losses were painful. The apostle was no stoic philosopher, ignoring his troubles with a stiff upper lip. Losing what he had gained in life was damaging. Nevertheless to him it was worth throwing it all away like trash. Why? Losing his identity in the old age was part and parcel of gaining Christ in the new. A Jewish kind of righteousness had been replaced by a righteousness that "comes from God," that is, a righteousness found in Christ. So Paul traded his reputable life in Judaism in order to be "found in him" (Phil 3:9)—not only in his resurrection glory but especially in the loss wrought by his cross. For him, sharing in the sufferings of Christ's cross revealed his true identity. Indeed, those opposed to this way of life were actually enemies of the cross (Phil 3:18). They missed the point of what it means to imitate Christ: loss by cross is gain.

Here's where we need to be very clear on what Paul is *not* saying. Paul didn't see "losing to gain" as an investment strategy. "I'll sacrifice this so I can get more of the same" (the mantra of the prosperity gospel). He did not give in order to get. He did not set aside Jewish privileges in order to win Christian privileges (he sacrificed those as well, 1 Cor 9:3-18). Nor did Paul reckon the benefits of the crucified life as divine payback for giving up what mattered most to him. His experience of Christ didn't work that way: "I'll give this up for Christ so that I can gain more of what I desire." No. As a matter of fact, for Paul just the opposite happened: from the Christophany to his death, Paul found that gaining Christ led to losing his life. The more he was conformed to the image of Christ, the more he recognized his loss as gain. Paul wasn't losing to gain more. He saw his loss *as gain*. And the only way he could see it that way was because of the cross of Christ. The cross turned losing into gain, shame into honor, death into life. The crucified life turned the world upside down, which made perfect sense to Paul. If death is the worst thing that can happen, but the *best* thing that can happen for a Christ believer, then no tragedy can overwhelm the good, no death can spoil life, no loss can erase what is gained—especially since loss is gain. The more Paul lost his life, the more he found it. Sacrifice does that. The more we sacrifice the more we realize what is important. Indeed, sacrifices reveal what matters most.

During our winter mini-term, I teach a course called "The Bible and American Culture." The class is designed to get students to see how the Bible functions as a protagonist and antagonist to American ideals revealed in cultural "texts," for example, films, plays and music. It takes a while for my students to see how Bible stories have informed movie scripts. What is even more difficult for them to see is their reflection in the Hollywood version of the biblical narrative, when the film functions like a mirror, revealing how American cultural texts have twisted gospel truth. The looks on their faces when they realized they've been duped by their culture—to prefer American convictions over biblical faith—is a pitiful site. Sometimes it's hard to think like an American and still follow Jesus.

One winter a student presented an analysis of his favorite film, *Braveheart*. He even came dressed for the part, looking just like William Wallace—painted face, wild hair, Scottish kilt, sword in hand. Wallace was his hero, a messianic figure bringing hope to the poor and oppressed of his homeland, just like Jesus. Illustrating his point, he played a clip from the film showing how Wallace sacrificed himself for the good of the people, inspiring followers to carry on with the mission of bringing freedom to the Scottish people. The student ended with a passionate plea, raising his sword for dramatic effect: "So, like William Wallace, we Christians must raise the sword of the Spirit and carry on the battle of bringing freedom in Christ to all." The air reeked of testosterone. The male students roared with delight; the ladies rolled their eyes.

Once the clamor died down, I asked the presenter, "What made you think Wallace's death was a sacrifice?" The answer seemed obvious to him; the sequence of events leading to Wallace's execution proved the point: he was betrayed by a close friend, beaten by the arresting officers, imprisoned by a wicked ruler; a woman offered Wallace a drink to ease the pain of his approaching death; strapped to a cross, the crowd mocked him as he was brought before his executioners; he was lifted up, suspended between heaven and earth with arms stretched out, screaming in great pain; his followers hid in the crowd, watching the spectacle in anonymity; a sword was thrust in his side; his last breath was a victorious cry. "Yes, his death portrayed in this film looks like a sacrifice," I said. "But we all know it wasn't. All who live by the sword, die by the sword, right? Wallace got what was coming to him. He was a murderer, and the law finally caught up with him. History does not give us the details of Wallace's execution. So why do you suppose Mel Gibson wanted Wallace's death to look like the death of Christ?"

At this point, some of the presenter's male compatriots rushed to his defense. Talk of "making the ultimate sacrifice," and "dying for freedom while fighting your enemies," and a "soldier's noble sacrifice" filled the room. Then I said bluntly, "Wallace didn't follow Jesus, did he? He didn't respond to injustice like Jesus did." Silence. "What if he did? How would the film be different if Wallace had followed the ways of Christ?" What happened next took everyone by surprise. A student said sarcastically, "Well, I suppose he would have visited all the villages, preaching peace and telling them to love their enemies. But we all know *that* doesn't work." An audible gasp could be heard from several students, followed by a pensive silence. The presenter's face fell, his eyes looking down, as if he were inspecting the floor. He sheathed his sword, looked up at the class and said, "Why didn't I see that before? I claim to be a disciple of Christ, and yet I would rather have a Messiah who kills his enemies than one who loves them." The irony of the moment hit us all like a ton of bricks: there stood a young man dressed like William Wallace talking about loving his enemies. After his presentation, several students thanked the presenter with a common confession, "You said what we were all were thinking, but we didn't have the guts to admit it. We all want a Messiah who kills his enemies."

Thinking like an American comes naturally to those of us who live in these United States. Thinking like a follower of Christ is far more challenging. In fact, American ideals often trump our Christian convictions, especially when it comes to living the crucified life. How are we supposed to love our enemies when we've been taught to kill them? How can I follow Christ, giving up my rights like he did, when I've been trained to protect my rights no matter what? Why does loyalty to America take precedent over loyalty to Christ, pledging allegiance to a flag over swearing allegiance to a cross? To what extent is our American citizenship more important than our Christian identity? How many Christians act as if patriotism is just as important as the gospel—or even worse, an expression of the gospel? In several ways the American way of life is at cross purposes with the crucified life; American politics cannot contain Christian faith. For example, politics makes enemies; Christians love enemies. Americans are taught to preserve national and personal interests at all costs. Paul taught his converts to prefer the interests of others. American consumerism is built on the idea that we should always want more. Paul was content with more or less. In light of these stark contrasts, one cannot help but wonder: if we were to live the crucified life like Paul—losing our identity in Christ—would our neighbors be compelled to accuse us of foolishness for forsaking the American way of life? Could we ever go as far as Paul did, referring to the advantages of American citizenship as "rubbish"? Would we sacrifice our American identity so that everyone would know for certain that we are a people of the cross? Could we risk it all to know Christ better, just like Paul? And, even more intriguing, even if we did, would we see our loss as *gain*?

## Reputation

This was the main problem Paul had with most of his converts: he had given up his identity, but they refused to give up theirs. He wanted them to be known as a people of the cross. But Paul's converts thought that was going too far. To them, Paul's magnificent obsession was myopic. They didn't center on the cross as the sole purpose for living like he did. To them Paul's vision was inconceivable. They didn't wear the spectacle of the cross as a lens to see a broken world made right. And yet it wasn't the message of the cross per se that offended Paul's converts. They knew the cross was the power of salvation for those who believe. It's just that they were repelled by the cross whenever they saw it mirrored in the life of Paul. That shocked Paul. "You foolish Galatians! Who has bewitched you? It was before your eyes that Jesus Christ was publicly exhibited as crucified!" (Gal 3:1). Paul's life was a picture of the crucifixion of Jesus—a public notice.[6] His identity was so wrapped up in the cross that everything he said and did was supposed to look like the cross of Christ in the eyes of his converts. Paul even bore on his body the stigmata of Jesus (Gal 6:17). In the beginning the Galatians welcomed Paul's unsightly "bodily condition" as if he were the crucified Christ himself (Gal 4:14)! But after Paul left, the Galatians decided the crucified life wasn't for them. Even though they started with the cross, they wanted to finish with the law (Gal 3:2-5)—a reputable standard that divided circumcised from the uncircumcised, Jew from Gentile, clean from unclean.

Paul could conceive of only one reason why his converts would do such a thing: to avoid persecution (Gal 6:12). They joined the circumcision because they were trying to make a "good showing in the flesh." They didn't want to be identified with the cross anymore. The cross was for lawbreakers. The cross invited persecution. The cross ruined good reputations. Who in their right mind would welcome such ridicule? Who would want to be identified with such failure? Who would point to a broken-down, beaten and bruised man and say with admiration, "I hope my life turns out like his"? The marks of a crucified life tattooed Paul's body—the evidence of an undesirable end. There was nothing about him that looked like success. I can imagine Paul's converts saying, "If that's what the cross does to a man, I'll try something else." Indeed, for those looking to make a "good showing in the flesh," only a gospel *without* a cross would be good news.

Today we face the same problem Paul tried to correct in Galatia. It's become rather fashionable to preach the gospel without the cross. I can see why. It's hard to draw a crowd when you're talking about sacrifice, the need for self-denial, that healing only comes with brokenness, that losing is the only measure of success. Americans can't tolerate such a message; it sounds like bad news to our ears. That's why most of us would rather hear about the benefits of the gospel, as if it were a product to satisfy consumers. Lonely? Poor? The gospel will supply what is lacking in your life. Depressed? Looking for more? The gospel will meet your every need. (I've discovered the gospel often has the *opposite* effect: it makes me needy.) Others see the gospel as therapeutic: it will fix whatever ails you. Preaching turns into group therapy to help congregants get over bad marriages, debilitating addictions and insurmountable financial problems. People become projects. Churches peddle programs. Members are left with the unmistakable impression that the ideal Christian life must be absent of trouble. Got problems? Get rid of them. And yet for Paul, trouble is the very place where the cross of Christ is most evident. But we don't want to hear that. Seems the marketing strategy of the church these days is: "You can have the life you've always wanted." But who would want a life that looks like a cross?

## Perspective

The gospel according to Paul brought trouble to Philippi. When these Roman colonists first heard the "good" message about a crucified man, they knew something smelled fishy. They had Paul arrested, charging him with preaching a message contrary to the Roman way of life (Acts 16:21)—you can't get more contrary to the Roman way of life than a Roman cross. But for Paul this contrary life, this paradox of the cross, was the only way to live: it marked the end of his life, which was death, and the beginning of his death, which was life. So whenever bad things happened to Paul, he embraced them as if he were experiencing the cross of Christ. This wasn't bad news; it was good news. The cross was never a burden. Paul didn't go around complaining about how preaching the gospel landed him in prison. Even when his converts tried to point out how bad things were, Paul was quick to correct their misgivings. This was no spin doctor trying to put on the brave face. Paul thoroughly believed he was living the good life even though he was in prison. "Rejoice!" he kept saying. "I'll say it again, Rejoice!" (see Phil 4:4). But all the Philippians could see was a man destined to die.

The letter to the Philippians has been called "the epistle of joy," and rightfully so because throughout the letter Paul sounds like a cheerleader as he tries to get his converts to join him in celebrating what God is doing in his life. The words "joy" and "rejoice" appear more times in this letter than any other written by Paul. Of course what makes Paul's diction even more intriguing is the reversal of expected roles played by Paul and his converts. Paul was in prison for preaching the gospel. His desperate situation should have driven him to melancholy madness, looking to his friends for comfort. The Philippians, known for their undying support of the apostle in previous situations, should have sent a letter of encouragement to Paul to get him through these tough times. What Paul wrote in his letter to the Philippians, however, reveals just the opposite. Paul was trying to encourage *them* that things were not as bad as they appeared.

Evidently the Philippians were convinced that Paul's imprisonment was a terrible tragedy. Paul's chains impeded the progress of the gospel. His imprisonment was an embarrassment to the cause of Christ. His death would be a huge loss; his execution would deal a significant blow to the church. Of course, nowhere in the letter does Paul quote the Philippians on these matters. But it seems that Paul goes to great lengths trying to convince his converts of the opposite: (1) Paul's imprisonment actually promotes the gospel (Phil 1:12-18); (2) his chains are not a source of shame but an opportunity to honor Christ by dying for him (Phil 1:19-20); (3) his death would mean "gain" for him not "loss," yet he believes that God will rescue him from prison and bring him back safely to the Philippians (Phil 1:21-26).

Such optimism must have sounded a bit naive to these Roman colonists. The Philippians knew how unforgiving Roman law could be. Had Paul forgotten? The first time he came to Philippi, he had been thrown in prison because he had preached a gospel that subverted the Roman way of life (Acts 16:21). At that time, God provided a miraculous means of escape for Paul—even though he didn't take it. This time things might not work out so well. They needed to do something for their apostle. So they sent money. What does a man in prison need money for? The answer seems obvious: to get him out of prison. Paul would need money for his legal defense, for daily provisions (Rome did not issue prison uniforms or offer daily rations—prisoners relied on outsiders to survive the ordeal), perhaps even for bribes (visitors had to get past the guard to offer any help). Paul thanks them for the gift but at the same time acts like he doesn't need it (Phil 4:10-13). Paul is content with his circumstances. He is finding strength by imitating Christ. But more than that, he wants the Philippians to have the same mindset (Phil 2:5), to "walk according to the same pattern" (Phil 3:17), to do the same thing: "Keep on doing the things that you have learned and received and heard and *seen* in me, and the God of peace will be with you" (Phil 4:9). What was the mindset, the pattern for living, the example the Philippians were to follow?

Paul's letter to the Philippians is one of the clearest explanations of the crucified life.[7] The only reason Paul can see the advantages of his imprisonment, the honor of his shameful chains, and the good in his death is due to the example of Christ Jesus (Phil 2:5-11). Jesus gave up equality with God and humbled himself by becoming a man, an obedient slave who died on a Roman cross. That Christ would stoop so low to redeem sinners is why God exalted him and gave him the most honorable name above all. This pattern of humiliation leading to exaltation is the essence of the gospel according to Paul. Messianic suffering must precede messianic glory. Death gives life. Loss becomes gain. Shame morphs into honor. The cross explains the resurrection.[8] This is the divine paradigm of the cruciform life. Paul sees it in the lives of Timothy and Epaphroditus (Phil 2:19-30). Timothy set his own preferences aside for the welfare of the Philippians. Epaphroditus risked his life trying to serve Paul and the Philippians. Paul sees the same gospel narrative being played out in his life too (Phil 3:1-14). I can imagine Paul saying to himself, "Jesus. Gospel. Procurator. Roman soldiers. Trial. Prison. I think I see a pattern here." He knew what was happening. He knew what was right around the corner. This cross would lead to resurrection glory, which is why he could say in all honesty, "I'm in prison. Rejoice, everyone!" He was following Christ.

When bad things happened to Paul, he interpreted them as opportunities to experience the cross of Christ. I must admit I have a hard

time looking at life the same way. I've been taught that good things
come to those who work hard, play by the rules, make the right choices
and avoid unwarranted risks—and I'm not the only one. Indeed, we're
all puzzled when bad things happen to good people. We automatically
look for ways to make sure the same doesn't happen to us. In fact, I
think most of us are obsessed with our own sense of well being. Americans manage risk, buy insurance, guard reputations, require warranties
to avoid loss. We go to great lengths to insulate ourselves from the
anxiety that accompanies disappointment. We build our lives on the
rock of our own sensibilities; we protect ourselves within the fortress of
our self-assurance. Ironically when bad times eventually crash through
our defense mechanisms, we cry out *to God* in bewilderment. "Why
me?" We are neither content with what we have (we always want more),
nor do we welcome loss as an opportunity to gain Christ. So here's the
question that haunts my soul: if I spend most of my time protecting my
interests and devote much of my energy trying to avoid loss, how will I
ever gain Christ? For those of us who prize comfort, will we ever experience the crucified life? We may see the cross in the lives of others—
especially those who have obviously given up everything to follow
him—but what about us? Can others see the cross of Christ in us?

What does the cross of Jesus look like today? There are obvious
places to look. Missionaries who sacrifice a comfortable life in America.
Single parents who ignore personal desires. Children who help their
parents take care of their brothers and sisters with special needs. A
devoted husband who spends every day in a nursing home, feeding his
demented wife her three square meals, holding her hand like a child,
hoping to find some glimmer of memory in her vacant eyes. Every day
they die a little. Every day they find more to live for. Their loss is gain.
By giving they receive. Their cross is a blessing. By dying they live. We
may see the cross of Christ in others. But we never see it in ourselves.
"What? Me? Sacrifice?"

Humility and crosses are very similar. Those who have it don't claim
it. When his converts pointed out how the cross brought great loss,
Paul could only see gain. I'm convinced the same thing happens today:
those who carry the cross of Christ don't see it in themselves. Try to

convince missionaries they're making a huge sacrifice, putting the welfare of their family at risk by living in a strange country, and the puzzled look on their faces will soon convince you that you're wasting your breath. You keep talking about what they've given up; they'll keep talking about what they've gained. You see a burden; they see a blessing. Their sacrifice looks like the cross of Christ. But all they can talk about is how fulfilling and rich their lives really are in Christ.

I've heard the same from other Christians going through trying times. Even though their cancer may not have resulted from sharing the gospel, I've seen these people embrace their weakness as strength. Dealing with their own "thorn in the flesh," I've even heard some Christians say, "I wouldn't wish this on anyone. But I'm grateful for my cancer. I know it sounds crazy, but I wouldn't trade the last few years for anything. This disease has taught me to rely on the Lord in ways I never would have imagined. I feel like I know him now more than ever." Even in sickness, believers find reasons to rejoice. That may sound foolish to the world, but I hear in their voice echoes of Paul's amazing testimony: "I want to know Christ and the power of his resurrection and the sharing of his sufferings by becoming like him in his death" (Phil 3:10).

Inside the church house wounded souls sing of God's healing, proclaiming the good news of Christ's cross, singing strained notes of blessed assurance, whispering prayers in defiance of a fallen world—a community of cross-shaped stories are bound together by their common pilgrimage. Driving by, a little girl asks her father, "Who lives there?" "Dead people live there, sweetheart," the father replies.

> I have been crucified with Christ; and it is no longer I who live, but it is Christ who lives in me. And the life I now live in the flesh I live by faith in the Son of God, who loved me and gave himself for me.
> St. Paul, from Antioch sometime after his first mission to Anatolia, to the Galatians (Gal 2:19-20)

# 2

# Living Sacrifice

*Crucifying the World*

✦

WITH THE SCENT OF CARNATIONS I think of death. Regardless of the occasion, whether marking the arrival of a baby or the beginning of marriage, the presence of that simple flower makes me think somebody died. It goes back to a time when I was very young, probably no more than four years old. My great-grandmother had died, and I remember sitting on the front pew of the church where our families were gathered for visitation the night before the funeral. As I recall, this was my first experience with death. I remember being a little confused. "Why all the fuss? Why is everyone hugging and crying and laughing? Who are these people?" And, most of all, "What's in that box?" As I think about it now, it must have been the first time I was overpowered by the fragrance of a room full of flowers. I'm sure my parents did their best to prepare the mind of a four-year-old for the strange world of funerals. But, as I sat on the front pew, taking it all in, I wasn't ready for what happened next. A woman came to me, asking me if I was all right. (I later found out this was one of my great aunts.) At this point—I don't know why she did it; maybe I asked, "What's in that box?"—my aunt ushered me to the open casket, picked me up and made me kiss my great-grandmother on the cheek. No one else saw us—my resistance and her insistence. I don't remember much after that. But the combination of a powerful aroma of flowers and a cold kiss indelibly etched on the mind of a little boy a memory of death that is unwillingly recalled by carnations.

Paul, too, equated the smell of flowers with death when he described himself as "the aroma of Christ" (2 Cor 2:14-16)—an analogy that has always fascinated me. It's one thing to say someone looks like a Christian or sounds like a Christian. It's quite something else to claim, "She smells like a Christian." Yet that's exactly what Paul was saying: "I'm a Christian because I smell like Christ." Really? And what does a Christian smell like?

According to Paul, a Christian smells like life and death all at the same time. To the saved and the perishing, Paul cast an odor of life and death (2 Cor 2:15-16). The imagery comes from the triumphal parade of Caesar as he entered Rome after a successful conquest. At the head of the parade, incense was burned and spectators threw flower petals for good luck. Subjects would thus smell the emperor before seeing him. Heading for the temple to Jupiter, Caesar and his soldiers marched through town with the vanquished in tow. The spectacle was meant for both subjects and citizens: a deathly reminder to the conquered and a lively celebration for the Romans. Playing on this imagery, Paul sees himself not only as one of the captives of Christ (that is, as a slave); he is also the "fragrance of Christ," the very odor of flowers and incense delivering the good news of Christ's triumph. To some, the gospel smell of Paul's life reminded them of death—specifically death on a cross. To others, the aroma cast the familiar scent of resurrection. Indeed, throughout 2 Corinthians Paul often sees himself as a moving picture of the death and resurrection of Christ. He believed he carried in his body the "dying of Jesus" so that the "life of Jesus" would be revealed to his converts (2 Cor 4:10). Paul found resurrection power in the cross of Christ. This mingling of life and death, scent and sight, was supposed to trigger in the minds of the Corinthians the essence of the gospel—cross and resurrection. The problem, however, was that the Corinthians were offended by what they saw in Paul. Indeed, Paul's life looked like death to them, and it didn't smell good.[1]

The smell of death casts an ugly scent. Is that why we surround the dead with flowers, hoping to overwhelm the odor? Cut flowers gathered for the deceased seems poetic. So much beauty, so much life cut short as death lingers in the room. In our part of the country, we even throw the flowers on top of the grave after the deceased has been buried. Once carefully arranged, now those lifeless beauties are tossed haphazardly on the mound of dirt, as if our attempts to preserve life were in vain. It seems we do everything we can to cover up death—hide it from our eyes; shield our senses at all costs. Paul, however, would have us embrace death as an act of living. To take in the smell of death—Christ's death and ours—is to declare that we are very much alive. Rather than hide from the inevitable, we choose death on his terms. Since all of us have to die, we might as well not die in vain. Most of us think we're put here on earth to learn how to live. In truth, Jesus taught us that the only way to live is to learn how to die, a little every day. Paul called it a "living sacrifice," a paradox that makes perfect sense to those who breathe deeply the aroma of Christ.

We were walking up to the place where we would soon bury his daughter when the grieving father stopped in his tracks. "Ron" stood a few yards away from the casket that held his daughter and her unborn son. "Alice" was a beautiful young woman, in her twenties, expecting her first child after only a few years of marriage. Tragically, she was suddenly taken from her husband, her family, her friends, due to a stroke that claimed her life. It all happened so fast. One day she's calling her mom and dad on the phone, excited about the plans she was making for the new arrival. The next day her parents are summoned to a hospital, arriving just in time to watch their daughter and grandchild die. Life changes like lightning flashes. So it didn't surprise me when Ron wasn't ready to say goodbye to his sweet, wonderful daughter on the day of her funeral. I walked up beside him, put my arm around his waist, and didn't say a word. His gaze never shifted away from the casket, surrounded by chairs and flowers, resting in the shadows, shielded from the sun by a tent. Then, as if he owed me an explanation for the delay, he said with deep sadness in his eyes, "I just need to take it all in. I want to stand here and take it all in—the moment, the pain, the sorrow, the heartache—all of it." After several minutes of standing in silence, soaking up the dreadful moment on that beautiful sunny day, we walked up to the tent, said prayers, read Scripture, wept and sang together. And I couldn't help but notice the smell of flowers.

Why do we dare to "take it all in" when our hearts are ready to explode with grief? Why do we sing when we mourn? Why do we adorn graves with flowers? Because we know death can only be recognized by the living, sorrow can only be shared by those who grieve, and there is no shame in dying. Death may look like failure to those who worship life. The grave may appear as a dark reminder for those who seek repose in the busyness of daily demands. But, for those of us who have died with Christ Jesus, if his death teaches us anything it's this: what looks like failure is really victory; what appears to be loss is actually gain; what seems to be shameful is the place where honor is found; and what sounds like mourning is true worship. Believers call it a "sacrifice of praise," for only those who are crucified with Christ can thank God for death, a fragrant aroma.

## Sounding Like a Fool

It's no wonder Paul saw the cross as the centerpiece of his preaching. For him it summed up all that was right and wrong with the world. The cross unmasked the weak and foolish things of the world: the quest for power and the pretense of wisdom (1 Cor 1:18–2:16). The cross revealed the ignorance of rulers and the vanity of intellectuals. Indeed, the way Paul saw it, the cross is a mystery to those who lust for powerful positions and boast of brilliant minds. For the power-hungry the cross of Jesus Christ is the epitome of weakness—a foolish way to save the world. To intellectual elitists, Christ crucified is sheer folly—nothing to brag about. But in the cross Paul saw the world crucified—both the presumption of making the world a better place via power and the pretense of solving the world's problems via wisdom. In short God doesn't do power and wisdom like the world. In fact the way God makes the world a better place looks completely pathetic and ineffective to the strong. And God's solution for what ails the world sounds like utter nonsense to the wise. What surprised Paul, however, is how many of his converts believed the same. It was evident in the way they treated Paul. Even though they had believed the gospel message, the Corinthians had come to despise the messenger. That's because Paul sounded like a fool to them. Why?

First of all, Paul decided against trying to sound like the educated elite when he preached the gospel in Corinth. According to the Corinthians the only way one could make a difference in the world was by Roman strength and Greek education. Several decades before Paul's time, Rome had destroyed the rebel Greek city of Corinth and then rebuilt it for the glory of Rome. Roman citizens (mostly retired military and recently freed slaves) were moved into the new colony to promote the Roman way of life. Sophists (literally "the wise guys" educated in Greek schools) came to the city to teach power-broker wannabes how to deliver powerful speeches. The art of public persuasion was crucial in politics. The sophists who taught rhetoric (how to structure an argument) and delivery (how to sound smart and look good) were making big money in this new town of movers and shakers.[2] But when Paul preached the gospel in Corinth, he determined not to use rhetoric even though the crowds were accustomed to fancy arguments. (We know Paul knew rhetoric because most of his letters include standard rhetorical forms and strategies—something his opponents recognized: "His letters are weighty and strong" [2 Cor 10:10].) In other words, even though he knew how to do it, Paul refused to use persuasive arguments conforming to conventional rhetoric when he preached the gospel. The world has nothing to offer a man on a cross. The ways of the world had been crucified; the new age of God's wisdom had been revealed. Therefore, Paul kept repeating the same message: Jesus Christ and him crucified. But that's not the only reason Paul sounded like a fool.

Paul was a poor speaker (1 Cor 2:1-5). He didn't make a very good impression either. Some of his detractors said, "His bodily presence is weak, and his speech contemptible" (2 Cor 10:10). That's not the image most of us have of the apostle Paul. To our way of thinking, he must have been a dynamic preacher, a powerful personality. But, quite obviously, that wasn't the case. He trembled when he spoke, voice quivering uncontrollably from fear. Paul was the incarnation of weakness. What amazes me, however, is how Paul responded to such criticism. I would have been tempted to defend myself: "Hey, I'm not so bad. I've heard worse. Besides, I was good enough to convince you of the gospel. If it weren't for me, you would have never heard of Jesus Christ!" But that's not what he did. Instead, he admitted his performance was pathetic. He believed his weakness was evidence of God's power. The fact that the Corinthians believed the gospel despite the poor delivery proved to Paul that their faith was due to the power of God and not the wisdom (sophistry!) of humanity.

Rather than make excuses for poor skills in public speaking, Paul embraced his pitiful preaching as evidence of his foolish message of the power of God found in weakness. The Corinthians preferred dramatic speakers who had mastered the art of public persuasion. Superb orators not only delivered well-crafted speeches, but they also had to think on their feet, offering clever comebacks to silence hecklers. If you couldn't hold your own in public debate, it was the sign of a weak mind. Imagine Paul trying to gain a hearing in a town where listening to public debates was a popular form of entertainment—C-Span for the ancients. (They must have been desperate for entertainment in those days.) With some of his converts looking on (Paul certainly continued to "preach the gospel" in the forum even after the house churches were formed), their apostle became the "spectacle to the world." He's stammering while the Corinthians roll their eyes in derision. He's trembling with fear as he speaks of the cross—a foolish death. When the crowd heckled him with insults, he "blessed" them (1 Cor 4:12). When he was slandered, Paul tried to make up with them (1 Cor 4:13). Where was the dignity, the honor, the self-respect? It must have been a pitiful sight. Before their very eyes, Paul had become "the scum of the world." And here's the really offensive part for the Corinthians: Paul wanted them to imitate him (1 Cor 4:16).

Paul refused to imitate the sophisticated Corinthians, taking the edge off this scandalous, offensive message. He *knew* he sounded like a fool delivering a foolish message. (Besides, who could have made a Roman cross sound good back then? It would have taken a dynamic speaker with all the powers of sophistry to talk these Roman colonists into believing that a crucified man was good news.) But that didn't bother Paul; he was convinced fancy words wouldn't make spiritual things sound good (1 Cor 2:12-14). Instead, he believed the wisdom of this foolish gospel had to be revealed by the Spirit of God. One wonders what the apostle would think of preaching today. We want our preachers to sound good and look good—handsome orators delivering entertaining messages. They must be brilliant, engaging, thrilling, relevant. Paul wouldn't have stood a chance in most of our churches. For him it would be like Corinth all over again. Can you imagine what he would say? "Where did you get the idea that the gospel is supposed to sound good to our ears? Who said we're supposed to make the gospel—a scandalous message—relevant?"

Indeed, I've often found the gospel to be *irrelevant*. That's because my definition of what is relevant, what is apropos, what is germane, what is applicable has more to do with my selfish expectations than the truth I need from God. Karl Barth was right: "The gospel is not a truth among other truths. Rather, it sets a question-mark against all truths."[3] The cross of Christ questions all my answers. I need the gospel—to shake me from my comfortable life, to rouse me from my desirable repose, to alarm me, to offend my sensibilities, my way of life, my selfish foolishness. Many times, when I hear the gospel according to Paul—the cross!—it doesn't sound good to my ears. I don't like it at all. It sounds impractical and unreasonable, even counterintuitive. "What? Give my life away? What? Boast about my weaknesses? What? Quit trying to get ahead? That doesn't sound right to me. I don't want to hear that." Neither did the Corinthians, but that didn't stop Paul: "Some of you, thinking that I am not coming to you, have become arrogant. But I will come to you soon, if the Lord wills, and I will find out not the talk of these arrogant people but their power. For the kingdom of God depends not on talk but on power. What would you prefer? Am I to come to you with a stick, or with love in a spirit of gentleness?" (1 Cor 4:18-21). As Paul later clarifies, "We are not *peddlers of God's word* like so many; but in Christ we speak as persons of sincerity, as persons sent from God and standing in his presence" (2 Cor 2:17).

When it came to the gospel, Paul knew he had nothing to sell. You either believe it or you don't; you see it or you're blind.

## Looking Like an Idiot

Paul was an idiot; he admitted as much. "I may be untrained *[idiōtēs]* in speech, but not in knowledge" (2 Cor 11:6). Of course for the Corinthians, if you sounded like an idiot, it meant you were an idiot. But the word didn't carry the same freight back then as it does today. In fact, we've lost the meaning of the word because we use it as a synonym for stupidity. To us, an idiot is someone who knows better but doesn't show it by their actions. "Look! Fred is running on the ice . . . oops! He fell and broke his arm. He's an idiot." In Paul's day an idiot was someone who rested on their own abilities, refusing to kowtow to the experts. The word *idiōtēs* literally meant "amateur" or "self-taught." Public speakers, though, were professionals. The pretense of public speaking revealed a confidence of expertise. To know what you're talking about you must *sound* like you know what you're talking about, *look* like you know what you're talking about, *act* like you know what you're talking about. Style exceeded content. Image was everything. Only a fool would try to command the attention of the public by talking like an idiot. Whenever that happened, a crowd would form to make sport of the stammering novice and enjoy the spectacle.

It's a good thing Paul wasn't looking for affirmation. He didn't get it, especially in Corinth. In fact Paul's opponents dismissed him as weak and ineffective. Meek and mild, self-taught and self-employed, Paul paled in comparison to the professionals (2 Cor 11:6-9). By his persistence in preaching the gospel—unskilled speaker that he was— Paul must have appeared as an obstinate and delusional man. Other preachers had fared far better in Corinth (especially Apollos), earning money for their craft. Paul, however, relied on menial labor to put food on the table. That offended the Corinthians, which explains why some traveling preachers used Paul as their "whipping boy"—a target of derision to make themselves look good as they tried to worm their way into the graces of their hosts: "That Paul. Sure is a lousy preacher, isn't he? No wonder he has to sow tents. Who would pay to listen to that fool?" (That's my paraphrase of the criticisms derived from 2 Cor 10:1–13:10.) The way they saw it, Paul couldn't get it through his thick skull that he was the poorest excuse for an apostle. Where was the gifting of God? (Paul didn't look good compared to other preachers.) Where was the blessing of God? (Paul was always needy.) To Corinthian eyes, Paul was a complete and utter failure.

Once again I'm surprised by Paul's response to these attacks. Rather than deny the charges, he affirmed them! "So, I sound like a fool, do I? Okay. I'll play the fool. Listen to the foolish tale of my foolish life. . . ." Thus scholars say that in 2 Corinthians 11:16-33 Paul delivers a "fool's speech," a satirical recounting of all the trouble he encountered preaching the gospel.[4] Of course, we miss the sarcasm in Paul's voice because his catalog of woes sounds to us like a hero's reticent boast. Beaten. Imprisoned. Stoned. Shipwrecked. Paul endured much at the hands of his opponents. They literally tried to beat the gospel out of him; but that wouldn't stop him. To us Paul is the picture of resilience—a dedicated man who preached the good news come hell or high water. But that's not the way the Corinthians saw it. In fact Paul knows his foolish boast is no claim to fame. Instead, when Paul lists all the bad things that have happened to him as an apostle, he's admitting his failures, his shameful past, his foolish ways, his stubborn streak, his idiocy. Many tried to get Paul to see the error of his ways: his own people, the Romans, even God. Beaten by Jewish leaders and condemned by Roman magistrates, Paul was a rebel who appeared to defy even God. Who controls the seas? God does. Who protects his servants from the enemy? God does. Who feeds the birds of the sky and clothes the grassy fields with flowers? God does. So here's the question any one could ask (one, I'm sure, his opponents relished): "Does it look to you like God is on Paul's side?"

If Paul was God's obedient servant, preaching the gospel of Jesus Christ, then shouldn't circumstances have worked out a little better? Shouldn't God make Paul's paths straight? Shouldn't God protect Paul from his enemies? Shouldn't God meet Paul's needs—especially the basics: food, drink, and clothing? Shouldn't Paul have a blessed life if he were an obedient servant of Christ? But that's not what happened. Paul admitted it. Time after time, city after city, it was the same story: beaten, shamed, run out of town. On to the next town: beaten, shamed, run out of town. He has been in "toil and hardship, through many a sleepless night, hungry and thirsty, often without food, cold and naked" (2 Cor 11:27). By land or by sea, Paul met opposition. Travel down a road: robbers. Get in a boat: storms. No one could get it through Paul's thick skull that he was headed the wrong way. The way Paul's opponents saw it, not even God could get through to the man. Think about it. What would it take to get Paul's attention? What would God need to do to convince Paul: WRONG WAY! Physical harm? That didn't stop him. Humiliating treatment? That didn't stop him. Shipwreck, abandoned at sea, poverty? No, nope, no way. Even the persistent problems in the churches started by this rogue missionary didn't clue him in to the fact that perhaps Paul was not the apostle he thought he was.

Allow me to sum up: Paul was a poor speaker. He worked with his hands to make a living. Bad things happened to him all the time. The churches he started were filled with problems. He was run out of nearly every town he visited. The Romans despised him. His own people abused him. Other missionaries mocked him. Given these circumstances, only a fool would say he was blessed by God. Can you hear it? "I know what you're thinking. Things look pretty grim. Embarrassing stuff. But, I *still* say God is on my side." Anyone with any sense at all couldn't help but ask, "Oh really? You're blessed by God? How do you figure?" This man sounds like he's in denial.

Paul knew he was a cracked pot (2 Cor 4:7). The fissures of his earthenware were obvious to all. Poor eyesight. Worn out hands. Scars all over his back. Paul looked like a mess of a man. Listen to how he put it: "Afflicted in every way . . . perplexed . . . persecuted . . . struck down . . . always being given up to death" (2 Cor 4:8-11); "through great endurance, in afflictions, hardships, calamities, beatings, imprisonments, riots, labors, sleepless nights, hunger" (2 Cor 6:4-5). Paul admitted that all of this looked very bad: dishonored by these shameful circumstances, he says, "we are treated as impostors . . . as dying . . . as *punished* . . . as sorrowful . . . as poor" (2 Cor 6:8-10). That one word leaps out at me, "regarded as *punished*." That's exactly what many of his own converts thought: all of the horrible things that happened to the apostle were God's punishment. God was disciplining this rebel whenever he was beaten, stoned and imprisoned. Even Paul was forced to confess that one problem in particular looked like punishment. He called it his "thorn in the flesh" (2 Cor 12:7). But Paul wouldn't blame God for the ordeal. The apostle attributed his chronic problem to a demon, what Paul called an "angel of Satan" (2 Cor 12:7). Indeed, this embarrassing problem, this thorn in his flesh, this devilish abuse must have been so bad that Paul begged God to take it away. The beatings he expected; the persecution he saw coming—all because he preached the gospel. But this? How could Paul live with this? What was it? Bad eyes? Malaria? Epilepsy? Many have speculated. We'll never identify Paul's thorn in the flesh, but one thing is certain: the problem was so bad even Paul could not pass it off as "slight momentary affliction" (2 Cor 4:17). It was horrible. It was offensive. It was persistent. It was demonic.

I think a clue may be found in the line, "as punished, and yet *not killed*" (2 Cor 6:9). There was only one time when Paul was punished to the point where everyone—even his companions—thought he was dead. Paul was nearly stoned to death at Lystra (Acts 14:19-22; 2 Cor 11:25). There's little doubt that Paul suffered head trauma from the stoning. The victims were often thrown to the ground, and massive stones were dropped on their heads and chest. Whether knocked out or comatose, one does not recover quickly from traumatic blows to the head. Paul was probably woozy on his feet, blurred vision, fuzzy-headed at the least—perhaps seriously wounded.[5] The aftereffects of head trauma linger, causing significant weaknesses and a debilitating condition. In fact it could explain why Paul describes his punishment as if it were an ongoing reality. (He uses a series of present participles in 2 Cor 6:9-10: dying, being punished, being sorrowful, being poor, having nothing.) Perhaps some symptoms of head trauma persisted. Maybe the demons in Paul's head never went away. It could very well be that Paul never fully recovered from nearly being stoned to death—his punishment seemed to linger.

Maybe it's because I live with a speech pathologist. For nearly thirty years I've heard my wife tell some amazing stories of patients who have recovered from head trauma. But this is what most people don't know. It doesn't happen overnight. The typical Hollywood scene of a comatose patient lying on a hospital bed suddenly opening his eyes and turning his head to look at his wife who's been patiently standing guard only to hear her husband say, "Hey there, sweetheart" is fiction. According to my wife, it *never* happens that way. Depending on the injury, many victims of head trauma have to learn how to speak again, walk again, eat again. Many suffer from personality changes, chronic mood swings, faulty memory, and monotone cadence. Some lack problem-solving skills; others have a hard time learning how to control their emotions. Eventually they get better. But it takes time. And sometimes those who have recovered from head trauma continue to deal with significant challenges: word-finding problems, seizures, facial ticks, verbosity, social impropriety, obsessive behavior. The untrained see these people as odd and eccentric; my wife will often say to me, "I wouldn't be surprised if he was once in a car wreck."

I can't help but wonder if Paul suffered from the lingering effects of head trauma. To the sophisticated, Paul was dismissed as odd and eccentric—a madman (Acts 17:18; 26:24). Paul was verbose. He wrote unusually long letters; sometimes Paul didn't know when to stop talking (Acts 20:7). He may have even been disfigured by the stoning (Gal 4:14; 2 Cor 10:10). Did Paul suffer from symptoms associated with head trauma? There's no way to tell. In fact, we'll never know for certain if Paul's verbosity or poor speech or disfigured appearance had anything to do with the stoning. At the same time, whatever the source of his shame—this "thorn in the flesh"—Paul was convinced that judging a person by "outward appearance" (2 Cor 10:7 KJV) was wrong. To be sure, Paul's life may have looked like failure (idiocy!) and he may have sounded like a fool, but as far as the apostle was concerned, all of this proved he was an undeniable expression of the wisdom and power of God: *strength is perfected in weakness* (2 Cor 12:9, my paraphrase). Where would Paul get such a crazy idea?

Some scholars believe that in 2 Corinthians 4:1-6 Paul is referring to his Damascus-road experience.[6] Paul couldn't preach the gospel without talking about himself—it sounded as if he were commending himself (2 Cor 4:2), that he was preaching himself (2 Cor 4:5) when he talked about his changed life after his face-to-face encounter with the "glory of Christ, who is the image of God." The problem was, his opponents couldn't see "the light of the gospel of the glory of Christ" in him because the "god of this world has blinded the minds of the unbelievers" (2 Cor 4:4). How did Satan blind them? Paul's thorn in the flesh must have looked like the curse of God. All of the bad things that happened to him—loss, shame, afflictions, punishments—convinced the Corinthians that Paul was a weak, broken, worn-out lantern. *This* is the glory of Christ? But, according to Paul, the weakness in his body, this clay jar, makes the glory of Christ more apparent:

> But we have this treasure in clay jars, so that it may be made clear that this extraordinary power belongs to God and does not come from us. We are afflicted in every way, but not crushed; perplexed, but not driven to despair; persecuted, but not forsaken; struck down, but not destroyed; always carrying in the body the death of Jesus, so that the life of Jesus may also be made visible in our bodies. (2 Cor 4:7-10)

Rather than hide his flaws or deny his weaknesses, Paul reveled in the power of Christ that was revealed through him when he was afflicted, perplexed, persecuted and struck down (ways of describing even his "thorn in the flesh"). Of course to the Corinthians it was sheer folly to boast about such things. Paul didn't care. He saw the essence of the gospel in his wounds, the wisdom of God in such foolishness, the power of God in human weakness. Where would he get an idiotic idea like that? Only one place: "Jesus Christ, and him crucified" (1 Cor 2:2). In what sounds like a confirmation of the cross, Paul heard God say, "My grace is sufficient for you" (2 Cor 12:9). That's why boasting in his weakness is the same as boasting in the cross. He freely admits there were times when he was "afflicted . . . perplexed . . . struck down" (2 Cor 4:8-9), even "depressed" (2 Cor 7:6 NASB). For Paul was convinced that weak believers reveal the strength of Christ's cross better than anyone.[7]

The problem today is we don't think Paul was right about that. In fact, in most of our churches we believe just the opposite: only the best and brightest are put on stage to teach the rest of us how to overcome our weaknesses. The strong, the powerful, the successful, the articulate, the chosen are the credible witnesses of what is true, what is believable, what is persuasive, what is commendable. Need to know how to have a successful marriage? Here's a couple who's been married for fifty years. Want your church to grow? Come hear this dynamic pastor whose church is now meeting in a basketball arena. Having a hard time overcoming your addiction? Buy the book from the Christian counselor who's written the latest bestseller. The message is undeniable: only the healthy, wealthy and wise have anything to say. The sick, poor and foolish should keep their mouths shut.

Recently a church was planning their annual marriage retreat and wondering which members should give their "testimony." A couple's name came up and someone said, "Wait. Should they be one of our speakers? They've both been divorced, you know. I don't think we need to hear from someone who's been divorced." Of course their names were passed over due to the veto power of the righteous. If the apostle Paul were there, I'm convinced he would have said: "On the contrary, divorced people are the very ones you need to listen to." In fact I think they could give us great advice about marriage, but that's not why I think we need to hear from them. I want to know how God's grace sustained them through their painful ordeal. How he helped them, surprised them, overwhelmed them by his grace. But we're so focused on our own definitions of success, overemphasizing results, that we miss the grace of God. Instead, those who fail at marriage are marginalized in our churches, sequestered from the body of Christ in their own "divorce recovery groups." Rather than ignore them, we should embrace their brokenness as a way of celebrating the grace of God, learning how God's power is perfected through weakness. That's where God's presence is most clearly seen—when everyone else thinks we've failed.

I've been to churches where miracles are celebrated with great bravado. A man stands before the congregation and testifies of God's healing. The test results confirm the miracle: a suspicious mass clearly seen on the MRI is now gone. The congregation breaks out in jubilation. They prayed for this man for weeks. The doctors can't explain it. The faithful understand it. The man boasts of God's miraculous healing hand. All declare with one voice, "God is good." The musicians play faster; the people sing louder; the pastor preaches harder; the church is triumphant. Later, at the end of the worship service, an announcement is made about funeral arrangements for the woman who died of cancer.

A hush falls over the congregation. There is no boast, no celebration, no declaration of God's miraculous work. A prayer is offered for those who grieve. The piano plays a somber postlude. The congregation files out of the auditorium in silence. Passing by, one of the parishioners says, "I wish we didn't have to end on such a downer."

Just once I'd like to hear someone boast of the miracle of God's grace for the one who died. Her courage as she celebrated life in the middle of dying. Her strength as she continued to serve food at the shelter for the homeless. Her grace as she puzzled over why God didn't answer our prayers for her healing. Her grief over the "bad" days outnumbering the good days. Her pain, her sorrow, her illness, her questions, her fears, her faith, her death. I wish we could learn to celebrate all of it—every bit of life—because the grace of God runs through it all. Don't we speak of Christ's death on the cross as the place of grace? Then why don't we boast about the believer's death as a graceful place? Paul did, for he knew better than anyone that we crucify the world when we claim the power of Jesus' cross. Indeed, the power and wisdom of God's grace is evident when a believer, dying from cancer, whispers on her deathbed in grateful defiance: "I wouldn't have made it this far without God."

When I think about Alice's death, it seemed like a horrible ending to a difficult life. When she was a toddler, she tipped an urn filled with hot coffee all over her chest and arms. Years of surgery and therapy brought constant pain and agony for this beautiful blond-haired, blue-eyed girl. When she was an adolescent, an airplane crash nearly took her life—insomnia accompanied "survivor guilt." Eventually things got better. It seemed like her life was just beginning—married, expecting her first-born. Then she died. I couldn't believe the news. Alice was a sweet, quiet, kind young woman. My first thought was, "Why would you do this, God? She's had it so hard. She's such a good person. Why all the trouble? Why all the heartache? And to end it all like this? This isn't right. It's not fair. She didn't bring any of this on herself. She wasn't a reckless person. She wasn't some hardened miscreant asking for trouble. All she did was try to quietly live her life. And this is the thanks she gets? It seems to me you owe her an apology—one *big* apology."

Sometimes, in my darkest moments, I pray some very heretical prayers. But when the family gathered around her casket the day we buried Alice, all I could think to pray was how much we needed God's grace. We confessed we were brokenhearted. We confessed we were wounded. We confessed we were perplexed. But in our weakness we tried to find the strength of God. Then, after the final amen, with the scent of carnations filling the air, I walked away from the tent only to hear the deep, heartfelt notes of a familiar song. Looking back I saw the whole family, father, mother, sister, husband, grandparents, all surrounding the casket, holding hands and singing defiantly, "When peace like a river attendeth my way, when sorrow like sea billows roll . . ." A sacrifice of praise. A sweet aroma of sorrow and joy, song and lament, life and death mingled together. On one hand, to those who are perishing, such praise sounds foolish; our faith reeks of weakness—the "opiate of the people," as Marx put it. We believers, on the other hand, call it the "fragrance of Christ"—the power and wisdom of God.

> May I never boast of anything except the cross of our Lord Jesus Christ, by which the world has been crucified to me, and I to the world. St. Paul, from Antioch, sometime after his first mission to Anatolia (Gal 6:14)

# 3

# Holy Temples

*Denying the Flesh*

✦

**WHY DID GOD** make food taste good?

The theological significance of that question didn't hit me until I was forty years old. Skinny all my life, I never thought I'd have to watch what I ate. Thin mint chocolate shakes. Boston cream pie. Root beer floats. Double fudge chocolate cake. No food was verboten. Then, after four decades of decadence, everything changed. It's like someone flipped a switch in my metabolic rate and ruined everything. I used to think Diet Cokes were for losers—a waste of money. (Why pay for nothing? No sugar, no protein, nothing to savor.) Now it's the only thing that comes close to satisfying my sweet tooth. But I know better: sugar substitute brings only a vague recollection of what used to taste good. "Tastes like sugar." Blah, who are they kidding? The truth of the matter is, I can't tell anymore. Sometimes I think the waitress has slipped me the "real thing." "Would you taste this?" My son or daughter takes a sip, recoils in disgust and says, "No, dad. It's not regular Coke. That's diet for sure." Then they give me that "poor-old-man" look of sympathy and whisper to each other, "His taste buds are shot." "I can still hear, you know?" Then I grumble to myself about how good taste (among other things) is wasted on youthful indulgences.

The tongue is one of the few organs built for more than one purpose. Eyes see; ears hear. But a tongue does more than taste. It is used for communication, both verbal (language) and nonverbal (what the Scriptures literally call "separating the lip," Ps 22:7). So why would God design the tongue to serve more than one purpose? It almost looks like an afterthought. "Let's see. Humans will need to be able to communicate. A tongue! That should do it. Now, we know they'll get hungry— their stomachs should growl loud enough to take care of that. But let's make it more interesting. Why don't we put some taste buds on their tongues? Then they'll get the message. Their hunger can never be satisfied by food alone. They'll want things to taste good too." Of course, I don't pretend to know the mind of God when it comes to divine purposes. But here's the part I *really* don't understand: it's the bad stuff that especially tastes good. If God were going to make us desire food for more than survival, then why did he make fat and sugar and starches and chocolate taste so good? Or turn the question the other way around. Since God wants what's best for us, shouldn't broccoli taste like ice cream and chicken taste like prime rib? "Okay. We've turned his tongue into a taste-mongering machine. Now, for the icing on the cake: let's make all the stuff that's bad for him taste *really* good—undeniably, irresistibly good."

Why would God make the world so good, so desirable, and then expect us to deny ourselves of these things that bring such basic pleasure? Why would God engineer sex to feel so good and then tell us, "Ah, ah, ah. Don't do it"? Why would he make us to feel so satisfied after we've stuffed ourselves with more food than we need? Why set us up as fleshly creatures, with all the urges and constant cravings, only to make us fall? On the one hand, denying fleshly appetites is hard. Constantly telling ourselves no feels like abdication. Self-denial wears a downcast countenance. Giving in, on the other hand, feels so good. Enjoying baser appetites comes naturally. Our bodies seem to be geared for greed. We always want more. Looking forward to dessert seems eschatological. Smacking our lips always breeds a smile.

Trying to solve the problem of our fleshly impulses has led many Christians to one extreme or the other. Some equate the flesh with evil. Fleshly desires seem good, but they're not good for us. Therefore, denying the flesh is the way we overcome evil. Others draw lessons from the creation account in Genesis: God created all things, and he declared them "good." Sex, food and drink are natural desires created by God for our pleasure. Evil promotes excess—a benchmark that varies with every person. Therefore one person's sin is another's pleasure. No one has the right to judge another. Interestingly enough, both camps call on Paul in defense of their positions. Yielding to the desires of the flesh is the antithesis to walking in the Spirit (Gal 5:16-17). And yet did not Paul say as long as we partake with thankfulness, all things are lawful and we should not be judged by any person (1 Cor 10:30-31)? The truth of the matter is, for Paul, the truth is somewhere in the middle.

## The Glory Maker

Paul was convinced that God put his glory in everything he made, which was a very Jewish way of looking at creation. A good God created everything and declared it was good—*everything* in heaven, on earth and under the earth. Evil does not exist by its own will. Evil cannot create anything. The only way evil can exist is to pervert what God has made. Paul's pagan neighbors, however, didn't see it that way. Some things exist because evil powers created them. Good gods and evil gods were locked in eternal battle over dominion of the whole world. Evil gods created sinister beings to wreak havoc and promote nefarious ways; good gods created benevolent powers to help influence flawed humans for divine purposes. Therefore, Greeks and Romans believed this cosmic battle between the forces of evil and good would never end. So what was one to do? What was the human fate? Some sought the virtuous life to overcome the destructive vices of the flesh; others gave in to the human condition: eat, drink and be merry, for tomorrow we die.

These dual responses put Paul in a difficult spot with his pagan converts. Who could be opposed to the virtuous life? Wisdom, honor, self-control and fortitude were desirable qualities, especially when overcoming human depravity. But Paul believed there was a higher power. Who could deny the simplest of human pleasures? Eating and drinking were as much a part of the good life as any other noble pursuit. But Paul believed in a higher purpose. In fact, whenever Paul tried to expose the impotence of virtue (humans can't help themselves!), he appeared to support the revelers. And every time he tried to rein in the libertines (all things are not profitable!), the moralists were vindicated. The problem, of course, was that Paul didn't share the dualistic "worldview" of his converts. He believed that God made everything good *and* that baser appetites can fulfill evil purposes. Of course he got both ideas from the foundational story of Israel's faith—the creation of the world and the fall of humanity (Gen 1:1–3:24).

Creation reflects God's glory. The art reveals the artist. Since humans are made in his image, we are able to reflect his glory in what we see and hear. In other words, the way Paul and his Jewish kin saw it, human capacity to see the glory of creation is a divine ability—we are able to see God in what he has made because we are made in his image. God creates because he is creator. Creation is beautiful because God is beauty. Therefore, whatever he creates is embedded with his glory. Why did he do it? Because he is good, he couldn't help but create what is good. Because he is glorious, he couldn't help but create what is glorious. Even God reflected on the glory of creation with the affirmation, "This is good." After six days, God marked the seventh day for reflection—a time when all creation would reflect the glory of God by glorifying God. That is to say, God put his glory in everything so that we would seek to know the Glory maker, worship the Creator of all things, glorify the God in whose image we are made.

This is why we are inspired by magnificent sunsets. This is why we are enchanted by the animal kingdom. This is why an overwhelming joy comes to parents when they hold their newborn baby in their arms. This is why weddings are happy occasions. This is why the simple act of sharing table with friends makes time stand still. This is why food tastes good. God put his glory in everything he created, invented, planned and shared. He thought that we, after taking in such glorious sights and sounds—waterfalls crashing, mountains imposing, birds migrating, puppy dogs playing, children laughing, lovers cuddling, friendships lasting—would want to know the one who made life so glorious. We are supposed to "taste and see that the LORD is good" (Ps 34:8). He did this. He made this. He shared this. This breathtaking, inspiration-making, mouth-gaping-open celebration of life we've been freely given by a very generous God—because of this grace—it was all supposed to compel us to give him glory, recognizing God as the source of every good gift. He knew we would need to give him glory because he is a glorious God.

This may sound crass, but that's why God made sex feel so good. God created sexual desire so that we couldn't help but fulfill the command "Be fruitful and multiply." Indeed, God created us to reflect him when we create so that we would find our purpose in glorifying God. But sex wasn't intended simply to make us feel good or to keep the human race going—it is supposed to point us to God. Even though we know "where babies come from," we are supposed to figure out that *God* is the one who gives life. I didn't become a father because of sex. God, our heavenly father, made me a father. I knew that better than anyone the day Andrew, Emma and Grace were born. Giddy with the pure joy of God-given life, I did some strange things, like mistakenly ordering a Whopper late at night at McDonalds. My stupid grin convinced the attendant I was playing a joke. All I said was, "I'm sorry. My daughter was born a few hours ago." I giggled as he gave me the burger, and I drove off. I kept laughing even as I scarfed down the burger at midnight.

Indeed, God made food taste good so that we would use the same tongues to give glory to a God who shared his power with us—to get dominion over the whole earth, planting gardens, drinking wine, sharing the bounty of what God has made. In celebrating life we give glory to God.

But here's where we've missed the whole point according to Paul. Even though we are made in God's image—we are powerful creatures—we tend to believe all of this comes from us. We create children. We make delicious food. We dominate the world. We seek our own glory. We think we're god. The Bible calls this idolatry, and we're eaten up with it.

Idolatry is our attempt to capture the glory of God for ourselves. Rather than desire the God who put his glory in creation, we settle for the glory by itself. We hunger for it. We thirst for it. We cast our affection on it. All of us want the glory, and we will do just about anything to trap it, preserve it and keep it for ourselves. The glory that was supposed to point us to God can so easily turn into an idol—an end unto itself.[1] It becomes our object of devotion, our quest for living, our purpose for being. It becomes our god. Indeed, the glory of creation acts like God, as transcendent and immanent as God himself. Sometimes we think we see it, we feel it, we find it—it is near, so close it feels undeniably divine. And yet, as soon as we try to capture it—reducing it to an object to hold, to embrace, to admire, to love—the glory is lost, gone like a fleeting thought. God's glory defies human control. Paul knew this all too well. In fact he saw the pursuit of trying to contain the illusive glory of God as foolish. Speaking of humanity in general, Paul wrote: "Though they knew God, they did not honor him as God or give thanks to him, but they became futile in their thinking, and their senseless minds were darkened. Claiming to be wise, they became fools; and they exchanged the glory of the immortal God for images resembling a mortal human being or birds or four-footed animals or reptiles" (Rom 1:21-23).

Idol-making is humanity's attempt to steal the glory of God. But we can't own it. We can't possess it. We can't control it. The glory of God's creation belongs to him. But that doesn't stop us from trying. In order to illustrate what I think Paul is talking about here, I'd like to use our rather innocuous attempt at preserving the glory of God—something we all do—when we take pictures. But then I'm going to explore the more sinister forms of idolatry that go on all around us.

How many times have you tried to capture a glorious moment on film? It could have been a magnificent mountain range or a special family occasion like a graduation. One is static, the other is fleeting. One is too big, too expansive to get on film; the other is too tender, too genuine to reduce to pictures. Capturing space and time seems illusionary. Even when we show our pictures to others, commentary always accompanies the presentation: "Well. This doesn't do it justice. The mountains were *huge*." Or, "We were having such a great time; you just had to be there." But, even though no photo album could contain all the glory, we'll still take pictures. We must have some record of the experience. We'll do everything we can to hold on to the glory of what we saw and how we felt.

It's always been a bit curious to me how Paul could transition so quickly from idolatry to sexual perversion in Romans 1:21-25. To his way of thinking, one naturally follows the other. The language of "exchange" runs throughout his argument. The foolish exchanged the glory of God for idols. The immoral exchanged the truth of God for *the* lie (most translations have "a lie," but the noun is articular—Paul was writing about "the lie," i.e., idolatry). Given to degrading passions, women and men exchanged natural desires for sexual deviance. All of this made God angry, which according to Paul, is evidenced by God's handing humanity over to the gods we worship. Humans were made to reflect God's glory. But when we try to keep it for ourselves, God takes it away. In other words, God gives us what we want—an idol of our own making incapable of containing the glory of God—but not what we are seeking. Indeed, what we are seeking (the glory of God) can only be found in glorifying God, something idolaters don't do because we want the glory for ourselves.

Now, two thousand years later, the transition from idolatry to sexual immorality makes perfect sense. Pornography, pictures of men and women trying to capture the glorious gift of sexuality, looks like a fitting illustration of Paul's argument in Romans 1. Whether or not Paul had in his head the pornographic murals in Roman bathhouses as he thought about the correlation of idolatry and sexual immorality is immaterial (even though a strong case could be made for the association since most bathhouses were filled with idols; but most scholars agree that Paul was relying on Jewish wisdom for his argument; cf. Wis 14:12, "For the idea of making idols was the beginning of fornication").[2] Indeed, worshiping the human body via sexually explicit pictures is idolatrous regardless of the time: ancient or contemporary. The intimate relations between a man and a woman are supposed to reveal the glory of God's image: be fruitful, multiply and fill the earth. The soulish union of a husband and wife in sexual intimacy is intended as a gift from God to reflect his glory. It is relational. It is incarnational. It is re-creational. Stripped of the glory of God, sex is reduced to a physical act absent of divine meaning and purpose. It is individualistic. It is mechanical. It is vacuous. Pornography is the foolish attempt to capture the glory of sex without God—an idolatry of human form and baser appetites.

The gifts of God are like prickly pears: if you don't handle them with care, you'll get hurt. That's the way it is with all things sacred. In fact the Scriptures are filled with warnings about taking the sacred for granted, purposing the divine for common utility. Abuse godly power and you do little more than set yourself up for abuse. The people of Paul's day knew this better than we do. They set up "taboos" to make sure divine gifts were employed with humility rather than arrogance. Sharing power with the Almighty was an ominous thing. With the greatest good comes the greatest risk. And of all the gifts God shared with humanity, "creator" was one of the riskiest. The power and the glory of sex are rife with both godly potential and devastating effect. God seemed to pour much glory into humans acting like creators. Psychologists know this; they try to help patients with the emotional baggage from bad relationships. Preachers know this; they sound the sirens of moral decay in our society as evidenced by domestic abuse in their congregations. Poets know this; they persist in writing about unrequited love between men and women—a seemingly vain pursuit that nearly always ends badly. Even people who don't believe in God know this. We all know this. Much seems to be at stake when man and woman copulate. From the time we are old enough to laugh at dirty ditties scribbled on bathroom walls, we've known that sex carries a powerful punch. It's no wonder the West is obsessed with sex; even our best minds can't sort out what it means. To me this makes Paul's warnings even more poignant. "For though they knew God, they did not honor him as God or give thanks to him, but they became futile in their thinking, and their senseless minds were darkened" (Rom 1:21). It's that one line that keeps turning over in my head as I think about how we abuse the gift of our made-in-the-image-of-God sexuality: "their senseless minds were darkened."

Without God, sex becomes a cipher—an empty and selfish pursuit. Degrading passions harden depraved minds. Rather than generate life that glorifies God, self-fulfillment inexorably leads to degenerate (as in, "the opposite of generating life") behavior. When sex is an idol, all we want to do is please ourselves. Indeed, the way Paul sees it, this unquenchable thirst for sexual fulfillment without God is a result of God's "handing them over to the desires of their darkened heart." The imagery is graphic. Paul talks about sexual vices as if these fleshly impulses were a prison, with God "handing them over"—a term often used in Paul's day to describe imprisonment—to the jailer. Imprisoned by their own cravings, they are chained to their baser appetites—a foolish, wasteful life. Finding sexual pleasure is their supreme quest. Sex becomes their raison d'être, their only purpose, the only thing they think about. Sex becomes their god.

Is there any doubt that sex is an American idol? Sexual attraction and sexual fulfillment are the twin themes of our culture, embedded in nearly everything we see and hear. It seems we bow in submission to Aphrodite every time we turn on the television or read an advertisement or listen to music. Shielding our eyes and plugging our ears doesn't seem to be a reasonable option. (The Amish might say different; withdrawing from society has some advantages—but even Amish communities have to deal with fleshly desires.) So what's a Christian to do? How do we deny ourselves in the land of plenty? It's no wonder a few years ago, during an open forum on our campus when we were discussing the impact of American culture on Christian spirituality, a student said bluntly: "Pornography is mainstream. Saying, 'I won't look at it' is naive. Today, it's not a matter of 'if.' It's a matter of 'how often.'" The silence in the room spoke volumes. None of the three-hundred-plus students in attendance felt obliged to offer a rebuttal. Consuming pornography was taken as a fait accompli. Sex is everywhere.

The Corinthians could have said the same thing: "It's not a matter of 'if' but 'how often.'" Roman bathhouses were filled with murals of hetero- and homoerotic scenes. One couldn't take a bath without taking in all the pornographic imagery. Sex trafficking was heavy in this Roman town too. Depending on a man's income or status, sex was readily available—and socially acceptable—via brothels, sex slaves, courtiers at public banquets, or priests and priestess serving in the temples of fertility gods and goddesses. Sex was everywhere. So what was a Corinthian Christ follower to do? Paul's response was simply, "Flee fornication!"

## Temples Are for Sacrifices

Paul's advice must have sounded a bit naive to the Corinthians. He had written to them previously in a letter (which we don't have) "not to associate with sexually immoral persons" (1 Cor 5:9)—a very Jewish way of dealing with such matters. His converts dismissed the directive as absurd: "So we're never supposed to leave our houses? Go to the bathhouse, you're bathing with sexually immoral Corinthians. Go to the public banquets, you're eating with sexually immoral Corinthians. Certainly Paul wasn't expecting his converts to withdraw from the world, was he?" No, obviously Paul didn't mean that (1 Cor 5:10). What's fascinating to me is how Paul refused to default to legalistic directives in this situation. He *didn't* say, "Don't go to the bathhouse!" or, "Don't go to the public banquets!" (Legalism would have made life much easier for them and for him—we'll save that discussion for the next chapter.) Instead, Paul employed what might be called a "poetic" strategy by conjuring up a metaphor that would relate to all of his converts. Rather than lay down the law, Paul tried to get these Corinthians to see that they were *temples* of the living God.

Food was sacrificed in all temples. Devotees offered meat, bread, grain and wine to show the gods/God how dependent they were on divine providence. Christians had no temples in which to sacrifice. How does a Christ follower show proper deference to the God who gives life? Such a question may not have been in the minds of the Corinthians, but one thing is certain. Released from their religious past of offering sacrifices in the idol's temple, Paul's converts had adopted the slogan: "Food is meant for the stomach and the stomach for food" (1 Cor 6:13). Interestingly Paul brings up the subject of food during his argument *against* sexual immorality (1 Cor 6:9-20). Of course, in Corinth, sex and food belonged together in temple worship like bread and wine in Christian Communion. So it shouldn't surprise us that Paul moves seamlessly from one subject to the other—food to sex—when trying to get his converts to see that their bodies are temples where sacrifices are supposed to be offered to God. Paul's argument goes something like this: "Yes, food is brought into your body like a temple. But your body is not meant merely for food. Your body belongs to God. Food alone cannot keep your body alive. God will raise it from the dead. Therefore, you owe your life to God. In the same way, your body is a temple of the Holy Spirit. In fact, every member of the body of Christ makes up the temple of God. So if you have sex with a prostitute you are not only defiling the temple of your own body but also the body of Christ. Your body is a temple that belongs to God. Your body is a temple for the glory of God. Therefore your body is the place where sacrifices are made so that the glory of God may be revealed. This is why I wrote, 'Flee fornication!'"

The key to overcoming sin, according to Paul, is sacrifice: both Christ's and ours. Christ's death worked like a temple sacrifice: atonement was made and the glory of God was revealed (cf. Rom 3:21-26; surprisingly, this part of the argument doesn't show up in 1 Corinthians). When we sacrifice ourselves, we reveal the glory of God's presence just like Christ because we are his temple. Indeed, Paul relied on Jewish imagery when he wrote about sin, the temple and the glory of God. Earlier in the letter, Paul had warned the Corinthians that since they were the temple of God, they would experience the presence of God as a purifying fire (1 Cor 3:10-17). The Corinthians had been acting very carnal, constantly yielding to the flesh (1 Cor 3:1-3). The evidence of their selfish life? They fought all the time. Some acted like they were more important than others. Incest was ignored. There were lawsuits among Christians. Men used prostitutes. There were food fights and worship wars. But Paul knew that God would "show up" one day, and his fiery presence would burn away all the stuff (wood, hay and stubble) the Corinthians dragged into the body of Christ (1 Cor 3:13). They would "suffer loss"—wasted effort and time spent on useless things—but their body/temple would be purified: "Do you not know that you are God's temple and that God's Spirit dwells in you?" (1 Cor 3:16). The way Paul saw it the presence of God (the Holy Spirit) is the fire that burns away selfish habits and fleshly desires—all temporal things—whether we like it or not. Since we are his holy temple, offering sacrifices to God, he wouldn't have it any other way: "If anyone destroys God's temple, God will destroy that person. For God's temple is holy, and you are that temple" (1 Cor 3:17). God can't tolerate what sin does to his temple. Indeed, when we read stories in the Old Testament where God "shows up" as a consuming fire, it's difficult to tell whether his presence is a good thing or a bad thing. It seems to depend upon who you are (cf. Mal 3:1-5).

I have heard things no one should hear; I've seen things no one should see. They are lodged in my brain, images I wish I could scrub away. That's what most members of churches don't know: pastors see the underbelly of the church, and it isn't pretty. It's a miracle ministers are able to mount the pulpit and speak of the church as the bride of Christ without breaking down in tears or lashing out in vindictive condemnation (which sadly enough happens all too often). When I was pastor of a good church in Jonesboro, Arkansas, members would come to me and share their stories—horrible instances of abuse suffered when they were children or dirty secrets of private sin that they couldn't seem to break free of. Every week, a new revelation. Every member, a different burden to carry. After a while, I wasn't shocked anymore. Because our worship services were on television, people who weren't members of our church thought of me as their pastor too. They came from all over the region: a deacon, a teacher, a minister—sin seemed to be no respecter of persons. (For example, a deacon wanted his paramour to move in with him and his wife, then acted incredulous that his wife objected to the idea. He brought her to me for counseling, thinking I would side with him and straighten out his wife! In another case, a young man couldn't understand why his wife was in an adulterous relationship with another man, but then admitted, "Well, maybe it has something to do with the fact that I wanted us to participate—despite her objection at first—in a ménage à trois." My jaw nearly hit the floor, and I wanted to say sarcastically, "Really? Do you think so?") Sin has a blinding effect; evil destroys everything it seeks to dwell in. And trying to help Christ believers deal with the devastating aftereffects of sin was overwhelming: marriages destroyed, addictions fostered, hearts crushed. Stubbornness reigned. The last thing many of them wanted to hear was the need for sacrifice. I found myself offering the same advice: "Perhaps you need to quit thinking about yourself and consider others for a change." Then I would talk about the sacrifice of Jesus, and how that should inspire us to sacrifice ourselves for others. Often their blank expressions told me such "preacher talk" wasn't helping at all. It was enough to drag my heart down to Sheol.

After a particularly hard week of endless confession, a member came up to me after Sunday services and said, "Pastor, it almost felt like God showed up today during worship," to which I replied, "I don't think we really want God to show up. Since our God is a consuming fire, it might not be a pretty picture." The shocked look on her face reminded me that she had no idea of what I had seen or heard that week; my response must have sounded very harsh. A few weeks later, that same woman came to me after Sunday services and said, "I don't know why God wants me to do this. But he told me to read this passage to you: 'My Spirit abides among you; do not fear. For thus says the LORD of hosts: Once again, in a little while, I will shake the heavens and the earth and the sea and the dry land; and I will shake all the nations, so that the treasure of all nations shall come, and I will fill this house with splendor, says the LORD of hosts. The silver is mine, and the gold is mine, says the Lord of hosts.'"

Then she read slowly, in somber tones, the rest of the passage (Hag 2:5-9): "The latter splendor of this house shall be greater than the former, says the LORD of hosts." After a long pause, she looked into my eyes and said, "I don't know what this means," then turned and walked away. That was March 22, 1998. The reason that date is fixed in my mind is two days later something happened that brought the nations—the whole world—to our little town. It felt like Haggai 2:5-9 was being fulfilled right before our eyes.

On March 24, 1998, two boys shot eleven classmates and two teachers, killing four twelve-year-old girls and one teacher. The tragedy made national and international headlines. The media swarmed into our town to get their own angle on the story. Many of us were interviewed—civic leaders, physicians, pastors, law-enforcement officers. But even as we were called on to answer all the questions—why did this happen? how did this happen?—we were trying to find answers for ourselves. What was especially troubling, as we tried to help the families of the victims, was the fact that this horrendous crime, this unspeakable atrocity, was perpetrated by two *young* boys; one was eleven and the other thirteen years old. I couldn't get that out of my mind: two sixth graders killed four sixth graders and a teacher. I used to think children were sacred space, that the devil could not use them for his evil purposes. "That's why children go to heaven when they die," my Baptist tradition told me, "because they are innocent; they haven't reached the age of accountability." But it's hard to believe *all* children are innocent when you're staring this undeniable reality in the face: two boys were held accountable for murder. We were all stunned—a town, a country, a world. It felt like our sacred space—all sacred space—was violated on March 24, 1998. Which is why, in the aftermath of the Westside tragedy, we *all* wanted to know: why did this happen?

The media blamed the residents of Jonesboro, using the typical caricature of Arkansas folk: a gun-toting town like ours would eventually pay for the reckless behavior of some parents who teach their children how to use guns. It seemed to us, however, that these East Coasters were trying to do more than report the story. They were out to prove we were different—that something like this would never happen in their neighborhood. (A reporter sheepishly admitted to me what he told his twelve-year-old daughter to comfort her. When she saw the story reported by her dad on television—seeing bullet holes in the walls of the school buildings—she couldn't sleep at night. So he called her on the telephone and said, "Don't worry sweetheart. It won't happen at your school because this town is not like our town.") Some experts attributed gun violence to video games and Hollywood films. Locals shunned the families of these two boys, accusing them of raising two bullies. Parents blamed the schools for tolerating bad behavior. School officials claimed this horrendous evil was the overflow of domestic violence. Counselors blamed absentee fathers. By the time everyone weighed in, there was only one, unmistakable inference to be drawn: it was *everyone's* fault. We did this. We caused this. We invited evil into our town, into our homes, into our souls. Indeed, as Aleksandr Solzhenitsyn concluded, "The line separating good and evil passes not through states, nor between classes, nor between political parties either—but right through every human heart—and through all human hearts."[3]

That's what it felt like; we all were violated. We all felt dirty. This was our problem. Evil desecrated the temple of our town; sin polluted the sanctuary of our souls. There was no getting around it. But I had to believe, like Haggai the prophet, that the glory of our temple would be restored. It happened bit by bit. As God's grace overwhelmed us—each one of us trying to find healing in his presence—the fire began to burn away what was unnecessary, what was temporal, what was selfish. Families of the victims organized to help others who suffered horrible violence. The community formed a committee to provide funds for the victims and their families. Parents spent more time with their children. Children made special efforts to include the marginalized during recess. Workers and employers banded together to remove hate speech from the workplace. Ministers decided to work together to help our community rather than be suspicious of each other. (Before the tragedy, there were two ministerial alliances.) Churches came together to help build a center for at-risk youth, volunteering many hours of service by spending time with teenagers who had nowhere to go after school. All of us were looking for cleansing. All of us needed to do something. We all wanted to overcome evil with good. Now more than ever we needed God's presence. All it took was sacrifice from every single one of us.

This is what Paul wanted the Corinthians to understand. Their fleshly desires were self-servingly regnant; they had invited sin to dwell among them. The deleterious effects were obvious: division, selfishness, immorality, sickness, even death (1 Cor 11:30). They needed two things to clean out their temple: God's purifying presence and the sacrifice of their fleshly desires. Sin feeds on selfishness; sacrifice brings God's glory. This is why Paul wanted the Corinthians to sacrifice food (1 Cor 8:10-13; 10:14-33) and sex (1 Cor 7:29-38), all the while putting each of themselves forward as the model worthy of imitation. If they sacrificed food and sex—good gifts that too easily serve selfish purposes and promote idolatry—it would be for their sakes as much as for the Lord's. God's gifts are meant to reveal his glory, and he is very jealous of his glory. To anchor the point, Paul uses the story of Israel in the desert, where idolatry, food and sex converged and invited God's judgment (1 Cor 10:6-14). "Flee idolatry!" functions, then, as a bookend to Paul's earlier injunction, "Flee fornication!"—tandem advice in overcoming fleshly selfishness. And in case they couldn't identify with Israel's story, Paul reminds them of the sacrifices he made while he was with them. He could have eaten whatever he wanted; he could have married and brought along a wife (1 Cor 9:4-5). Instead, Paul chose to sacrifice both—for the Corinthians and for the Lord (1 Cor 9:12-23). He purposed to give up food, drink and sex for the sake of his converts in order to imitate Christ (1 Cor 7:7; 8:13; 9:15, 18, 27; 10:23). This is why Paul sums up his teaching with, "Whether you eat or drink, or whatever you do, do everything for the *glory* of God" (1 Cor 10:31, emphasis mine). All things—especially the basic desires of sex and food—are gifts of God meant to reveal his glory. To use them for any other purpose is selfish idolatry. Sex and food were never meant solely for our pleasure. Since they give life, we are supposed to dedicate them to the one who gives life. And to use them for divine purposes takes sacrifice. "Do not seek your own advantage, but that of the other" (1 Cor 10:24). If they could do that, Paul was convinced the Corinthians would be able to overcome evil with good and see themselves as temples of the living God, where sacrifices are made and his glory is revealed—just like Paul and Christ.

On the one hand, using food and sex for selfish pleasure ironically leads to abuse: of others and of ourselves (addiction!). To enjoy food and sex as glorious gifts of God, on the other hand, leads to sacrifice: for others and for ourselves. Sharing table means sharing food; parents sacrifice for their children. Paul knew this all too well. This is why he encourages his converts to give up food for their brothers and sisters. This is why he sacrificed fleshly desires for his Corinthian children. Indeed, according to Paul, if we are to see God's glory in our fleshly creatureliness (we are *temples* of the Holy Spirit), we will be compelled to glorify God as "living sacrifices" (Rom 12:1).[4] In giving, we would give glory to God. In fact, whenever we sacrifice, we immediately acknowledge the origin and purpose of all things. When we sacrifice to

God, we remember that we are neither the beginning nor end of all things. What do we have except that which was given to us—all things come from God (1 Cor 4:7)? For whom shall we live except the one who sacrificed himself for us—all things end in Jesus Christ (1 Cor 6:20)? And yet it seems that we are caught somewhere in the middle: between the beginning and the end, the Spirit and the flesh, eating and sacrificing. So in the meantime Paul wanted his converts to remember that "as often as you eat this bread and drink the cup, you proclaim the Lord's death until he comes" (1 Cor 11:26). Indeed, at the table of our Lord, all of these things intersect: food, drink, sacrifice and temple. For Paul knew that, gathered for worship as temples of the living God, we would "taste and see that the Lord is good."

Indeed, God makes life taste good.

May the God of steadfastness and encouragement grant you to live in harmony with one another, in accordance with Christ Jesus, so that together you may with one voice [tongue!] glorify the God and Father of our Lord Jesus Christ.

St. Paul, from Corinth, before his final trip to Jerusalem (Rom 15:5-6)

# 4

# Free Slaves

## *Graceful Obedience*

✿

"**THERE IS A PATH** to freedom. Its milestones are: obedience, honesty, cleanliness, sobriety, hard work, discipline, sacrifice, truthfulness, love of your homeland." Words to live by. Some might even say, words to die by. The first time I read them, I was struck by the strength of these words, the soundness of these words, the rightness of these words. "Many people might find their life's purpose in this creed," I muttered to myself. "You could build a nation on these ideals then teach citizens to defend them at all costs." Then I thought of how many people died under the banner of these words.

In fact, that's exactly what happened to thousands of people—they died with these words hanging over their heads. That's because this saying was painted on the roof of the long, narrow maintenance building at the Nazi concentration camp at Dachau. Every sighted prisoner saw it as they entered the building—the beginning of horrors of what we call the Holocaust. The maintenance building housed the *Schubraum* (literally "shoving room"), where new prisoners were stripped of their clothes and dignity, where humans were treated like animals prepared for torture and slaughter. The victims were Jews, German priests, Jehovah's Witnesses and homosexuals. The Nazis rounded up these "misfits" and imprisoned them in their concentration camps all over Germany in order to clean up the neighborhood and reorient these prisoners to the "proper" way of life. What happened behind those

prison walls is well known. The atrocities suffered by Jews, priests, Jehovah's Witnesses and homosexuals at the hands of their tormentors
were hell on earth. What I couldn't understand, as I stood there one
summer day in front of the maintenance building at this notorious concentration camp, was how the men who did such horrible things could
believe they were living up to this creed. Why not be honest, tell the
truth? The sign should have read: "Obey or not: we will kill you anyway." Instead, these murderers acted like they were doing something
noble, something virtuous, something lawful—the sign proved it. How
could words that sound so right lead people to do such wrong?

It must have seemed like a cruel joke to the prisoners inside. The
ultimate bait and switch. The big lie. "Work hard and you will find
freedom." Instead, what these prisoners were forced to do was not work,
and the end for most of them was not freedom. Even the entrance to
the camp—a gate through which every prisoner passed—had iron bars
bent to shape the words *Arbeit macht frei* ("Work makes freedom").
Such words may have made sense when they entered the prison. Yet,
viewed from inside the concentration camp, the words must have appeared completely backward—figuratively and literally. No matter how
hard the prisoners tried, regardless of how much they obeyed their
taskmasters, all they got was more slavery, more abuse, more death—
especially if they were sent to the extermination camps. Inside the
prison, "work makes freedom" makes no sense at all, no matter how
many times you read the sign.

How do we explain the atrocities that took place behind these prison
walls? The starvation, the torture, the sadistic experiments, the bar-
baric treatment. How could one human being treat another with such
hatred, such heartless cruelty, such hellish intention? Evil. We blame
evil. We blame sinister forces. We blame the devil. But Paul wouldn't.
Paul didn't blame the horrendous evil of sinful humanity on Satan—
especially when he considered his own horrible past. A one-time persecutor, Paul never said, "The devil made me do it." He never shifted the
blame of his sinful behavior to the evil one. Rather, when dealing with
the unrelenting power of sin, Paul blamed two agents. First of all, sin
resides in the flesh—the baser appetites of humanity. For Paul the root

of the problem of human sin is the flesh. And yet, as pervasive as Paul's talk is about the flesh, he will not attribute the cause of all sin to human selfishness. The flesh has a partner in crime, a co-conspirator. As a divine agent of such great potential, many have been fooled by its universal appeal. It is a power that was supposed to make things better but actually made things worse. Rather than curb sin, it increases it. Instead of taming the flesh, it provokes it. Paul saw the *law* as the main instigator, a manipulated tool, the provocateur of human sin. In fact Paul goes so far as to suggest that "apart from the law sin lies dead" (Rom 7:8). That which was supposed to be the solution turned out to be the problem.

Paul didn't have very many kind words for the law. And that's rather surprising when we remember the law is God's Word. The law is supposed to be a "lamp unto our feet, and a light unto our path; that if we hide its words in our heart, we will not sin against God"—at least that's the pledge we recited as children during Vacation Bible School. Paul heard similar accolades his entire life. The Psalms are filled with praise for the law: it is a lamp (Ps 119:105); it tastes good like honey (Ps 19:10). The law is a life-giving river (Ps 1:2-3); the law is liberty (Ps 119:45)—can you imagine Paul ever saying the law is liberating (cf. Jas 1:25)? Instead, Paul describes the law—at its worst—as a cruel taskmaster, enslaving those who tried to keep the rules (Rom 7:6; Gal 5:1). Or more respectfully, the law was a disciplinarian, forcing children who didn't know any better to do the right thing (Gal 3:24)—a school that felt like a prison (Gal 3:23). Even when Paul was compelled to speak positively about the law (Rom 7:7-16), his praise looks like a counterbalancing act—almost as if he were on the horns of a dilemma, trying to hold on to two contradictory ideas: even though the law "is holy and good," it sure seems to lead to a bunch of unholy and bad behavior. And even though he shifts the blame of our inability to obey the law ultimately to "sin"—as if it were a power unto itself ("sin used the law against me!")—the negative undertone of Paul's critique of the law is quite apparent. Paul sprinkles words like "dead" and "old" and "captive" and "slave" throughout his argument, associating them with the law and making it sound bad (Rom 7:1-25). Whatever one makes of

Paul's colorful language, one thing is certain: law and righteousness were mutually exclusive in his mind. Such a pessimistic view of the law is a far cry from the triumphant claims of the psalmist: "Happy are those whose way is blameless, who walk in the law of the LORD" (Ps 119:1).

At one time Paul knew what it felt like to walk blamelessly in the righteousness of the law (Phil 3:6). But then, after his encounter with Christ, Paul found righteousness apart from the law—a righteousness based on the cross of Jesus Christ. In fact, according to Paul, the cross of Jesus revealed why the law didn't work anymore. The law was supposed to generate life but brought death (Rom 7:5; Gal 2:19; 3:21). The law was supposed to be a gift that advanced God's blessing, but it effected a curse instead (Gal 3:10-13). The law was supposed to give the Jews an advantage on the judgment day, but it condemned all just the same (Rom 3:1-23). Believe it or not, this was *good news* according to Paul. That's because he believed the cross of Jesus did what the law could not do. Jesus' death brought life (Rom 5:17, 19). Christ's redemptive work was God's gift of justification (Rom 3:24; 5:15). Through Christ, God condemned sin "in the flesh" to make *all* human flesh— Jews and Gentiles—righteous because they "walk not according to the flesh but according to the Spirit" (Rom 8:4; cf. Rom 5:15-19). This led Paul to dispense with the righteousness that is found in the law, "for if justification comes through the law, then Christ died for nothing" (Gal 2:21). And if Christ died in vain, then all is in vain (1 Cor 15:14)—for Christ as well as for Paul and his converts. Therefore, the way Paul saw it, he could never go back to the law. Since he was crucified with Christ, to return to the law would be the same as coming down from Christ's cross and admitting he was wrong. That would make Christ a "servant of sin" and Paul a perpetual lawbreaker (Gal 2:18), always falling short of God's glory. So when it came to the law—for Paul as well as others— faith in Christ was the point of no return. In more ways than one, Christ was the end of the law for all who believe (Rom 10:4).

Paul couldn't believe it, therefore, when his converts wanted to do the right thing according to the law and therefore be right according to the law. "You foolish Galatians! Who has bewitched you? It was before your eyes that Jesus Christ was publicly exhibited as crucified!" (Gal 3:1). If Christ's cross was enough, why look elsewhere? Evidently the Galatians found something very appealing about the law, what with all the promises of blessings and rewards. This put Paul in a difficult spot. He probably referenced the law when he preached the gospel. He probably used the Hebrew Scriptures (especially the Psalms) for worship and instruction. Other "apostles" had evidently encouraged obedience to the law. The only thing left for Paul to do was to show his converts the downside of the law, which was ironically attested by the law: "Tell me, you who desire to be subject to the law, will you not listen to the law?" (Gal 4:21). They were about to get an earful.

## Why the Law Didn't Work

In his letter to the Galatians, Paul gives three reasons why the law didn't work. First, he appeals to the Galatians' experience.[1] When they believed the gospel according to Paul, they received the Spirit's power to overcome the flesh and work miracles (Gal 3:2-5). The Spirit didn't come due to "works of law," whether performed by them or by Paul. Second, Paul explains how his Gentile converts received the promises God made to Abraham without the law. This is a crucial part of his argument, for Jews believed that only those who were seminally present in the loins of Abraham were blessed by God's word of promise (when God speaks, there is life). Obviously Gentiles were excluded (they didn't "hear" God's word) because they were not of Abraham's seed (the word Paul uses is *sperma*). But didn't God promise Abraham that he would be the father of *many* nations, not just Israel? How would this happen? Conventional wisdom in Paul's day taught that Gentiles who obeyed the law would be included in God's blessing to Israel. That's because even Abraham was required to "walk blamelessly" before God to receive covenant blessings (Gen 17:1-2). "To walk blamelessly" had become synonymous with obeying the law (Ps 119:1; Phil 3:6). Circumcising the flesh—an act of obedience to the law—would seal the deal for future generations, Jews as well as Gentiles (Gen 17:3-14; Sir 44:19-21). Paul, however, circumvents the whole process by claiming that his uncircumcised converts are children of Abraham because they have the faith of Abraham—belief in the promises of God is what made Abraham righteous (Gal 3:6-9, 15-18). Besides, the fact that the law brought a curse to those who failed to live up to its requirements worked against the fulfillment of God's promised blessings (Gal 3:10-15). The law was a temporary provision for Israel, mediated by angels. It was added, Paul claims, "because of transgressions" to "imprison sin," that is, to limit the power of sin. All of this was in preparation for the fulfillment of the promise, that is, to guide all to faith in the Messiah, the God-blessed seed of Abraham (Gal 3:15-29). Therefore, when it comes to the fulfillment of God's promises to Abraham, the law had done its job, guarding children until the time they were to receive the inheritance from their father—an inheritance that comes through Christ (Gal 4:1-5).

The third reason why Paul believes the law doesn't work has more to do with the broken relationship between the apostle and the Galatians. As far as Paul is concerned, his converts are no longer acting like friends (Gal 4:12-18) or family (Gal 4:19-20). Paul feels betrayed because some of them were influenced by outsiders to keep the law, observing the religious calendar and getting circumcised. That makes it appear as though Paul's gospel were not enough, that their apostle had not given them everything they needed. After reminding the Galatians of their one-time affection for him ("we were once good friends, what happened?"), Paul attacks the interlopers by questioning their deceitful intentions (Gal 4:12-18). But, when he turns to consider how his converts are no longer acting like his children, Paul sounds more exasperated. He even calls attention to his maternal tone as he begins to scold the Galatians (Gal 4:19-20). Paul "the mother" piles on warnings by highlighting the personal harm that could come to his children. By submitting to the law, Paul's children are ignoring their pedigree and associating with the wrong children, risking persecution and enslavement (Gal 4:21-31). Handling the law is like playing with a sharp knife: "Circumcision? Don't do it! You'll hurt yourself, or maybe someone else!" (Gal 5:4, 12). The law has no power over the flesh (Gal 5:16-24). In fact his children are fighting all the time, competing with each other (Gal 5:15, 26). It's as if Paul were saying: "Look at what's happened since you began to obey the law. It only made things worse." Indeed, Paul's frustration is palpable at the end of the letter, when he sounds like a parent issuing their final warning: "Quit making trouble for me! My enemies have caused enough problems for me" (my paraphrase of Gal 6:17).

Throughout Galatians, Paul sees the cross of Jesus as mutually exclusive to the law. There are those who boast in the law and thereby avoid the persecution of the cross (Gal 6:12-14). For Paul it was just the opposite. He boasted in the cross and was persecuted because he didn't submit to the law. Scholars wonder which came first: persecution because of the cross or punishment because of the law. Paul definitely saw a correlation between his refusing to promote circumcision and the persecution he endured (Gal 5:11). At the same time, he accused his adversaries of avoiding the persecution that came with the cross of Jesus (Gal 6:12). Both the cross and circumcision had social consequences. But what scholars want to know is whether Paul arrived at his negative view of the law because of the difficulties he encountered by preaching a law-free gospel. In fact debate over the order of Paul's logic regarding the law usually ends with two conclusions. Either Paul saw the law as a problem, perhaps even before the Christophany, and began to see the cross of Jesus as the solution. Seeing the Crucified One on the Damascus road confirmed his suspicions that the law inevitably led to a curse. Or it was only after accepting the cross of Jesus as the solution to the human condition that Paul began to see problems with the law. Since Christ defines the righteousness of God, then the law can no longer serve that purpose. In other words, which came first: problem or solution?[2] The answer depends on how we read Romans 7.

Living under the law is like a prison. Submitting to the law is slavery. Why did Paul speak of the law in such pejorative terms? When he wrote these things, was Paul revealing his own experience or someone else's? In other words, did the law feel like a prison to Paul? Or was Paul using polemical language to convince his converts not to submit to it; in other words, for Jews the law is a good thing, but for Gentiles, unaccustomed to its demands, the law would only turn out to be a bad thing—something that enslaves? Was Paul speaking autobiographically (my struggle) or biographically (our struggle) in Romans 7? No doubt, there are several places where Paul seems to identify with the plight of his Gentile converts (Gal 4:3-5)—as if Jews and Gentiles face the same situation. In other places, he marks the difference of their religious past: his converts were once enslaved to idols (Gal 4:8). So when he uses the pronoun "our," it's difficult to tell whether Paul is telling Israel's story or Adam's story. In other words, when Paul uses inclusive language, is he identifying with his Jewish kinspeople or with all humanity? This is what makes Romans 7 so difficult to interpret—especially when it comes to sorting out Paul's spirituality. For, if we know for certain that Paul is talking about his own struggle with the law, then some suggest we would merely have to decide whether he is referring to his pre- or post-Christophany experience; that is, is Paul recounting his problems as a law-abiding Jew or a free-from-the-law apostle? But if his description of trying to keep the law is not autobiographical, then Paul is simply speaking theoretically—and so, what we read in Romans 7 is not indicative of Paul's experience. But if that is the case, how do we make sense of statements that sound so personal, like: "For I delight in the law of God in my inmost self, but I see in my members another law at war with the law of my mind, making me captive to the law of sin that dwells in my members. Wretched man that I am! Who will rescue me from this body of death?" To the average reader, Paul sounds like he's sharing his innermost thoughts—his secret, torturous struggle.

This is where a great divide exists between scholars and laity. It should come as no surprise that many Christians assume Paul was talking about himself in Romans 7, especially Romans 7:7-25. They identify with Paul's struggle as if it were their own. When Paul admits that he knows what's right but has a hard time doing what's right, readers resonate with his plight. So, when I try to share scholarly opinion that Paul was probably not talking about himself as a frustrated Jew or impotent Christian, church people tend to look incredulous, as if I were ignoring what is obvious. The arguments, however, are well known among scholars; commentaries on Romans explain how Paul used a rhetorical device to speak of the human condition—"I" means "we."[3] Otherwise, how could Paul the Jew ever describe himself as being "once alive apart from the law" (Rom 7:9)? Or, especially in light of what he wrote in Romans 6:14 ("You are not under law but under grace"), how could Paul the apostle ever say he is currently "sold into slavery under sin" (Rom 7:14)? But such nuances are lost on most readers of Paul's letters today. For them, Paul's shorthand reference to the failure of law, "the law of sin and death" (Rom 8:2), aptly sums up the dilemma of Romans 7, especially for Christians.

To be sure, the complexities of Romans 7 also divide scholarly opinion. For example, when Paul refers to the law, is he always talking about Jewish law, or is he speaking of a general principle (especially Rom 7:21-25)?[4] Even though we may not consider at this point all the interpretive issues of Romans 7, the fact that Paul can identify with the plight of his readers reveals more insight into his spirituality than we previously thought.[5] Perhaps it's wrong to ask, "Which came first, the problem or the solution?" as if Paul worked within such a linear category, as if the "problem" went away and never returned. ("Whew! Now that I'm a Christ believer I don't have to deal with the law.") Maybe Paul was revealing a struggle that was cyclical, one that was true for Jews and Gentiles. In other words, Romans 7 may be autobiographical in that Paul is describing his experience with the law both prior to and after the Christophany; and it is biographical inasmuch as Paul is describing "everyman's" struggle to do what is right, whether Jew or Gentile.

On the one hand, Paul knew that the law didn't keep Jews from breaking the law—himself included (Rom 2:17-24; 7:7-11). But that didn't stop him from trying to keep it. Even after his encounter with Christ, Paul kept the law at times (1 Cor 9:20). Yet Paul discovered that only when he "set his mind on the Spirit" were the requirements of the law fulfilled in him. (When Paul wrote in Rom 8:4 that "the just requirement of the law might be fulfilled in *us*," he was certainly including himself.) On the other hand, if he ever tried to please God "in the flesh"—that is, submitting to the law rather than the Spirit's power—then he found he was unable to do what is right (Rom 8:4-8). This is what he meant when he warned his converts not to live as if they were "debtors . . . to the flesh, to live according to the flesh" (Rom 8:12). To live according to the flesh was the same as life under the law. (Notice the same parallel antinomies in Gal 3:2-3; 5:16-18, i.e., faith/Spirit vs. law/flesh.) Indeed, for Paul "life in the flesh" was synonymous with performing "deeds in the body" (Rom 8:13), referring to something more than blatant immoral acts, for how could anyone say that they were able to "please God in the flesh"?

To try to please God in the flesh is what Paul called having "confidence in the flesh," that is, not only rites performed in the flesh (circumcision) but also deeds accomplished by the individual (obeying the law, cf. Phil 3:4-6). These "works of the flesh/deeds in the body" were attempts at doing the right thing without the Spirit—a life that resulted in death because a fleshly mind is "hostile to God" (Rom 8:6-8).[6] Since the law and the flesh were under the power of sin, then it was only through the Spirit's power, according to Paul, that one could "please God," whether Jew or Gentile. That's because the Spirit's power overcomes the law of sin and death, producing in Christ believers a "lawful" life even though they are not subject to the law. Paul's converts received the Spirit without obeying the law, *and* they were not required to keep the law because of the Spirit.[7] In fact Paul believed that his converts were free to keep only one law, the law of Christ (Rom 8:2; 1 Cor 9:21), because the whole law is summed up in the commandment: "Love your neighbor as yourself" (Gal 5:14; Rom 13:8-10)—a commandment that could only be kept by the power of Christ's Spirit, whether Jew or Gentile (Rom 8:9-10; 13:14; 15:1-13). So Paul could not write about the problem of the law without talking about the weakness of the flesh and the power of the Spirit. In other words, the problem was more than, what do we do with the law? but also entailed, how do we keep from living according to the flesh? and, how do we live according to the Spirit?

## Life in the Spirit

The most common question I hear from former students and current friends has to do with the law. I have received numerous inquiries, especially via email, posing the same question: what role does the law play in the life of a Christian? Whenever I try to give Paul's answer, "Christians don't have to keep the law," many are puzzled. My response doesn't seem right to them. In fact, "freedom from the law" sounds like anarchy, especially to American ears. We can only imagine how difficult it must have sounded to Jewish ears, especially since they believed—and rightfully so—that their law came from God.

I think it is telling that Americans prize law and order. (How many detective/law/CSI television shows are there?) We believe in the law because we want justice for all. In fact justice only comes when lawbreakers get what they deserve. (The plot of *every* detective/law/CSI program.) Some may argue that we are just as zealous in our allegiance to "law" as Paul's kinspeople, which is why many American Christians have a hard time taking Paul at his word. He preached a gospel of grace and mercy: grace gives us what we don't deserve, and mercy keeps us from getting what we deserve. We hear that all the time in church. Nevertheless, whenever I emphasize one aspect of Paul's teaching on grace—that we are free from the law—eyebrows are raised and worried looks abound. A recent discussion I had in class illustrates the typical conversation:

Student: "What about the Ten Commandments? Aren't we supposed to keep the Ten Commandments?"

Me: "Not according to Jesus and Paul. They said you only need to keep one: love your neighbor as yourself. Besides, you can't keep all ten commandments anyway."

Student: "So, you're saying we shouldn't try? The commandments are God's Word, you know."

Me: "Oh, so you want to keep the commandments? Why just ten?"

Student: "What do you mean?"

Me: "There aren't just ten commandments. Why not keep all of them, since you're wanting to obey God."

Student: (now acting a little reserved) "How many commandments are there?"

Me: "Six hundred thirteen." (Pause) "Let me ask you this: 'do you like catfish'?"

Student: "Yes."

Me:      "Do you eat shrimp? Do you like your steak medium, or per-
         haps even rare?"

Student: (somewhat reticently) "I eat shrimp and steak—medium
         rare."

Me:      "Sinner."

Student: "I get it. So, if we don't have to keep the Ten Commandments,
         how will we know if we're living right? What are we supposed
         to do?"

Me:      "Live by the Spirit."

Student: "That's it? That's all we need to do? That sounds like a license
         to sin."

Me:      "And that's exactly the charge leveled against Paul by those
         who kept the law."

It sounds too good to be true: the only thing we need to live a holy
life is the Spirit. I can imagine many of Paul's kinspeople (and perhaps
even some of his converts) echoing the same response: "Is that it?"
Many in Paul's day had similar reservations, especially given the religious background of Paul's converts. Remember: Paul didn't start
churches with disgruntled Baptists, Presbyterians or Methodists. Paul's
churches were filled with one-time godless, immoral pagans; surely
they needed some guidance, some way of marking their progress in
their new faith. Paul wouldn't have it. He held his ground, for he was
convinced the same power that enabled him to live a crucified life was
the power who lived in every Christ believer, regardless of their background. It is the Spirit's power whereby Christ believers overcome sin
and the flesh. So Paul would say: "We don't need the law to help us do
what is right; the Spirit does that." In fact, according to Paul, the *only*
way a believer is able to live a life pleasing to God is by a circumcised
heart, not circumcised flesh (Rom 2:29). The law is unyielding and
cold as stone, but the Spirit writes a living letter (2 Cor 3:2-3). The letter of the law fosters death ("the letter kills"), but the Spirit creates life

(2 Cor 3:5-6). The glory of the law was condemnation, but the glory of the Spirit is transformation (2 Cor 3:7-18). Indeed, the law was an old covenant that fades with time. The Spirit, however, makes all things new because it is eternal (2 Cor 5:17).

We must remember the reason Paul could say these things about the law was that he believed he was experiencing the end of the world—the cross and the resurrection proved it. The Spirit's powerful presence in the life of a Christ believer was one more bit of evidence that the messianic age had dawned on Paul's generation. Prophets like Joel, Isaiah and Jeremiah anticipated the time; the new age of Messiah's kingdom would be revealed by: (1) the Spirit falling on "all flesh" so that "everyone who calls on the name of the Lord shall be saved" (Joel 2:28-32; Rom 10:13); (2) Israel rejecting the one bringing the "good news" and Gentiles seeking the God of Israel because of the gospel proclaimed to them (Is 65:1-2; Rom 10:20-21); and (3) a new covenant with the law of God written on the hearts of his people (Jer 31:31-34; 2 Cor 3:3-6). All of these things (and more) were coming true in Paul's time; they were witnessing the end of the old age. This is why Paul could make such seemingly disparaging remarks about the law. It's old. It's passing away. It's dead—all because the law was part of the old age. The advent of the Spirit, however, was God's undeniable revelation that the new age had come. So Paul encouraged his converts to think of the law like a widower thinks of her marriage—dead and gone: "But now we are discharged from the law, dead to that which held us captive, so that we are slaves not under the old written code but in the new life of the Spirit" (Rom 7:6). Indeed, according to Paul, life in the Spirit was the beginning of the end of all things, even the law.

Paul had much confidence in the power of the Spirit. Vague expressions like "walk in the Spirit" or "be filled with the Spirit" or "live in the Spirit" should have been enough, as far as Paul was concerned, to guide his converts to do the right thing. For him life in the Spirit was as simple as putting on new clothes, wearing Christ like an armor (Rom 13:12-14; Col 3:10). It was a matter of making up your mind that you were going to have the mind of Christ in all things (Phil 2:1-16; Eph 4:17-24). Indeed, for Paul the life of the mind is a spiritual pursuit

(Rom 12:2; Phil 4:8). But what happens when Spirit-filled, Spirit-guided believers have a different mind on a particular matter? What if the Spirit convinces some Christians to drink wine or eat idol meat or treat the Sabbath like any other day—violating one of the Ten Commandments (Rom 14:2, 5; 1 Cor 8:7)? What about those who were convinced that such behavior was the complete opposite of what God desired? Even in Paul's day, teetotalers and vegetarians and Sabbath observers could chapter-and-verse their opponents with enough Scripture to prove they were more righteous than their eat-drink-and-be-merry counterparts. Who's right and who's wrong?

This is where Paul was at his best—getting people of diverse backgrounds to learn how to get along with each other (the topic of the next four chapters). And that's rather surprising given the fact that Paul himself was such a provocative figure in the early church. Indeed, Paul refused to answer questions in a way that would give credence to one side or the other. He never sided with the legalists, even though it would have made it much easier on Paul. It's easy to tell who's obeying and who's not when you have a black-and-white standard by which to judge all. But the freedom he experienced in Christ meant too much to him; he refused to be judged (1 Cor 4:3-5; 9:1-12). At the same time, Paul would not countenance a gospel that promoted the lifestyle "all things are lawful for me." Such a me-centered, selfish approach to spirituality would profit no one, neither the libertine nor his or her community. Neither extreme revealed the Spirit-led life. Legalists turn gray issues into black-and-white realities; libertines interpret freedom from the law as anything goes. How would Paul get these competing ideologies to find common ground in the gospel he lived and proclaimed?

Paul presented himself as the exemplar of a Spirit-filled life. He learned how to sacrifice personal convictions for the welfare of the group. When he spent time with law-abiding people, he kept the law. When he shared table with the law-free crowd, he probably enjoyed all kinds of food. This was living according to what Paul called the "law of Christ," sacrificing yourself for others (1 Cor 9:19-21). To become "all things to all people" to "save some" is to follow the pattern of Christ. Love is the commandment that trumps judgment, and love cannot exist without sacrifice. If legalists loved their brothers there would be no judgment; libertines must sacrifice themselves to love others. "Each of us must please our neighbor for the good purpose of building up the neighbor. For Christ did not please himself" (Rom 15:2-3). That's what Paul did; he set aside his Jewish ways when he was with Gentiles, and he submitted to the law when he was with his Jewish brothers and sisters. He was convinced that if his converts would imitate him, then the Spirit's work would unify people of such diverse opinions because of the love of Christ. But what happens in mixed company, when legalists and libertines eat at the same table? Shouldn't libertines encourage legalists to loosen up a bit and enjoy the good life of freedom in Christ? Or would it be irresponsible for legalists to compromise their convictions and join the party? Besides, don't libertines need to learn a little self-discipline? Which group should sacrifice for the other? And, even more fascinating, since Paul saw himself as a model to be imitated, which end of the table would he join, the meat eaters or the vegetarians?

In certain respects, Paul put the onus on both groups (Rom 14:1-23). He expected those who had liberty to eat meat to restrain themselves in the presence of the "weak" because the weak might be tempted to eat and violate their conscience. And he expected those who operated according to certain self-imposed rules to refrain from judging their liberated brothers, even encouraging the "strong" as they enjoyed their carnivorous ways. Both groups were to hold to their own convictions (Rom 14:22); both groups were doing the right thing because their convictions were based on faith (not law; Rom 14:23). The problem came when one group tried to enforce compliance on the other, which compromised the peace and joy that comes "in the Holy Spirit" (Rom 14:17). Rather, Paul taught that when the house churches gathered as one, they should "welcome one another" just as Christ welcomed them (Rom 15:7). In this scenario the meat eaters would encourage the vegetarians in their diet, and the weak would encourage the strong in their liberty. Both are free to hold to their own convictions without judgment; and only in that freedom would they be able to encourage the other. In this way they would be "walking in love" by building up the *whole* body of Christ (Rom 14:15-21).

"I'm not being a legalist, but . . ." Those words fell from the lips of one of the most legalistic Christians I've ever met. He was criticizing his church during one of their business meetings for supporting "family programming" on television. The church he attended had its own cable television channel. They produced several overtly Christian programs. But they also decided to include certain syndicated programs that were "family friendly." Even he admitted there was nothing offensive about the shows. But according to his way of thinking whatever is not for the gospel is against the gospel. The church should allow only explicitly Christian programs—and not every so-called Christian program was truly Christian. If the program never mentioned "Jesus Christ" or explicitly gave the "plan of salvation," it wasn't Christian as far as he was concerned. When the pastor tried to take issue with his argument, the man interrupted him and began to declare in prophetic tones a warning of God's imminent curse upon the whole congregation for supporting "Hollywood." I couldn't resist trying to speak with the man after the confrontation. "I noticed you said that you weren't being a legalist when you raked the church over the coals for having G-rated programming on their cable channel. Well, if that's not legalism, what is?" To which he replied, "Legalism is when someone tries to tell me what to do." "But isn't that what you were doing? Trying to tell everyone here what to do?" "Oh, that's different," he said. "God sent me to warn the church."

And there's the rub. All legalists believe they're doing the work of God. But the question remains: are they walking in the Spirit?

Who's walking in the Spirit? Paul pointed to all kinds of evidence, what he called "fruit of the Spirit" (Gal 5:22-23): love, joy, peace, patience, humility and so on. According to Paul these were not "virtues" achieved by the self. (Indeed, Greeks and Romans never would have considered "humility" as virtuous—humiliation is something that is done to you.) These qualities were evident in the life of one who was empowered by the Spirit; that is, fruit must be produced in a believer by a divine source. But that is not to say that believers were completely passive in the process; Paul's converts were supposed to "walk in the Spirit." They crucified the desires of the flesh (Gal 5:24).

They helped restore transgressors (Gal 6:1). They persisted in doing good (Gal 6:8-10). There was no law against these things (Gal 5:23). Indeed, Paul could speak of the obedience of his converts *without* the law, which explains why the apostle used the metaphor of slavery when he wrote about service to God and to others. As far as Paul was concerned, those who serve others are compelled by the Spirit of God. They serve one another because they are slaves of Christ; they have been "bought with a price" (1 Cor 7:22-23). Of course for both Jews and Gentiles, slavery wasn't a desirable thing at all. The Roman Empire turned conquered peoples into slaves. The Jewish people were once a slave nation whom God freed from Egyptian bondage. But Paul was convinced his converts would want to live as slaves of the Lord because of what Christ had done for them—he "emptied himself, taking the form of a slave. . . . He humbled himself, and became obedient to the point of death—even death on a cross" (Phil 2:7-8). Service to God, then, was a matter of imitating Christ, empowered by the Spirit to serve others (Phil 2:1-4). And yet ironically this kind of slavery was liberating for Paul. Slavery to God meant freedom from the enslaving powers of the law, sin and flesh (Rom 6:17-22). In other words, life in the Spirit brought grace to others (service) and freedom to the individual (obedience). So Paul could say: if you were called as a slave, you are free in Christ; and if you were called as a free man, you are a slave of Christ (1 Cor 7:22). To be like Christ is to be a slave of Christ. Thus Paul the slave of Christ was free to become a servant of all (1 Cor 9:19; 2 Cor 4:5), even when that service led to a prison (Phil 1:1-18).

"The Church is her true self only when she exists for humanity." Dietrich Bonhoeffer was sketching ideas for a book he wanted to write once he was released from a Nazi concentration camp. He didn't know it then, but he would never get to write that book. A few months later, having spent nearly two years in prison, Dietrich Bonhoeffer was executed by German soldiers—just a few weeks before Allied forces liberated prisoners in southern Germany. There is so much to admire about this man: his courage, his resilient faith, his tireless efforts for the Confessing Church, his brilliance, his steely resolve, his passion for Christ.

But what I admire most about him is that, even in prison, Bonhoeffer was thinking about others—how he would help rebuild the church in Germany after the war, how he would encourage his brothers and sisters to rediscover what it meant to be a genuine disciple of Jesus Christ. He outlined what it would take to bring reconciliation to his war-torn country, setting out milestones of discipline, action, suffering and death on what he called "the road to freedom."[8] He would write of the need for spiritual vitality in the church; of the decadence of dead religion; and of faith as participation in the incarnation, cross and resurrection of Jesus. The church would need a fresh start, proclaiming the Word of God with new power:

> She must tell men, whatever their calling, what it means to live in Christ, to exist for others. . . . She will have to speak of moderation, purity, confidence, loyalty, steadfastness, patience, discipline, humility, content and modesty. She must not underestimate the importance of human example, which has its origins in the humanity of Jesus, and which is so important in the teaching of St. Paul. *It is not abstract argument, but concrete example which gives her word emphasis and power.* I hope to take up later this subject of example.[9]

Indeed, he did—not with words written on paper but as an example of the Word written on "fleshy hearts," as Paul would say. For Dietrich Bonhoeffer not only wrote about the cost of discipleship; but he also lived it to the end, hung from the gallows on April 9, 1945. What Bonhoeffer experienced, Paul knew all too well: "the letter kills"—even virtuous words written on the roof of Nazi prison camps—"but the Spirit gives life," especially to slaves who have been set free from the law of sin and death. Bonhoeffer echoed Paul's sentiments in a farewell message to a friend. Just before they took him away to be executed—stripped naked and hung—he said: "This is the end—for me the beginning of life."[10] On that day it should have been obvious to everyone that the famous sign at Dachau was wrong. Submission to German law only brought death. The path to freedom—for Dietrich Bonhoeffer, Paul the apostle and every slave of God—is Jesus Christ.

Remember Jesus Christ, raised from the dead, a descendant of David—
that is my gospel, for which I suffer hardship, even to the point of being
chained like a criminal. But the word of God is not chained. Therefore
I endure everything for the sake of the elect, so that they may also ob-
tain the salvation that is in Christ Jesus, with eternal glory."
St. Paul, awaiting execution, from a prison cell in Rome (2 Tim 2:8-
10)

PART TWO
*Buried with Christ*

# 5

# Whole Body

*One Faith*

✣

"HERE'S THE CHURCH; here's the steeple. Open the door and see all the people." The hand gestures that go along with the familiar childhood saying cemented in my mind the simplistic idea that church is a time and a place. When I was around ten years old, my pastor tried to correct this preschool hand game by giving a new version of the saying, one that would be more "biblical." "Here's the *building*; here's the steeple. Open the door and see the *church*." (He even wiggled his fingers for effect.) But, I didn't like it. His version didn't rhyme. Besides, our common vocabulary confirmed what I had been taught as a little kid. Nearly every Sunday morning, during the weekly ritual of shining shoes and fastening clip-on ties, my parents would sound the alarm, "Hurry up; we're going to be late for church." During the week, if we happened to drive by the modest stucco building in Compton, California, we'd say to our friends, "There's our church!" We had "church" at particular time and we went to "church" at a particular place. Of course over the years I heard enough sermons to know that "church" referred to a group of people; our pastor loved to use Paul's term *ekklēsia* to describe us—we were the "called out ones." But the idea that church is a collection of people only made sense to me on Sunday morning, when I could look around and see who was there for worship.

To be sure there were other times when the church of my childhood could be seen and heard. Sometimes we ate together. (We called these meetings "fellowship suppers"; for the longest time I thought "fellowship" could only happen if we were eating and drinking.) We gathered for weddings and funerals. We also came together for special events like Vacation Bible School and Christmas pageants. But that wasn't the same as having church on Sunday morning. Sitting together on wooden pews, singing old songs with strange lyrics ("Here I raise mine Ebenezer"), watching adults fall asleep in the choir loft, counting ceiling tiles during the sermon, finding strange things stuck under the pews, longing for the final "amen" and the postlude (always played with great exuberance by my mother, the church organist)—if it didn't include these things, then it wasn't church. Once it was all over, filing out of the auditorium and taking in the rich irony of hearing my mom play "To God Be the Glory," we would *leave* church and go home.

For Paul, to leave church would be the same as leaving home—that's because to him church was home. He was the family father; his converts were brothers and sisters. In most regions they gathered *in homes* to worship, to eat, to pray, to read, to give, to talk, to counsel, to deliberate, to grieve, to remember. Sometimes they met in synagogues and lecture halls. For the most part they gathered for worship on Sunday but also met on Saturday and other days of the week. Church was neither a time nor a place. Rather, for Paul and his converts, church was family. Church was not only a collection of individuals; but it was also a person. Church was not simply a religious function; but it was also an identity. Church was not just an earthly society; but it was also a colony of heaven. Paul called the group many things: an assembly and a fellowship, a temple and a household, a body and a family. It was hard to describe. No term seemed to fit. Members came from every walk of life: mostly poor but some rich, mostly common but some nobility, mostly Gentile but some Jews. They were one of the most diverse collections of humanity at the time. And yet, for all of its amorphous, unidentifiable qualities, one thing was certain as far as Paul was concerned: the church was one people called by one God because they worshiped one Lord and were initiated into one faith by one baptism.

That idea—one church, one faith, one baptism—sounds idealistic today. Baptists, Presbyterians, Lutherans, Methodists, Pentecostals,

Catholics and Anglicans would be quick to remind us of our differences (especially during their conferences and conventions). Besides, the church in West Africa doesn't look anything like the church in the West. The church south of the equator doesn't act anything like the church in the deep south of the United States. East Coasters think differently than believers of the Near East. Thus it would be easy to say, "Only a dreamer would claim we are one church." In fact that's the way Paul's axiom is often described; to say, "There is no longer Jew or Greek, there is no longer slave or free, there is no longer male and female; for all of you are one in Christ Jesus" (Gal 3:28) is a dream that will only become reality in heaven. As long as we're living in the real world, the church will always be divided: ethnically, economically, politically, theologically. For many, there is too much that divides us to call us "united." But here's the real surprise: they could have said the same thing in Paul's day. The factions in Corinth, the Judaizers' campaign in Galatia, fights between the "weak" and the "strong" in Rome—Paul's efforts at unifying the house churches notwithstanding—this was a divided church. Indeed, the diversity of the church in Paul's day probably made his talk about "one faith, one baptism" sound just as foreign to first-century believers as it does to us today. Even though we're no longer debating whether circumcision is a requirement for faith (wouldn't Paul be relieved?), we have to admit the church doesn't subscribe to "one baptism." Sprinkle or immerse? Water and Spirit? Cleansing or confession? Initiation and membership? Ordinance or sacrament? Children and adults? Every Christian group has it own ideas about baptism because the New Testament does not present a unified picture of the meaning and practice of baptism. And ironically, as much as any one else, we have Paul to blame for that.

## Baptism as Burial

For some reason Paul thought baptism was a way of participating in the burial of Christ (Rom 6:4; Col 2:12). That idea is found nowhere else in the New Testament. Of course almost all of the other writers mention baptism—Luke, Peter, John, Matthew, even the author of Hebrews. And in most places baptism is referenced as a given, as if readers didn't need a description of the practice or its significance. Indeed, we are left to infer the logistics (who? where? what? when? how?) and theology (why?) of the ritual. And when it comes to Paul, things get more complicated. That's because Paul used baptism—with all of its vagaries and mystifying qualities—in order to make a point about something else. In fact, in every case but one (Rom 6:1-4), Paul refers to baptism when he is trying to get his converts to learn how to get along with each other (Gal 3:28; 1 Cor 1:13-17; 12:13; 15:29; Eph 4:5; Col 2:12). In other words, Paul never tried to put on paper his theology of baptism; he never felt obliged to explain it. And yet baptism was a very important touchstone for Paul—especially when he wanted to remind his converts of what they had already committed themselves to from the beginning.

In Paul's mind, water baptism and the baptism of the Spirit were mingled together. Furthermore when Paul referred to baptism "in Christ" we can't tell if the apostle was speaking christologically or ecclesiologically; that is, were we baptized into Jesus in heaven or into his body, the church, on earth? Of course scholars try to help us sort out the difference, especially in places like Romans 6:1-11. Most will argue that baptism "into Christ" has to do with being identified with Christ, either baptized in his name or joined with him in his death[1] and resurrection, "seated in the heavenly places" (Eph 2:6).[2] Others claim Paul was writing about membership—being baptized into the Body of Christ—to encourage the church in Rome to "present your members to God as instruments of righteousness" (Rom 6:13). Some argue that Paul was referring only to Spirit baptism; others say he was recalling the water ritual every time he wrote about baptism.[3] The problem, of course, is that Paul used the word "baptism" to describe both experiences. Were they connected or not? No doubt, there is much to consider when we try to unwrap Paul's baptismal imagery. Indeed, some of it may be crucial to understanding Paul's spirituality, especially if we are to believe that Paul tied Spirit baptism to water baptism. But I would prefer to set those questions aside for the moment and consider instead the implications of Paul's claim that baptism is our participation in the burial of Christ, a rather strange idea that we don't typically spend much time thinking about.

Even though I grew up in a Baptist church, baptism was the strangest thing I ever saw. The thought of someone shoving me underwater was frightful. Then to see the baptized brought back to the surface, coughing, sputtering and wiping their eyes made me question the whole process. What was all of this about? Why did adults submit to this torturous rite? At the same, it was quite an entertaining event, especially in the 1960s. When my friends and I would hear the announcement, "we're going to have a baptismal service tonight," we giggled with delight knowing that "church" was going to be different. When the time came the pastor always entered the water fully clothed (shirt and tie!), wearing a white robe. To a boy and his friends, seeing a grown-up "swimming" in street clothes was especially bizarre. Then, one by one, the candidates—also donning white robes—stepped into the baptistery. The robes would often balloon as they waded into the water, forcing a modest woman to nearly re-create the notorious image of Marilyn Monroe holding down her dress. If she were wearing the high-class beehive hairdo (think bride of Frankenstein), then we cackled with great anticipation to see which way her hair would flop when she was brought up from the water. Sometimes there was great resistance, a fearful candidate wrestling with the pastor trying to keep their head above water. Every now and then a leg would surface as if the baptized were signaling for help. Once it was all over, the convert would leave the baptistery looking like a wet cat and eventually reappear before the congregation with proper clothes and wet hair.

As entertaining as baptisms were to a grade-school boy, I was always struck by the seriousness of the ritual when our pastor said, "Buried with Christ," and placed the candidates underwater, eyes closed and arms crossed over their chest like a corpse. At that moment baptism looked like burial. We were left with the unmistakable impression that baptism is not something we do for ourselves; everyone has to *be baptized*. Like burial, baptism is something that is done to you. No one can bury themselves; no one can baptize themselves. Dead persons rely on the living to take care of their bodies for proper burial. At that point the dead have nothing to say. They are entrusted to the care of their family.

In the same way, the baptized lean into the arms of the church. Placed under water, believers are buried with Christ, entrusted to the care of their new family—to bring them out of the water and to a new way of living. They couldn't do this on their own. They must *be buried* with Christ. Indeed, burial by baptism is a passive event performed by a community of faith. We're so used to thinking about our spirituality as something we actively pursue. But Paul would have us consider that spiritual development is sometimes done to us and for us—which is why he kept bringing up baptism whenever he addressed church conflict in his letters. As far as Paul was concerned, whenever his converts witnessed baptism, they were supposed to be reminded of the commitment they had made to each other. They were dead to themselves and alive to God. Paul believed that baptism pictured their reliance on Christ as they depended upon each other. Buried with Christ in baptism, they were sealing their alliance as a new family of needy people in matters of life and death. They were united in Christ.

If a man like Paul died in the big city he had to rely upon friends to make sure he received an honorable burial (cf. Mt 27:57-60).[4] That's because most merchants and craftsmen who worked in the city left their hometowns in order to ply their trade. (Notice how often we hear of Paul's associates in one city, then the next; e.g., Prisca and Aquila lived and worked in Ephesus, Corinth and Rome.) In fact, in most cities there were burial clubs, a volunteer society of poor working-class members who promised to bury their dead friends with honors, even holding memorial services on the birthday of the deceased. Sometimes they would gather at the tomb of their dead friend to share a drink or even a memorial meal. To the Corinthians, Galatians, Colossians and Romans, the church probably sounded like another burial society, what with all of its talk about members being buried with Christ and sharing table in memorial.[5] In fact within a century early Christians began the practice of being buried together in shared tombs—having "died in Christ" they were therefore "buried with Christ." Or it could also be that to some of Paul's contemporaries, baptism may have resembled certain pagan rituals that were performed in order to ensure safe passage in the afterlife for the deceased. Some scholars suggest such influences from their religious past may explain the bizarre Corinthian practice of baptizing for the dead (1 Cor 15:29).[6] In that case Paul's converts had simply misunderstood the significance of the ritual; that is, even though baptism was a rite of passage from death to life, Paul was talking about a different kind of death and life, at a different time. Indeed, according to Paul, being buried with Christ through baptism pictures both the death and new life of the convert in Christ *before* the grave. Some of the Corinthians thought they could help their friends *after* the grave by being baptized for them (like the Mormons do). But when it came to his Corinthian converts, what concerned Paul more than the misapplied ritual was their confusion over what they died *to* and who they were to live *for* when they were buried with Christ.

Paul often used the rite of baptism to explain how the rights of an individual are sacrificed for the welfare of the church. We often speak of Christ's death and resurrection as a theological starting place for understanding our spirituality. Indeed, most books on Paul's spirituality skip over the significance of being buried with Christ. That's because we tend to emphasize our personal experience as the locus of spiritual formation. So individual preferences end up governing spiritual development. I determine what is vital and what is harmful; my experiences govern what is useful and what is irrelevant. In such an individualistic pursuit, church becomes a place (not a people!) where my spiritual palate is satisfied, where I get what I think I need to grow spiritually. Thus my experience of the Spirit is determined by my choices, my desires, my expectations, my efforts. I really don't need anyone else (especially if they try to tell me what to do—as if I don't know what's best for myself). If a church doesn't give me what I think I need, I'll find another that will.

But Paul would have us consider the implications of Christ's burial through baptism as the initiatory experience of the Spirit-led life—something that must be developed within the community of faith. We received the Spirit from others, so we can't walk in the Spirit alone. To emphasize our solidarity, Paul was inclined to prefix some of his favorite words describing the Christian life with *syn* (the Greek preposition meaning "together"). Our fellowship is not only a *koinōnia* but a *synkoi-*

*nōnia*—a shared life in Christ (Phil 1:5-7); we are heirs of God (*klē-ronomoi*) but more significantly coheirs (*sygklēronomoi*) because we suffer *together* (*sympaschomen*) and will be glorified *together* (*syndoxas-thōmen*) in Christ (Rom 8:17). Indeed, because our spirituality depends on our shared participation in Christ, Paul worked with the presumption that none of us can be Christians by ourselves.

I was asked to perform the funeral for a girl who had been viciously murdered. The victim of a jealous boyfriend's rage, the young lady had been brutally stabbed to death in her college apartment. Her mother was in my office, perhaps looking for consolation but especially needing a minister to conduct the memorial services for her only child. She apologized that she had never found much use for church. Occasionally she would attend worship services—especially on Easter Sunday—taking her daughter along. "It never became a habit," she said nearly weeping uncontrollably. Then after a long pause, she asked: "Do you think my daughter is in heaven?" But before I could respond, she read several lines from a poem written by her daughter—verses that spoke of her undying hope in the resurrection of Christ. Then she said, "That says something, doesn't it? She did believe in God. She had hope. It says so right here." This is one of those moments every minister dreads—when grieving souls want you to answer questions you have no business trying to answer. "How would I know?" I thought to myself. "Do I tell her what she wants to hear? Or do I speculate on her daughter's eternal destiny with words that may fall too easily from my lips?" As I watched this grieving mother with her head down, slowly folding the sheet of paper as if there were nothing left to say, I said, "That poem certainly gives you hope, doesn't it?" "Yes. Yes, it does," she said, trying to convince herself.

When we gathered at the cemetery to bury the girl, her friends refused to draw near the casket. They were easy to identify because all of them looked the same: dressed in black, but with a peculiar style. At that time the "gothic" look was popular among those who preferred to contemplate the darker side of life. Their faces were caked with white makeup, dark circles under their eyes. Their hair was disheveled, dyed jet black. They preferred to stand several yards away, huddled together, separate from the mourners. When I finished my remarks at the graveside, the mother sobbed uncontrollably. At this point I would normally encourage church members to gather around the bereaved and offer comfort with words and warm embrace. But she didn't have church family. She appeared so alone, wailing for her dead daughter. After a few family members and I tried to comfort her, I asked the crowd of onlookers, "Please. Come comfort your friend's mother." None of them even looked up at me. Thinking they didn't hear, I said loudly, "Listen to me. Please come and express your sympathy." They didn't move. "I mean. Please come and comfort her—give her a hug, tell her you're hurting too." I was stunned by their response. They didn't move. A couple of young ladies finally broke away from the crowd and approached their friend's mother. She embraced them as if they were her own, sobbing and holding them tight. The rest of the crowd looked on with no emotion, keeping a safe distance from the death they resembled.

If there were ever a time someone needs the church, it's when they bury family. And for those of us who are buried in Christ, there is comfort at the grave because we are family. It's often been said that death is the great equalizer. Regardless of fame or fortune the grave awaits every single one of us. But for those who have been buried with Christ in baptism, the grave has already been visited—the great equalizer has already happened. Regardless of fame or fortune, we come out of the baptismal grave the same: old things have passed away; everything has become new. That's why Paul kept bringing up baptism whenever his converts appeared to have forgotten what they had already given up. Before they were buried with Christ, they saw themselves as either Jews or Greeks, slaves or free, male or female. After baptism, they were supposed to be one people, dead to the things that divided them in the world. Notice how often Paul wrote, "You used to be . . ." or, "You once were . . . " (Gal 4:8-9; Eph 2:11-13; 1 Thess 1:9). Then he would use the "but now" phrase over and over again, reminding his converts of their new identity, their new humanity, their new allegiance, their new family. In fact Paul saw the church as an end-of-the-world work that had already happened in time. (We don't have to wait for heaven!) In other words, rather than think of themselves as Gentiles who happened to belong to a church of mixed ethnicity that will one day be united in heaven, Paul wanted his converts to see themselves as one people who lived as if the world—divided by ethnicities—had already come to an end. The church was supposed to picture to the world what a heavenly family looks like on earth, now. Ethnicities will not be erased in heaven (Rev 13:7 emphasizes that "every tribe and people and language and nation" will be gathered around God's throne), nor should they be on earth. Indeed, God is the author of diversity. But this divine diversity was supposed to reveal *together* the glorious work of God. Instead, differences create division on earth. Therefore to see all relationships through the lens of being one in Christ should mean that the church couldn't exist *without* Jews and Gentiles, slave and free, male or female *and* shouldn't be divided *because* of Jews and Gentiles, slave and free, male and female.

That was the main problem in Paul's day, especially in a place like Corinth. His converts were divided by ethnicity, by status and perhaps even by gender; it was evident by the house groups they joined (1 Cor 1:12). Birds of a feather tend to flock together. The Jews met in one house, claiming "Cephas" (Peter's Aramaic name) as their leader. High-status Gentiles, those of noble birth (1 Cor 1:26), met together under the direct leadership of Christ—they needed no human leader! The "wise" claimed Apollos, probably because of his speaking skills; others were loyal to Paul—they were probably the riff-raff, the common merchants, the weak and shameful and poor (which is the way Paul characterized himself, 1 Cor 4:10-13). Indeed, when they came together as "the church," it revealed how divided they were—that they were not one people, one family, one body (1 Cor 11:18-19). According to Paul, these divisions (*schismata*, from which we get the word "schism") were factions (*haireseis*, from which we get the word "heresy") that threatened to destroy the work of God. *God* had put them together, arranging the body of Christ with Jews and Greeks, rich and poor, strong and weak, so that there would be *no divisions* (1 Cor 12:24-25). They were supposed to realize how much they needed each other, like a body needs hands and feet. Indeed, to separate the body into different parts would be just as foolish and unhealthy as to dismember a human body, tearing it limb from limb (1 Cor 12:14-18). It was heresy. It was unholy. The Lord's day was supposed to be a time to celebrate what God had joined together; they were buried with Christ. Instead, the body of Christ in Corinth looked more like a hacked up corpse, with body parts strewn all over town.

Now we see why Paul keeps bringing up baptism throughout his letter to the Corinthians. When he first writes about the factions in Corinth, he implies it has something to do with the fact that they have misunderstood the significance of baptism (1 Cor 1:13-17). Isn't it ironic that—since Paul saw the rite as a way of illustrating their unity—the Corinthians used baptism as a benchmark to distinguish the differences among them? Divisions in Corinth were so bad that they were taking each other to court to settle disagreements. To Paul, this was B.C. behavior: "This is what you used to be. But you were *washed*, you were sanctified, you were justified in the name of the Lord Jesus Christ and in the Spirit of our God" (1 Cor 6:11). Even when they worshiped God they were divided (1 Cor 11:17–14:40). Thus, in the middle of this lengthy argument about spiritual gifts, Paul uses his favorite term to describe the church, the "body of Christ," in order to remind the Corinthians of what happened to them when they were baptized:

> For just as the body is one and has many members, and all the members of the body, though many, are one body, so it is with Christ. For in the one Spirit we were all baptized into one body—Jews or Greeks, slaves or free—and we were all made to drink of one Spirit.
>
> Indeed, the body does not consist of one member but many. (1 Cor 12:12-14)

Bodies—whether Jews or Greeks, slaves or free—were baptized into one body. The transformation was supposed to be evident when they gathered as one church. What divided them in the world—ethnicity, economics, gender—had been united in Christ. The problem, of course, was that the church in Corinth looked more like the world than a sneak preview of heaven.

## One God, One Body

Sometimes the world appears more unified than the church. My wife recorded the closing ceremony of the Vancouver Olympic games, wanting me to see the comedic routine accompanying the presentation of the Olympic torch. But what caught my eye was the ritual celebration that officially closed the winter games of 2010. I said offhandedly, "A visitor from the first-century Mediterranean world would see this and ask, 'What god are you worshiping?'" Indeed, the celebration had all the necessary parts: the fiery altar in the center, the indigenous people in native dress looking like priests, the celebrants parading, songs lifted in praise to the Spirit of the Olympics, the stadium filled with joyous revelers. Talk of sacrifice and the offering of much money would convince any first-century visitor that this god was worthy of veneration. What's fascinating to me is how many of us would never describe the Olympics in religious terms. In fact it would be offensive to most of us to suggest that all of this was nothing more than a modern form of idolatry. Perhaps it would take a visitor from the first-century to point out the obvious. Then again, maybe a first-century visitor like Paul would have mistaken the gathering as the church. Indeed, the Olympic scene looked like it came straight out of Revelation 4–5—people of every tribe, tongue and nation gathered for one purpose. I can imagine Paul saying as he watched television that night, "If the 'Olympic Spirit' can attract such a unified crowd, how much more should the Holy Spirit draw a people of every tribe, tongue and nation together to worship the one, true God?"

Martin Luther King Jr. has often been quoted as saying: "Sunday morning is the most segregated hour of the week." At the time he was referring to the problem of a church divided ethnically. For the most part the color of our skin determines where we worship. What's so sad is how little things have changed in half a century. Indeed, it may be safe to say that the church is even more divided now than it was then— especially if you believe the signs. I have the privilege of speaking in many churches; most of the time the congregation meets in a building that's within driving distance. When I drive to speak on Sunday mornings, I pass by many church buildings and their signs. It seems like, in the quest of distinctive identity, there's an unspoken contest going on. Many churches claim to be "first"; others identify with famous saints (like Paul or Peter) or important places (like Gethsemane or Calvary). Some call themselves an "assembly," others a "community." Then I can't help but notice the eye-catching marquees, "New Life Church" or "The Truth Church"—as if these groups were advertising the ultimate pay-off. All along my heart is strangely grieved and warmed all at the same time. On the one hand, I think of all the places Christ believers are gathering for worship. The church is spread across the world like a net. No one can travel any distance in our country without seeing the signs. On the other hand, I wonder how we could call ourselves "one church" when we're so obviously divided—doesn't the competition reveal bias? "You need to worship with us because we're better than the rest!" I wish I could put a moratorium on all church signs. In fact, wouldn't it be great if *all* churches had the exact same sign? Then the unmistakable impression travelers would get would be: "Look. The church meets there . . . and there . . . and there . . . even there."

Of course, I'm not so naive to think that signs are the whole problem. And neither was Paul. To be sure the Corinthian slogans, "we're of Paul" and "we belong to Peter" revealed divisions within the body of Christ. And it wasn't only the Corinthian house churches that had a hard time getting along with each other. Visitors to Corinth from other cities—even Jerusalem—had particular ways of doing the gospel that were foreign to Paul and his converts. Sometimes Paul encouraged the Corinthians to receive them as family (2 Cor 8:16-24). Other times he singled out the visitors as interlopers who were distorting the "truth of the gospel" (1 Cor 11:3-15). Therefore some of us who love our signs (especially the part that says "Baptist" or "Presbyterian") might say, "See there? Even Paul warned his churches about the false teachers who perverted his gospel. So we are imitating Paul when we separate ourselves from the heretical teachings of other denominations." Yes, Paul warned his converts about false teaching—his letters are filled with such instructions. But if we are genuinely going to imitate Paul in this matter, let's look more carefully at what he found so offensive about these visitors who were preaching another Jesus (2 Cor 11:4).

According to Paul these "foreign" missionaries were "boasting according to the flesh" (2 Cor 11:18 NASB). Indeed, they were claiming to be superior apostles—greater than Paul!—due to their ethnicity (2 Cor 11:22) and status (2 Cor 5:12; 10:12; 11:5-12, 20). Because they were Jews (with letters of commendation probably from Jerusalem) they acted as though they were superior to the Corinthian Gentiles. Because they were impressive preachers, they said they were superior apostles compared to Paul. And, even worse, because they claimed this superior status "according to the flesh," the Corinthians bowed down to them as if *they* (as well as Paul) were inferior to these "super-apostles" (2 Cor 12:11). The icing on the cake was when Paul's converts paid money to these men for their services (2 Cor 11:7). Paul refused to accept payment for preaching the gospel to the Corinthians (1 Cor 9:11-18), and they despised him for it (2 Cor 12:13-18)! Why? Because at this very time Paul was trying to collect money from the Corinthians (as well as other churches) for impoverished *Jewish Christians in Jerusalem!* "See?" the Corinthians could have said, "Even Paul acts like these super-apostles deserve royal treatment. Even he is collecting money for them." But Paul didn't see it that way at all. Because they emphasized their superior status "according to the flesh," Paul accused these super-apostles of subverting the heart of the gospel: "In Christ there is neither Jew nor Gentile!" In other words these men were preaching "another Jesus," a "Christ according to the flesh" (2 Cor 5:16)—certainly not Christ according to the Spirit. For the Spirit unites what the flesh divides. Indeed, Paul tried to convince his converts to imitate him and "recognize no one according to the flesh" (2 Cor 5:16 NASB). To do otherwise would be to preach and practice *another* gospel.

That's why Paul kept reminding his converts of their common baptism: they shared one Spirit. Paul kept proclaiming their common faith: they worshiped one God. Paul kept insisting on their common confession: Jesus is Lord. Paul could speak of one church with many members (what we would call "diversity") because he confessed one God, one Lord, one Spirit (what we would call a "trinitarian" faith). In fact scholars hear echoes of trinitarian faith in the baptismal confessions of early Christians—what the baptized said to the crowd gathered to witness the water ritual. The apostle was probably including baptismal confessions when he reminded the Corinthians that "no one can say, 'Jesus is Lord' except by the Holy Spirit" (1 Cor 12:3), setting up his argument regarding the significance of baptism (1 Cor 12:4-13). Some converts may have shouted out, "Abba," as they were brought up out of the water—a moment that pictured their "adoption" as sons and daughters (Gal 4:6). Some scholars suggest that during the ritual the baptizer may have pronounced: "Sleeper, awake! Rise from the dead, and Christ will shine on you" (Eph 5:14).[7] These confessions reveal as much about the baptized as they do about God. Baptism is theological and ecclesiological. Indeed, Paul wanted his converts to realize that when we make statements about God we're also talking about ourselves. God is one; we are one. The Spirit is poured out on all flesh; we will judge no man according to the flesh. Buried with Christ in baptism, we are all awakened to new life in him.

Paul wouldn't promote a particular church or denomination (even though some church signs say, "St. Paul's Methodist" or "St Paul's Episcopal"). He would probably feel compelled to remind us that no congregation has more of the Holy Spirit than another. He would say that no one can claim to be God's best church. That's because, whether we admit it or not, we are *all* the church. The lesson Paul wanted the Corinthians to learn was rather simple: it didn't matter where your house church met or who attended your house church. When you put all the house churches together in Corinth, only *together* do they reveal the body of Christ. Status has nothing to do with importance. Sure, certain spiritual gifts might be more predominant here or there; certain individuals may operate with higher-profile gifts compared to others. But God arranged the different members of the body—each with different gifts—for the good of everyone, the entire church in Corinth (1 Cor 12:4-30). In fact he wanted them to value each other, acknowledging how much they needed each other in order to be the body of Christ for each other and the world. But the Corinthian house churches were too busy competing with each other—contests that showed up especially when they met together for their so-called love feasts—to notice the damage they were doing to the church and the world. They ap-

peared as though they were gathering more to reveal their differences
than their common faith (1 Cor 11:17-20). "When you come together it
is not for the better but for the worse" (1 Cor 11:17)—a rather incrimi-
nating thing for Paul to say about Christians.

Would Paul say the same is true today? When we gather to worship
God in our different buildings is it as much to reveal our differences as
our common faith? When different churches gather as one—especially
under the banner of one denomination—is it for the better or the worse?
The truth of the matter is: we are all baptized by one Spirit; we are all
buried in Christ; we are all children of God. In fact the body of Christ
would be incomplete without Pentecostals, evangelicals, mainline Protestants, Catholics and Anglicans. We tend to limit the diverse gifting
of the Spirit within our own congregations. Perhaps the diversity of the
gifts of the Holy Spirit is more evident when we cross denominational
lines, when we consider the *whole* church. Pentecostals have much to
teach all of us about the Holy Spirit. Evangelicals need to share their
zeal for evangelism with all of us. Mainline Protestants can help all of
us rediscover the great doctrines of our faith. Catholics can teach all of
us how to live the crucified life, the *imitatio Christi*. Anglicans need to
remind us all that church is community, a parish of sharing life together. Indeed, maybe we should take to heart Paul's instruction to the
segregated Corinthian house churches and celebrate *all* spiritual gifts,
truly believing that God has so arranged the body of Christ—Pentecostals, mainline Protestants, evangelicals, Catholics, Anglicans—for
the common good of every single one of us. Yes, we're different. And
those differences should reveal how much we need each other. After
all, we are family.

Paul never talks about his immediate family in his letters. As far as
we can tell, he never mentions his parents or his brothers or sisters if he
had them; he never refers to his grandparents, aunts, uncles, nephews
or nieces. That is startling to me. That's because, like all of us, I can't
help but talk about my family. They come up in daily conversation all
the time. However, I rarely talk about our church. And predictably,
when I do, it normally has something to do with what's happening on
Sundays—the worship service, different programs, Sunday school

classes, musical events. I never think about what my church is doing on Monday, or Tuesday, or any other day of the week (unless there is a special activity). In other words, I see the world through the eyes of my family—"wonder how the day is going for Sheri"—and church is ancillary to my life, something that supports my life, my family. And many churches gladly assume this assigned role; they even market themselves as "family friendly."

Paul would have us view things the other way around. To him church is family, a people that consumes our daily thoughts and conversations. What if we saw the world like he did? What if we acted as if church were family? What if we talked about members as if they were our brothers and sisters? What if the welfare of the church were the most important concern in our lives—more than our work, more than our friends, more than our spouses or children or parents? In other words, what if we were to imitate Paul? What would that look like today? Some of us might be tempted to dismiss the idea as "cultic." But then again, if church is supposed to be more than a time and a place, then what are we supposed to do? If church is our family, how should that affect our everyday lives? If Paul, the apostle to Gentiles, is our father in the faith, then how should we behave as his children? Perhaps we could start by teaching our children a new hand game. Rather than relying on the hands of one person to picture the church, we need to join hands with one another and say, "Here's the church; it is our family. There are no doors because we are one people."

> Greet Andronicus and Junia, my relatives who were in prison with me; they are prominent among the apostles, and they were in Christ before I was. Greet Ampliatus, my beloved in the Lord. Greet Urbanus, our co-worker in Christ, and my beloved Stachys. Greet Apelles, who is approved in Christ. Greet those who belong to the family of Aristobulus. Greet my relative Herodion. Greet those in the Lord who belong to the family of Narcissus. Greet those workers in the Lord, Tryphaena and Tryphosa. Greet the beloved Persis, who has worked hard in the Lord. Greet Rufus, chosen in the Lord; and greet his mother—a mother to me also.

> St. Paul, from Corinth, to his family in Rome (Rom 16:7-13)

# 6

# Common Bonds

*Worship as Corporate Reality*

⁂

**WE NEED EACH OTHER** to worship God. I cannot worship God by myself.

I slipped into the memorial service just before it started at 10:30 in the morning. Sitting on the back row was a retired professor from the university where I teach. We were both there to mourn the death of his friend, our colleague, my former professor. "May I join you?" I whispered. "Yes, but I may need to leave a little early," he said. A very distinguished gentlemen, "Dr. Cline" was sitting alone because his wife has Alzheimer's disease. For the last ten years, he has visited her every day—especially during breakfast, lunch and dinner. She can't feed herself; she doesn't talk. There may be faint signs of recognition in her eyes. But for the most part her husband of more than forty years is a complete stranger to her—a woman who can't remember.

During the memorial service, we heard testimony of a life well lived. Common words kept appearing in the eulogy: patience, gentleness, kindness, faithfulness. As we were remembering the deceased, I couldn't help but think about the man sitting next to me . . . and my future. I'm getting to the age where I'm surrounded by my past and future all at the same time. We have new faculty members, young men just beginning their careers and family. When I see their "little ones" visit daddy in his office, it brings back fond memories of when Sheri and I were starting our careers—balancing work and the daily demands of taking care of our children. Oh the joy! I've also been attending several funerals lately; some of my professors have died. It's hard to put into words the grief of hearing the significance of a person who meant so much to you reduced to a few words. Once the service was over, I couldn't help but say to myself, "Is that it? Is that all we have to say? This is all that we could remember? He was so much more than that!"—all the while thinking about my own future.

Before the end of the funeral service the congregation joined in singing the great hymn—one of my favorites—"Great Is Thy Faithfulness." Singing the song I know by heart, Dr. Cline offered to share the hymnal with me. There we stood, each man holding half of the book and singing of God's faithfulness. All of the sudden I was overcome with emotion when we sang the line "summer and winter, and springtime and harvest." I had sung that line hundreds of times before. But now, thinking about this faithful husband in the winter season of his life, the song meant much more. Dr. Cline sang the bass line with resolve, but I could barely "join with all nature in manifold witness" to God's great faithfulness. My emotions had gotten the best of me. Once the song was over I embraced the unsuspecting man and whispered in his ear, "Dr. Cline, you are a blessing to me," after which he bowed his head in somber reflection. Then he checked his watch, asked to be excused and left the service. It was 11:30, and at that moment, I pictured a woman being fed by a man she couldn't remember, and then I saw—I remembered—God's faithfulness to me.

I've always been intrigued by Paul's idea that when we worship God we're "speaking to one another in psalms, hymns, and spiritual songs" (Eph 5:19 NASB). Even though worship is supposed to be directed toward God, Paul claimed there was a "horizontal" aspect, a social significance to our worship of God. And in certain respects I identify with Paul's sentiment. Many times during a congregational hymn, I find myself looking around at people as we sing. I take in the peculiar site of everyone saying the same thing—no small miracle, especially when it comes to religious convictions. Ask a group of people, "What do you believe about God?" and the responses are endless. Yet when we sing—all saying the same thing about God, "Holy, holy, holy, Lord God

Almighty"—it seems we're in complete agreement. It also appears that our songs are directed to no one in particular. Some watch the worship leader; others cast their gaze on common Christian symbols. Some close their eyes; others watch the choir—all the while I'm looking around at all of these people mouthing the same words. Sometimes I wonder, "Why are we doing this? Compared to everyday experiences, this is a rather odd thing to do."

The earliest reputation of the church, the first things Christians were known for were hospitality (a topic we will take up in chapter eight) and their strange way of worship. Eighty years after the death of Christ, Pliny the Younger (the Roman governor of Bithynia) complained to Caesar about a growing menace: Christians who assembled on Sunday in order to sing together a hymn to Christ as if they were singing to a god.[1] Even back then the practice seemed odd. Of course in those days singing praise to human rulers was a common occurrence; Caesar was more than willing to receive such accolades. And songs of praise were offered in temples to gods all over the empire. But to gather in a room (not a temple!) without an idol (where is the god?) and sing to one another as offering praise to God was considered bizarre. And especially to Pliny, *what* these Christians were singing was even more peculiar.

## Singing Is Subversive

To worship a man crucified by the Romans was sinister behavior according to imperial rulers. Only great men like Caesar were enrolled as gods after they died. But a man who died on a cross? Such a fate was the opposite end of a great life. Only a fool would worship such a fool— a rebel who dared to resist Roman power. In fact the cross was supposed to be a deterrent, a horrible death reserved only for those who committed treason. Rome's final verdict should have put enough fear into the heart of any reasonable person not to make the same mistake. Imagine Pliny's confusion when he hears that some Gentiles in his province are gathering on a certain day to worship a Jewish messiah who was crucified—just one man among thousands who were put to death by Rome. No wonder Pliny was suspicious of these people; it must have seemed to him like they had lost their minds.

Magistrates said the same thing about Paul (Acts 26:24). The apostle was always getting into trouble with Roman rulers because he declared Jesus as Lord—a very foolish thing to do in the face of Roman power. Indeed, claiming "Jesus is Lord" was the same as saying "Caesar is a fool." Rome had made a huge mistake by crucifying Christ; but God corrected Rome's mistake by raising Jesus from the dead. Despite Paul's best efforts of convincing Festus of the "truth of the gospel" the Roman prefect dismissed the story as the tale of a madman. It must have been Paul's favorite part of the story, "Jesus is coming again," that especially sounded like a foolish man offering an empty threat: Christ would return soon to deal out rewards and retribution. (A few years later, the same threat would be made against Nero's enemies. Rumor had it that Caesar Nero would return one day from the east; having cheated death, he would be accompanied by a massive army from Persia—Rome's most feared enemy—to exact revenge against his assassins and the citizens of Rome. Most, however, dismissed the rumor as foolish nonsense.) Once Festus shipped Paul off to Rome to be tried by Caesar, the apostle found himself in a Roman prison, writing letters to his converts and persistently claiming the lordship of Christ. Defiantly he quoted lines from a hymn sung by the first Christians—a song that declared Christ's victory over *all* enemies:

> He who was in the form of God
> did not regard equality with God
> as something to be held onto,
> but emptied himself
> taking the form of a slave,
> born in the likeness of men;
> And being found as a man
> he humbled himself
> becoming obedient to death
> (even death on a cross).
>
> Therefore God raised him up
> and gave him the name

above every name
so that, at the name of Jesus,
every knee should bow
in heaven and on earth and under the earth
and every tongue should say the same thing:
"Jesus is Christ and Lord
to the Glory of God the Father." (Phil 2:6-11, my translation)

Paul was reminding the Philippians (*Roman* colonists) of the significance of the lyrics they sang during worship—a claim that one day *every* tongue would sing the same song, even Caesar.[2] I can imagine a smile breaking out across the faces of the Philippians—did they relish the thought?—when they sang the line, "Every knee should bow . . . and every tongue should say the same thing." What a day that will be when even the emperor has to say, "Jesus is Lord."

Yet, I'm troubled by the idea that one day God will force everyone to sing the same song. That's because singing must come from the heart to be a song. It can't be compulsory. You can't force someone to sing. And no one knew that better than the Jewish people—especially the author of Psalm 137. Six hundred years before Paul's imprisonment, in the aftermath of the destruction of Jerusalem, the psalmist talks about how the Jewish people hung their harps in the tree limbs when they got to Babylon. Remembering what they lost (everything!), all they could do was sit down and cry. Their captors goaded them, "Sing us one of the songs of Zion!" No doubt, when the Babylonian army surrounded the holy city, the people must have offered songs of loud praise, counting on God Almighty to save them. As Nebuchadnezzar's forces prepared to sack Jerusalem, perhaps they heard a psalm like this one rising from within the walls:

God is in the midst of the city; it shall not be moved;
God will help it when the morning dawns. (Ps 46:5)

But the reality of the morning brought death and destruction to Jerusalem. So once it was all over and the ruin of war was painfully obvious, the Babylonians taunted the vanquished, wanting to rub their noses in the obvious defeat of YHWH: "Sing us one of those songs about your Almighty God and the strong tower of Zion!"—to which the psalmist cries out, "How could we sing the LORD's song in a foreign land?" Of course the irony is palpable: this is a song about why they refused to sing. It must have sounded odd to their captors, singing a song about why they can't sing anymore. But to the exiles, those who sang the unsingable song, it made perfect sense because the Jews were used to singing subversive songs. It was in their worship DNA.

Everyone knows that songs of praise are supposed to build up God's reputation as good and great. But consider how many psalms are laments, songs of complaint to God. Indeed, complaining was an act of worship—something the Almighty God inspired—because the Psalms are filled with lines like "Why have You abandoned us, God?" and "Why don't you listen when we cry for help?" and "Where are you?" This amazes me. God didn't merely tolerate Israel's frustration as they whined and fussed about how YHWH let them down, but he also *inspired* them to sing these songs; after all, these songs became their Scripture. I think it says as much about Israel as it does about God. Israel didn't want songs that merely praised God for the good times, as if his ego were so fragile that he couldn't handle the truth. They told him what they thought of him regardless of their circumstances. They knew he could handle it. In fact they believed he wanted to hear it because worshipful complaint revealed how big they believed their God really was. The only way to worship the Almighty God was to be honest with him, sing a song that actually came from the heart, tell him the truth. Only a small god couldn't handle the truth.

Sometimes it feels like we Christians worship a very small god. Our praise is carefully crafted to sing only about the good things that God has done. But sometimes it's not very honest. What happens when your world comes crashing down? What happens when Babylon takes over Jerusalem? When God's apostle is thrown into prison? When evil seems to run amok, when the godless have run of the place, when death steals away the saint who did nothing more than give his whole life to God? It makes me angry. It makes me want to tell God what I really think. The last thing I want to do is sing a song about how everything is fine; nothing is wrong; we're all okay. Well, sometimes I'm not okay.

Sometimes I can barely drag my heart into a worship service and sing about our God Almighty, especially when it feels like he let me down. "Why did You let this happen? I thought You loved my friend. He was the best Christian I've ever known. Now his wife and children must go on without him. Why did he have to suffer so? The indignity, the pain, the lingering death. It seems like you didn't care for him at all. You let us down." I wish I had a song to sing about that.

I think that's exactly what Caesar will do on the last day. He will complain to God about the end of his world because Jesus is Lord and Caesar is not. Savor the thought! Our songs of praise will be his song of complaint. Jesus is Lord and we are not. This never changes. What God has done he will do again—whether we like it or not. Don't we all need to be reminded of that, especially when we worship God? Songs of praise and songs of complaint. What God has done is what God will do. The exalted will be humbled and the humbled will be exalted. Some will complain about it and others will praise God for it. And it will *all* be worship to the glory of God our Father *because* a crucified Christ is Lord.

That is what makes Israel's worship so compelling. Singing was an act of remembering the past and claiming the future all at the same time. Notice how often—especially in their songs of complaint—the psalmist recites what God has done, as if both YHWH and Israel needed to be reminded of the greatness and goodness of God. Indeed, Israel knew that if they ever forgot their songs, they would forget their history:

> If I forget you, O Jerusalem,
>     let my right hand wither!
> Let my tongue cling to the roof of my mouth,
>     if I do not remember you. (Ps 137:5-6)

Singing was remembering. But also notice how, in the midst of Israel's sorrow, the psalmist calls on God to bring about a glorious future— that the past should be an indication of what will happen. When they sang about the good old days, they were making claims about their future. That's because they believed God never changes. God loved

Israel. He would never give up on them. Who he was defines who he will always be. What he did for Israel ensured what he would do. So their worship of God would never be confined by present circumstances because God is eternal. The people of Israel were making claims for themselves as well as for YHWH. He was their God and they were his people. And nothing would change that.

That's what Paul wanted his converts to see. When they gathered to sing psalms, they were claiming their history too. That's because Paul believed his Gentile converts were grafted into the tree of Israel (Rom 11:17-24). So when they sang the line "We are being killed all day long, and accounted as sheep for the slaughter" (Ps 44:22), they were singing about themselves. Or when they sang, "Blessed be the Lord, who daily bears us up; God is our salvation. Our God is a God of salvation, and to GOD, the Lord, belongs escape from death" (Ps 68:19-20), they were claiming the gospel of Israel's hope as their own. Indeed, Paul makes it very plain that Israel's songs belonged to his converts as well:

"Blessed are those whose iniquities are forgiven,
    and whose sins are covered;
blessed is the one against whom the Lord will not reckon sin."

Is this blessedness, then, pronounced only on the circumcised, or also on the uncircumcised? (Rom 4:7-9)

When the Gentiles sang these psalms to God, they were singing to each other, talking to each other, reminding each other, remembering what God had done for them. And when they read from Israel's scripture, they were hearing the word of the Lord as if he were speaking to them too: "As I live, says the Lord, every knee shall bow to me, and every tongue shall give praise to God" (Is 45:23, as quoted by Paul in Rom 14:11). This is what Paul meant when he encouraged his Ephesian converts to speak to each other in psalms, hymns and spiritual songs (Eph 5:19). Their singing was subversive. By singing these songs these Gentiles were claiming they were the Israel of God. By singing these songs, these Roman colonists were claiming the crucified man was their Lord. By singing these songs their worship became their reality—

they were one people, both Jews and Gentiles, slave and free, men and women—and the walls that divided them came tumbling down:

> So then, *remember* that at one time you Gentiles by birth, called "the uncircumcision" by those who are called "the circumcision"—a physical circumcision made in the flesh by human hands—*remember* that you were at that time without Christ, being aliens from the commonwealth of Israel, and strangers to the covenants of promise, having no hope and without God in the world. But now in Christ Jesus you who once were far off have been brought near by the blood of Christ. For he is our peace; in his flesh he has made both groups into one and has broken down the dividing wall, that is, the hostility between us. (Eph 2:11-14, italics added)

In song, Paul's Gentile converts needed to be reminded of their identity. In song, Paul's Gentile converts needed to be reminded of their history. In song, Paul's Gentile converts needed to be reminded of what God had done through Christ Jesus. They were speaking to one another in worship. In fact, when they were singing about the work of Christ, they were singing about themselves: "He is our peace, who has broken down every wall." No more ethnic hatred. No more "us versus them." No more "haves and have-nots." No more aliens and citizens. These people were singing a new song, for songs about Christ sung by his people in worship directed to the God of Israel made peace where there was no peace.

## Let Us Break Bread Together

When we sang "Negro spirituals" during worship services when I was a child, I always felt a bit uncomfortable. First of all a bunch of white people trying to sing soulful music never sounded good to me. It always felt constrained, like we were trying to do something we couldn't do, or hold back something that couldn't be tamed. (I could always tell the difference when I would hear Negro spirituals sung by the people who composed them—they would set free the beat that was embedded in the song, released to the rhythms we tried to harness.) I also didn't care for the term "Negro spiritual" printed on the bottom of the page in the hymnal. Growing up in southern California in the 1960s, I knew it was wrong to use any form of the word; "Negro" was just one step away from the curse word nobody should use. But what bothered me more than all of that, every time I would hear these songs, I would visualize black slaves singing them in the presence of their white masters. The sentiment behind their words haunted me:

> Let us break bread together on our knees,
> Let us break bread together on our knees;
> When I fall on my knees,
> With my face to the rising sun,
> O Lord, have mercy on me.

Every time we sang this song I would see a black man forced to his knees early in the morning, performing some menial task at the command of his overlord. Then I would marvel over the invitation extended—it was a thoroughly Christian image—of the black man inviting his white brother to join him in humble adoration of the God who gave both of them this new day. I was strangely warmed and sickened to my stomach all at the same time. Looking around at our mostly white congregation, I felt like a hypocrite singing the song. Perhaps the imagination of a grade-school boy was working overtime, but I always read between the lines and saw these images while we tried to sing those songs. We were singing their songs as if they were our songs (they were supposed to be!), and it didn't feel right.

I wonder if Paul's converts (especially Roman citizens) felt uncomfortable singing Israel's songs—especially since Jews in certain regions of the empire were persecuted by their Gentile neighbors. Or were Jewish Christians jealous of their Scripture, offended when Gentiles handled the Psalter in worship, especially if they were women? Jews were pretty fanatical about who could handle their sacred texts. The way the rabbis saw it, God gave commandments to men, not women (Gen 2:16-17). God gave the law to Israel, not Gentiles (Deut 5:1-4). Indeed, Israel's worship was a segregated service, where priests had access to the inner sanctuary, roped off from the rest of the Jews, men were separated from the women and children, and the court of the Gentiles (the front porch of God's temple—"Welcome, everyone! But you can't go in") was

the farthest removed from the holy of holies. But what the law divided
was supposed to be united in Christ according to Paul (Eph 2:14-22).
The church, a new holy temple, was built by Christ—with his own
flesh and blood he took away the hatred of the cross and turned it into
a gathering point, uniting two people into one. But that was easier said
than done. Can you imagine how difficult it must have been for Jews to
sit down next to Gentiles and worship God? Or for Jewish Christians
to see Gentile women handle the sacred Scriptures? Or for Roman
Christians to hear their Jewish "brothers and sisters" sing certain psalms
(perhaps with great bravado since "Babylon" was the nickname Jews
had given to Rome)?

> O daughter Babylon, you devastator!
>     Happy shall they be who pay you back
>     what you have done to us!
> Happy shall they be who take your little ones
>     and dash them against the rock! (Ps 137:8-9)

Perhaps it's no wonder, especially in cities like Rome and Corinth, that
Jewish Christians didn't gather with Gentiles nor did the social elite
worship with slaves in the poor part of town.[3]

But that didn't stop Paul from encouraging his converts to come together to worship God. Isn't it fascinating that Paul presumed the different house churches would come together to worship, especially when
they shared the Lord's Supper? He never entertained the idea that each
group would be content to keep to themselves, to observe the Lord's
Table among their own kind. They had to come together for Communion. He kept telling them that they needed each other, that they belonged together—that Jews needed to hear Gentiles praise the God of
Israel and that Gentiles needed to hear Jews invite them to join in worship. And it should come as no surprise that Paul quotes the Psalter to
make his point (Rom 15:7-12). Paul counted on the joyful reunion of
these house churches, imploring the Roman Christians to "greet one
another with a holy kiss" (Rom 16:16) when they came together. But
when the Corinthians gathered in one place for their "joint worship
service," they needed to do more than offer the kiss of hospitality. In

fact their total lack of *Christian* hospitality had created a huge problem in Corinth. And of all places, it was at the Lord's Table where their inhospitable behavior showed up the most.

Early Christian worship was modeled after Sabbath services of the synagogue. They offered prayers and recited Scriptures, teachers offered comments about the readings of the day, and they intoned songs of praise. (Some scholars question whether synagogue worship included singing—but what about the Psalter?) What made the Christian version of these weekly services unique was the addition of a meal. In fact the Jewish people were known for refusing to eat on the Sabbath; their pagan neighbors mistook their abstaining from cooking as fasting. In quite the opposite direction early Christians were known for their "love feasts," a celebration of food and drink on their day of worship. In a city like Corinth, where there were several house churches, it would take a large house to accommodate the entire group when they gathered for Communion. And according to Roman custom (Corinth was a Roman colony), the owner of the house was expected to provide the meal. This is where the trouble began.

There are certain dynamics of church life in the first-century world that are lost on us simply because most Western Christians do not meet in homes to worship God. Domestic customs were a necessary part of religious life for Christians in Paul's day. For example, imagine how the social rules that governed behavior between a husband and wife were blurred when their private domicile was turned into a "public" gathering and their marital relationship was redefined as "brother and sister." The simple issue of whether a wife should cover her head (which was expected of her when she went outside) and keep quiet in the church (when it was perfectly acceptable for her to speak to her husband in her own home) must have created significant problems for Paul's converts (see 1 Cor 11:1-16; 14:26-40). In both cases the honor of her husband was at stake. And even though Paul was the first to emphasize that there is neither male/husband nor female/wife in the body of Christ, the apostle deferred to the husbands, requiring wives to subvert domestic practices by covering their heads and not talking to their husbands in their own homes. They could pray (talk to God) and prophesy (talk to the church) but only with veiled heads. In this case, Paul protected the honor of the husbands when the Corinthians gathered for worship. But when it came to the wealthy, Paul changed the rules and expected patrons to give up their claims to honor, especially in their own homes, because their house had become a synagogue and their family had become a church.[4]

It was customary for patrons to host meals in their homes in order to maintain contact with their clients, who were obliged to promote the honor of their "family father." The meal was held in the back part of the house, the table situated on a raised floor, where the best portions of food and the finest wine were served to the more honorable members (men only!), who were invited to the high table to eat with the patron. The rest of the clients were served smaller portions and cheap wine as they sat at tables in the front of the house or stood outside in the courtyard. Of course the lowest members of the household—the slaves—served the meal to family members and clients. Once the meal was over and the patron left the house with his entourage of clients (as many as two dozen persons), the slaves ate the leftovers. It is quite apparent that the Corinthians were following these social customs when they met for their love feasts (1 Cor 11:17-34)—this was proper hospitality according to the Roman way—and it made Paul very angry.

Picture the scene: mostly poor, low-status Christians are filing into the house of a wealthy man (1 Cor 1:26). Inside they find fifty men and women standing in the courtyard, greeting, talking, waiting for the meal to begin. Then the patron begins the meal by taking his seat at the high table, where male members of his family and other high-status friends take their rightful place and join him. The host offers a blessing, thanking God for the bread and the wine—the body and blood of Christ. Christian slaves begin to serve the food and wine. The high table guests have the best portions of food placed before them; their cups are filled to the brim with superb wine. The rest of the group watches the spectacle from the family room, adjacent to the dining room with the raised floor. Once the high table is nearly finished, the rest of the group is served—some are seated, most are standing and consuming small portions of food and wine. Once the meal is over the slaves clear off the tables and eat the scraps of bread and drink what is strained from the dregs. Afterward, they read Scriptures and sing psalms—eating and drinking, praying and singing—all to the glory of God. But according to Paul this was not for the glory of God but for the honor of men; they were eating and drinking judgment against themselves (1 Cor 11:29):

> When you come together, it is not really to eat the Lord's supper. For when the time comes to eat, each of you goes ahead with your own supper, and one goes hungry and another becomes drunk. What! Do you not have homes to eat and drink in? Or do you show contempt for the church of God and humiliate those who have nothing? What should I say to you? Should I commend you? In this matter I do not commend you! (1 Cor 11:20-22)

Corinthian ways had eclipsed Christian practice when it came to sharing table. Even though proper acts of Roman hospitality were shown to those who deserved it, by their actions the Corinthians had canceled out the significance of the meal, having set aside the very essence of hospitality embedded in the Lord's Supper. The way they celebrated communion revealed how poorly they understood themselves (one body) as well as the meaning of the feast (his death for all).[5] According to Paul they had not "judged the body rightly" and were consequently eating the bread and drinking the cup in an "unworthy manner"; that is, ironically in their attempts to show honor they were observing the Lord's Supper in a dishonorable way (1 Cor 11:27). This was why, according to Paul, some of their members had experienced the judgment of God—sickness and death (1 Cor 11:30). This is where, as scholars point out, Paul's words have been grossly misunderstood. Paul wasn't saying that Christians must confess their sin—get right with God—to become "worthy" to partake of the supper. (Indeed, all of us come to the Lord's Table because we are *unworthy* sinners!) When Paul wrote, "For all who eat and drink without discerning *the body*, eat and drink judgment against *themselves*" (1 Cor 11:29), he was talking about the body of Christ. (Notice the plural pronoun is coterminous with "the body.") The way they observed Communion revealed that they had judged the body of Christ wrongly.[6] The Corinthians were acting like some members deserved better treatment at the Lord's Table because they were privileged, more respectable, more desirable. By following their honor code they were actually eating the supper in an "unworthy" or "dishonorable" manner. The elements of Communion (one loaf, one cup, see 1 Cor 10:16-17) should have taught the Corinthians that some members were not more worthy than others—there are no VIPs at the Lord's Table. They all shared one loaf of bread; they all drank from the same cup because they *all* needed the body and blood of Jesus Christ. The ground at the Communion table was supposed to be level; no one had the right to act like the host and raise a toast for the Lord. By serving each other and eating together, they were supposed to memorialize the work of Christ—he died for *all*.

Instead, the way the Corinthians observed the Lord's Supper was to show which members—which house churches—were more important than others (1 Cor 11:18-19). Communion had become a social contest. Paul says, therefore, that when they come together for Communion it is "not for the better but for the worse" (1 Cor 11:17). The incarnation was supposed to be God's ultimate act of hospitality: God became man so that man could dine with God. But the Corinthians had turned the Lord's Table into a country club, where certain members received preferential treatment and others were marginalized. What a horrific irony! The very place where Christians were supposed to see their common confession—we are all sinners who need Christ—had become a method of revealing first- and second-class members, as if some members deserved the supper and others should only get leftovers. Now we see why Paul was so angry. "It's no wonder some of you are sick and dying! God is punishing you because you don't see the body of Christ as it really is: we are one body eating one loaf because we worship one God who offered his one Son for every single one of us" (my paraphrase of 1 Cor 11:17-34).

Some things never change. The *only* thing the Lord gave us to memorialize his sacrifice for us—Communion—proves to be anything but communal. There are certain Baptist churches that will not serve the Lord's Supper to you if you're not a member of their church. Go to most Roman Catholic churches, and the priest will pass over you when it comes time to receive the Eucharist. The reason is the same. We are imitating the Corinthians. We're trying to show which "house churches" are more important than others. "Oh, so you've come to our house, have you? Well, you stand over there while we worship our Lord." So Baptists gather in their Baptist churches in order to have Baptist Communion; Catholics observe the Eucharist for other Catholics. If you think this is a small matter, try to share the table of our Lord at an ecumenical meeting, where the whole church gathers to worship God. You will soon discover what Paul meant when he said, "When you come together, it is not for the better but for the worse." We've made the same mistake as the Corinthians; we are not "discerning the body rightly." So should Paul's warning alarm us? Is this why some of us are "weak and ill, and some have died" (1 Cor 11:30)? No, we know better than that (I say sarcastically): "Sickness and death has nothing to do with sin. People die because they get old."

A nursing home is the place where tales of classic Greek comedy and tragedy are rolled up into one. Occasionally my wife will visit patients at the "old folks" home and see enough in one day to make a woman laugh for hours and cry for days. Having heard many of Sheri's stories during dinner, our family has often said that the nursing home is a sitcom waiting to be written. For example, she told us about the time someone noticed—day after day—that decorations were slowly disappearing from the lower half of the Christmas tree. Come to find out, the resident "kleptomaniac" (an elderly man with brain atrophy) had stuffed the ornaments in his pajamas and wheeled the contraband back to his room. His dresser drawer was packed full not only with Christmas ornaments but also Thanksgiving, Halloween and Fourth of July decorations. The image of the elderly gentlemen with Christmas ornaments stuffed in his pants "jingling all the way" down the hallway in his wheelchair gave us quite a laugh that night as we sat around our family table.

At other times Sheri recounts more poignant moments at the nursing home. Like the time she stepped inside on a winter Sunday morning. Most of the residents were gathered around the piano in the common room listening to an elderly woman play church hymns. The lady, who was well into her seventies, said to my wife, "I love coming to play for these *old* people. They really seem to appreciate the songs." Sheri had noticed the same, all of them nodding their heads to the beat, some of the singing, many humming the tune. Even the patients with advanced Alzheimer's seemed to brighten up, almost as if they were fully present in worship of the God they once served so faithfully. Then one of the local ministers served Communion to this makeshift congregation, which represented many denominations: Baptists, Methodists, Episcopalians, Assemblies of God, perhaps even Catholics and members of no particular denomination. The preacher read from Scripture, prayed and then distributed the elements without fanfare. There was no commotion. No objection. Slowly but surely they ate the bread and drank from the cup. Holy Communion. The body of Christ. A gathering of saints knocking on heaven's door.

When I'm served Communion, I don't think about the senior citizens down the road celebrating the Eucharist in wheelchairs. I don't remember that Methodists and Catholics and Pentecostals are eating from the same table that day. I don't think about believers in South Africa or South America, Korea or Kenya sharing Communion with me. I don't think about the body of Christ all over the world partaking of the Lord's Supper. Rather, when I'm given the broken piece of bread and hold it in my hands, I think about my sin. He was broken because of my sin, our sin. When I drink from the cup, I think about his sacrifice. He died for me, for every one of us. So I open my mouth, receive what is given and try to remember what God has done for me, for us. I need to be fed. I need to be reminded. I need to hear someone say, "The body of Christ broken for you." I need to hear someone sing, "All I have needed, thy hand hath provided." We need each other to celebrate Communion. I cannot worship God by myself.

The more I pictured Dr. Cline feeding his wife that day, the more I wept. Sometimes it feels like we all suffer from spiritual Alzheimer's disease. We forget who we are; we forget whose we are. But the Lord, like a faithful husband, shows up and feeds his bride every day. At times there may be faint recognition in our eyes. We are the church, every single one of us. We are his holy bride, all dressed in the purity of his righteousness. We are lovely in his eyes. He adores us. He gave his body for us, all of us. He feeds us. He shed his blood for us, all of us sinners. He died for us. And even though we may not realize it, he is here, taking care of us, loving us, holding us, faithfully—because we are his. I couldn't get that picture out of my mind: like a woman in a nursing home wearing a vacant stare, I open my mouth and receive what he gives me. And he, with a smile on his face, catches a faint glimmer of recognition in my eyes when I sing: "Great is thy faithfulness, Lord, unto me."

> But God has so arranged the body, giving the greater honor to the inferior member, that there may be no dissension within the body, but the members may have the same care for one another.
> St. Paul, from Ephesus before he was run out of town, to the Corinthians (1 Cor 12:24-25)

# 7

# Sacred Community

## *Sex and Marriage*

⚜

THE UNPREDICTABLE RETURN of Christ has inspired some predictably strange behavior among believers. Thomas Müntzer (1525) led peasants to war against German princes and nobility, believing that Christ would intervene in the midst of the great battle and defeat their common, earthly adversaries. William Miller predicted that Christ would return to earth on October 22, 1844, inspiring many followers to leave their crops unharvested, forgive all debts, sell their property and give away all their possessions to unbelievers. Edgar Whisenant gave "88 reasons why the rapture will be in 1988," setting up a window of opportunity for Christians to enjoy their last days on earth. (The "body snatching" event was supposed to occur during Rosh Hashanah, September 11-13.) Convinced that the "end is near," some believers took summer dream vacations, ran up huge debts on their credit cards, quit their jobs and hosted "Rapture watch parties" as they counted down the days of Christ's return. Over the years the imminent return of Christ seems to have convinced many to cast off concern for the long term, believing that heaven is right around the corner. Some have risked their lives (like Müntzer's followers), others their financial future (the Millerites and the "Whisenantists"), throwing themselves under the wheels of history to prove their faith. But time marches on, and the foolishness of these fanatics convinces most Christians not to make the same mistake, getting caught up in the sensationalism that often surrounds end-time scenarios. In fact most of us are embarrassed by these chapters in church history when overly zealous prophets have made outlandish claims about the end of the world.

I don't know very many Christians who live like the "end is near." Instead, most of us make plans for the future, absent of any notion that Jesus could come back any moment. (Who in their right mind would sell all they have, give to the poor and wait for Christ?) In fact I'm ashamed to admit that I rarely think about the return of Christ. There was a time, however, when I thought about it all the time—back in the 1970s, when Hal Lindsey's books were bestsellers and we were singing Larry Norman's song "I Wish We'd All Been Ready," and every other sermon I heard was about end times. Our pastor would interpret current events in the Middle East as "signs of the times," convincing us with illustrated charts and graphs that the prophecies of Daniel, Jesus, Paul and John were coming true. But after a few years of eager expectation, the hype gave way to fatigue. End-time predictions offered by alarmists began to sound shrill; I went away to college to study the Bible and lost faith in dispensationalism. The same old saw, "People get ready, Jesus is coming," no longer excited me. The earliest prayer of the first Christians, "Maranatha," seemed wistfully sentimental. On the other hand, the skeptics taunt, "Where is the promise of his coming? . . . All things continue as they were from the beginning" (2 Pet 3:4), sounded more honest than any sermon on the last days.

About this time, I was asked to lead a bible study for the youth group of my home church. Before I started, one of the students asked, "Are we going to study about end times?" "No," I said, "I'd like to talk about something a little more relevant. Let's focus on Paul's teaching regarding marriage in 1 Corinthians 7." The girls' eyes brightened up; the guys acted totally disinterested. But as I read through the entire chapter, they all began to lean in and try to take in all that Paul was saying. Reveling in being a bachelor, I especially enjoyed emphasizing the part where Paul tried to convince young men not to marry because they would be preoccupied with trying to please their wives, "worried . . . about the affairs . . . of the world," I said slowly, relishing every word (1 Cor 7:34). As we worked through the argument, I quickly discovered that questioning the virtue of marriage in the evangelical world was the same as if I were promoting Communism. (Of course, I had an agenda—more interested in provocation than inspiration—but who could question my motives as long as I had proof texts to back up my claim?) Some of the teenage girls took umbrage; the guys giggled nervously. But I held my ground. Digging into the text, the young ladies quickly pointed out that this was merely "Paul's opinion." Even the apostle admitted he was not offering the Lord's command (1 Cor 7:25). So they declared triumphantly, "We won't take his advice on the matter, thank you very much." "But it's in the Bible," I retorted. "Paul says, 'imitate me.' Shouldn't we take him at his word and try to imitate him, remaining single so that we can be solely devoted to Christ?"—perhaps being a little disingenuous (I married a few years later). But it didn't matter. The discussion was over; there was no argument. The girls closed their Bibles; the guys were ready to leave. And neither I nor St. Paul had anything else to say about the matter.

## Marriage at the End of the World

Even though I didn't realize it at the time, we *were* studying about the last days when we read 1 Corinthians 7. That's because the main reason Paul thought his converts shouldn't get married was due to his firm belief that Jesus was coming back any moment. As a matter of fact we often misunderstand (or completely ignore) his advice about marriage because we don't share Paul's eschatological outlook. He preached the "end is near" because he believed everyone's time on earth was nearly over; to his way of thinking that should change everything. Two thousand years later, we know different. As a matter of fact this is where Paul's spirituality is completely different from ours—especially when it comes to marriage. We don't teach our children to "imitate Paul." ("Sweetheart, I hope you grow up and remain single the rest of your life!"—hardly). Paul's ways are not our ways. He thought celibacy was a gift from God; we see it as a curse. Paul thought married couples' devotion to Christ was suspect; we're suspicious of singles, considering them failures ("What's wrong with them?"). Instead, the church places marriage at the top of the list, the ultimate demonstration of devotion to

Christian ideals. Ministry to singles, therefore, is ancillary to the main purpose of today's church: to support the family.

But Paul had different ideas about family and marriage because he was a man of his time, not ours. Not only did he see the world differently, but also like other first-century people he had a completely different set of priorities regarding marriage than we do. And the difference can be most clearly seen in the presumptions behind Paul's argument in 1 Corinthians 7. In fact the main reasons why people get married today—companionship, love, sexual satisfaction—were pretty much at the bottom of the list as to why couples married in Paul's day. Rather, most first-century people were married primarily for two reasons: economics and status.[1] Marriages were arranged by the men of the house in order to ensure the economic and social welfare of the family. Bride prices in the East, dowries in the West—a lot of money changed hands when man and woman became husband and wife. Marriage was a delicate balance of guarding investments and planning for the future. High-status families married off their daughters to sons of equal or higher social standing. These arranged marriages thus preserved the honor of the family name and carefully guarded family fortunes. But the economic advantages didn't end at the wedding. Couples got married to have children (free labor!)—boys to help with the family business, daughters to help with domestic chores. This was their social security; parents raised children to help secure their collective financial future and to take care of them when they got old. Marriage and economics went hand in hand.

In certain respects this explains why Paul didn't see the need for his converts to marry. Since marriage is about securing resources for an uncertain future, and children are the surest means of social security, then why would a believer waste time by getting married when Jesus is coming back any moment? In fact Paul operates with several presumptions as he offers "timely" advice for his converts: (1) the last grains of sand are slipping through the hour glass ("the appointed time has grown short" [1 Cor 7:29]); (2) the things that are important to the world—money, marriage, honor—are fading fast ("the present form of this world is passing away" [1 Cor 7:31]); (3) so making a better life for yourself—upward mobility or a change of status—is unnecessary ("let each of you remain in the condition in which you were called" [1 Cor 7:20]); (4) the highest priority of any believer is Christ ("I say this for your own benefit . . . to promote . . . unhindered devotion to the Lord" [1 Cor 7:35]); therefore (5) the purpose of all relationships is to promote the work of the Lord ("wife, for all you know, you might save your husband" [1 Cor 7:16]; and, "if the husband dies, she is free to marry anyone she wishes, only in the Lord" [1 Cor 7:39]). This is what Paul believed; this is what guided his life. Indeed, he wanted his converts to imitate him even in remaining single: "I wish that all were as I myself am" (1 Cor 7:7).

It's not that Paul was against marriage per se. He encouraged married people to act like married people (1 Cor 7:3-5) and to stay married, even if the husband or wife were not a Christian (1 Cor 7:10-16). And even though he encouraged his converts to remain single, if they chose to get married Paul consented: "If you marry, you do not sin" (1 Cor 7:28). In fact, as far as Paul was concerned, the only reason he gave for a Christian to marry at the time was to keep from sinning, "for it is better to marry than to be aflame with passion" (lust? 1 Cor 7:9). In other words one of the driving forces for marriage was Paul's conviction that sexual satisfaction could only be found between a husband and a wife. Paul certainly didn't entertain the idea that sex and the single life were coterminous. Instead, he presumed that for his converts to be single meant a life of celibacy. (In our day being single means you're either undesirable, irresponsible or gay—it certainly doesn't mean "no sex.") Even Paul knew that a man may not be able to control himself because "his passions are strong, and so it has to be, let him marry" (1 Cor 7:36). But this was by way of concession. He really wanted a man to "stand firm in his resolve" and not get married, even if he was already engaged (1 Cor 7:37). Therefore it is quite obvious that Paul did not see marriage as the ultimate goal of every Christian. Rather, he believed that anything that would distract a believer from being completely devoted to Christ—even marriage—should be set aside for the sake of this higher priority, his highest calling: "I mean, brothers and sisters, the appointed time has grown short; from now on, let even those who have wives be as though they had none" (1 Cor 7:29).

This is where many of us might be tempted to rehabilitate Paul's position and say, "He didn't mean *that*"—especially in light of the positive statements the apostle makes about marriage and families, not only here but also in other places, like Ephesians 5 and Colossians 3. Besides, if husbands were to take Paul at his word, acting like they don't have wives, the apostle could be accused of being a home wrecker. As a matter of fact, because of statements like these and others (e.g., 1 Cor 14:34-35), Paul has been labeled a misogynist. But to accuse Paul of missing the point of marriage (he sounds like a typical single man!) or to say that he saw women as nothing more than a man's lustful distraction (chauvinist) is to question the sincerity of the apostle's devotion to Christ—a sincerity he believed *every* believer shared. That's what makes Paul's advice on marriage sound rather naive to our ears. He presumes that a man will love Christ more than any woman. He thinks that women won't look for fulfillment in a man because they find everything they need in Christ. And, even more shocking for our culture, he doesn't act like sex is the highest good in our common pursuit of satisfaction. In other words he believed that our desire for sex and marriage should take second place to the pressing reality that Jesus is coming back any moment. Paul thought about marriage in terms of how it would serve the church in its mission, how it would benefit the faith.[2] That sure is a strange way to view marriage, especially in our time, when we think the church exists to benefit our families, our purposes, our future. Indeed, compared to Paul we see things completely upside down. Or perhaps we should say, Paul saw things right side up because he had the same view as Jesus.

Everyone knows you shouldn't take marital advice from a single man. But it is an undeniable fact that both the founder of our faith and the apostle to the Gentiles were single men.[3] And to make matters worse, Jesus had some pretty harsh things to say about family relations (Lk 9:57-62; 12:51-53; 14:26). In a radical departure from the norms of his day (where family identity meant everything), Jesus redefined his earthly family in light of his kingdom mission: "My mother and my brothers are those who hear the word of God and do it" (Lk 8:21). His behavior proved he meant it; he treated his disciples more like brothers than his own family. Paul certainly believed the same. He acted like his converts were his family; he was especially fond of using familial terms to describe their relationship ("Though you might have ten thousand guardians in Christ, you do not have many fathers. Indeed, in Christ Jesus I became your father through the gospel. I appeal to you, then, be imitators of me" [1 Cor 4:15-16]). So when Paul gave advice to his converts about marriage, he thought he was acting like their family father, arranging marriages (or discouraging them) for their own good—being completely devoted to Christ. Marriage that compromised such devotion would be nothing but trouble, "and I would spare you that" (1 Cor 7:28). This concern of Paul's is one more reason why he sent his "son" Timothy to remind his Corinthian children of "his ways" in Christ, "as I teach them everywhere in every church" (1 Cor 4:17).

But what would Paul say to us, two thousand years later? Would he give us the same advice?[4] Some might say, "Absolutely, because the American family has become an idol in the church," and in certain respects, I can see why. We know families have been in crisis for quite some time: Christian marriages end in divorce about the same rate as the national average. One can draw the startling inference that our faith makes no difference when it comes to husbands and wives living together. (Or could it be Paul was right? Perhaps these Christian couples should have remained single.) This led some, especially in the evangelical world, to "focus on the family," to save the institution from adversarial forces, making it our number one priority. The concerned parties launched parachurch ministries, formed political alliances, targeted enemies, addressed problems and gathered resources to preserve family values. Marquee issues (abortion, euthanasia, ERA, teenage pregnancy, public versus private education, school curricula, gay marriage) came and went in order to rally the troops during the battle to protect the family. Other countermeasures were installed to make sure the church was doing everything it could to make Christian marriages strong: premarital counseling, preschool programs, parenting classes, marriage seminars, men's ministries, women's ministries. The implication was unmistakable: the American family was under assault, and we should do whatever it takes to save this sacred institution. But in our attempts to make Christian families ideal, we forgot our most important obligation: devotion to Christ (not the family) is what makes a man or a woman a Christian.[5]

Imagine, therefore, what Paul would say to couples whose marriages are falling apart:

Paul:      "I'm so glad you came to see me today; I think I can help."

Husband: "Well, I have to tell you, sir, that I didn't want to come today. I don't think I'm the one who needs counseling. I'm doing everything I can to save this marriage."

Wife:      "Oh really? You're doing everything? Please." Turning to Paul for sympathy, "Don't you think it takes two people—two loving, dedicated people—to make a marriage work? Love and sacrifice, right? Well, there's only one person in this marriage who's making sacrifices, and it's not him."

Husband: "You don't think working sixty hours a week to provide for this family isn't a sacrifice?" Looking at Paul, "See what I mean? Now, you tell me, who's got the problem?"

Paul:      "Well, you see . . ."

Wife:      "Oh, so you think what I do every day is a vacation? I'm trying to work part time to help make ends meet, and then I come home to a filthy house, where I pick up his clothes that are thrown all over the place, get some laundry started, do the dishes (which by the way includes all the cups and day-old dishes he's left here and there), I try to get something ready for dinner before 'prince charming' walks through the door and heads downstairs to sit on the sofa, turn on the TV and watch sports all night long."

Husband: "Well, sometimes a man needs a little peace and quiet, right Paul?"

Wife:      "But what about my needs, huh? What about my needs?" Nodding to the apostle, "Isn't love about meeting needs?" She begins to cry, "This isn't what I thought marriage was supposed to be. He doesn't care about me. He's more interested in what he wants than what I need."

Husband: "I'm trying. I'm trying real hard. It's just that . . . well there's just so much expected of me—at work, at home, my parents . . ."

Wife:     "Oh yes. And we haven't even begun to talk about his parents. That will take another day of counseling."

Paul:     "Yes, you're right. We have plenty to talk about. But, let's start with this question, 'Would either of you say that you are completely devoted to Christ?'"

Husband and Wife (looking very confused): "What? Well, yes, we think so."

Husband: "No disrespect, sir, but what's that got to do with anything?"

Paul:     "My main concern has to do with your relationship with Christ. That's more important than anything—even your marriage."

Husband: "We come in here and pour out our hearts to you and that's all you care about, whether we're being good Christians?"

Paul:     "The way I see it, if you were devoted to Christ then you would know" (talking to the wife) "that no man could meet all of your needs, and you would know" (talking to the husband) "what it means to have a grateful heart. Besides," (speaking to both) "don't you believe that sacrificing yourself for Christ and his work is our first priority? . . . Look. None of us know how much time we have on earth. There's so much work to do for the kingdom and so little time. You need to quit thinking about yourselves and think about others for a change."

Husband (turning to the wife): "See? I told you this wouldn't help. Let's go."

Wife:     "And to think we had 1 Corinthians 13 read at our wedding."

It's one of the great ironies of our time: the famous "love chapter" written by Paul is commonly recited during wedding ceremonies. I think the apostle would find the custom very strange. That's because he wrote 1 Corinthians 13 to remind his converts that true love is how the church reveals we are the body of Christ. (It comes in the middle of his teaching on spiritual gifts not marriage.) As far as Paul was concerned, true love isn't found in marriage or in family, in words or in miracles, in knowledge or even in self-sacrifice. (See 1 Cor 13:1-3.) True love is found in Christ. Therefore true love is to be found in his body, the church. Really? Not marriage, not romance, not children, not parents—true love, pure love, godly love is found only in Christ and his church? That's hard to swallow (especially for those who have endured abuse not only in marriage but also in church). All the more reason Paul believed we all need to change our perspective, not looking at things "from a human point of view": "For the love of Christ urges us on, because we are convinced that one has died for all; therefore all have died. And he died for all, so that those who live might live no longer for themselves, but for him who died and was raised for them. From now on, therefore, we regard no one from a human point of view" (2 Cor 5:14-16). That's the difference between us and the apostle Paul. He saw all things—yes, even love and marriage—through the lens of the new creation.[6] Husbands were to see their wives as members of the body of Christ—when they loved their wives, it was the same as Christ loving the church (Eph 5:25). Wives were to submit to their husbands as members of the church submitting to Christ (Eph 5:22). This was life in the Spirit; this was how members of the church submitted to each other "out of reverence for Christ" (Eph 5:21). They didn't do this to make their marriages better (even though that is often the case—I have noticed that I'm a lousy husband when I've lost my first love). Rather, husbands and wives are to love each other because they are brothers and sisters in Christ. We love because he first loved us. Christ and his church define the marriage relationship. In fact, that's why Paul found sex outside of marriage so reprehensible: it polluted the body of Christ.

## Sex in the Church

As foreign as Paul's advice regarding marriage sounds to us, what is even more bizarre is what the Corinthians had written to Paul in their own letter. Evidently they believed that a husband shouldn't have sex with his wife (probably the best way to translate, "It is well for a man not to touch a woman" [1 Cor 7:1]). Where did the Corinthians get such a strange idea? Scholars think one of two places: either from Paul or from Roman culture. Some of Paul's female converts had taken the apostle's baptismal teaching—neither male nor female—to heart. Since these sexual distinctions don't exist in the resurrection, then these "eschatological women" believed that they should no longer be treated as wives; they had already become "like the angels," perhaps harking back to Jesus' teaching (Mk 12:25).[7] But where would they get the idea that the resurrection—an end-of-the-world event—had already taken place? From Paul, who taught his converts that they were a "new creation," where old identities (gender, ethnic, social) had been eclipsed by their participation in the resurrection of Christ in the here and now. In fact the Corinthians had already given up on the idea of a physical resurrection, a notion Paul had to straighten out later in the letter (1 Cor 15). Indeed, Paul's emphasis on experiencing the resurrection of Christ by living a Spirit-filled life would later inspire false teachers who "swerved from the truth by claiming that the resurrection has already taken place" (2 Tim 2:18) and "forbid marriage" (1 Tim 4:3). In other words these women were the first to take Paul's teaching regarding the "already" of the resurrection to the extreme that they no longer believed in the "not yet."

Other scholars think it was the men, not the women, who proposed that husbands shouldn't use their wives for sexual pleasure. It had nothing to do with misunderstanding Paul's teaching but reflected the Roman sex ethic, which was borrowed from the Greeks.[8] Among the Roman elite it was believed that husbands were to honor their wives by making them the mothers of their children, and so they considered it shameful to use them as vessels of fleshly indulgence. As a result it became socially acceptable for Roman men to find other means of sexual satisfaction, for example, brothels, slaves, mistresses, courtiers and young men (under the auspices of "training" them for love). This explains why Paul had to deal with the problem of sexual behavior of men (1 Cor 6) before addressing the question: "It is well for a man not to

touch a woman" (which at face value sounds incredibly contradictory—
if they believed men shouldn't have sex with women, then why were
they seeking the services of prostitutes?). In this case Paul was dealing
with two problems that resulted from one issue: the way Romans understood sex and marriage.

To be sure, the baptismal confession "There is neither male nor female, Jew nor Gentile, slave nor free" seems to be on Paul's mind, serving the substructure of his argument as he answers the Corinthian letter. Relations between husbands and wives (1 Cor 5–7), between Jews
and Gentiles (idolatry and dietary issues [1 Cor 8–10]), and between
slave and free (status issues at the table and during worship [1 Cor 11–
14]) proved to be contentious among the house churches of this Roman
colony. The main problem was that Paul's converts had a hard time living the confession; the body of Christ was supposed to be a group of
people where unity would be enhanced by diversity *because all were buried in Christ, all were baptized by the same Spirit, all were serving the same
Lord.* All that they were, all that they did was supposed to be for the
sake of the body of Christ, the church. There can be no selfish agenda,
no individualistic pursuit of personal desires when the main goal of the
house churches is the welfare of the whole body. This conviction is
what guided Paul when he dealt with divisions over spiritual gifts, eating idol meat, sharing the Lord's Table and family relations. Indeed,
whether the Corinthians had confused Paul's teaching regarding the
resurrection life or had imported Roman ways into Christian family
relations, the apostle's goal was the same: when it comes to Christ and
his church, all things are for the common good. Therefore, especially
when it came to sex, Paul had to discipline the Corinthians for their
own good.

The notorious problem in Corinth was that a man was living with
his father's wife (1 Cor 5:1). We don't know whether the father was
dead or alive; but it really doesn't change the onerous state of affairs.
Paul is quick to point out that even pagans find incest objectionable,
and he is incredulous to find out that most of the Corinthians are arrogant and proud of this egregious behavior (1 Cor 5:2, 6)—evidently
Chloe's house church had objected to it, for they were the ones who

reported this as well as other problems to the apostle (1 Cor 1:11). Once again we don't know enough details to answer the obvious question: why would most of the house churches accept such an abominable practice? Perhaps the woman was a wealthy patroness of the church, and no one wanted to challenge her influence. Maybe this is another example of the influence of the "eschatological women"; since sexual identity doesn't matter anymore, then sexual behavior has become irrelevant at the end of the age. Or it could be that the young man had come into the power of his dead father's estate, deciding to keep his stepmother as his paramour. Whatever the circumstances, what distressed Paul more than the sexual immorality of the incestuous couple was the approval of the Corinthians. Since sexual deviance affects the entire church, then the Corinthians should have "mourned, so that he who has done this would have been removed from among you" (1 Cor 5:2). Instead, they boasted about it. So Paul had to discipline the church.

That's the point of Paul's instruction: he is disciplining the *entire* church because their sin is a corporate reality.[9] Many have misunderstood Paul's teaching at this point, thinking that church discipline means kicking out members who are involved in terrible sins. But if that were the case, Paul should have instructed the Corinthians to kick out the men who were going to prostitutes or the VIPs who were getting drunk at the Lord's Table. So what's the difference? First, even pagans knew the sin of incest was wrong. Therefore members of the Corinthian church were engaging in behavior that was reprehensible even by the world's standards. But even more shocking than that, Paul's converts didn't see anything wrong with incest. It wasn't that they were trying to hide it (the typical response of those trying to justify their sin—Adam!). In fact the Corinthians were proud of it. So by requiring his converts to shun the incestuous couple, Paul was disciplining the entire church. They shared the blame because sexual sin infected the whole church (1 Cor 5:6; 6:15-20). They should have already taken care of the matter. But how? By grieving over their sin (1 Cor 5:2). Paul assumes that when the house churches assembled as one, they would have grieved over their corporate sin, taking responsibility for their shame.

Instead, they were shameless, acting arrogant, as if nothing were wrong. So Paul had to discipline the entire church by making them do the right thing—shunning the man and his stepmother would have been a powerful tool in Paul's day, where honor (the social approval of your group) meant everything. Indeed, Paul claimed he would be there "in spirit" when they turned the man (not the woman?) over to Satan "for the destruction of his flesh" (1 Cor 5:5)—a very painful thing for the Corinthians to do since they did not see anything wrong with the man's behavior.

Paul's instructions regarding church discipline provoke many difficult questions. For example, what does it mean to turn someone over to Satan for the destruction of his flesh? Is this a reference to the Job story? And if so, wouldn't that place Paul and his converts on the side of the false comforters? Did Paul expect the Corinthians to take his advice literally, that is, not to eat with dastardly sinners like the sexually immoral, idolaters and drunkards (1 Cor 5:11)? If that were the case, then why didn't he require his converts to abstain from sharing table with those who were inebriated at the Lord's Table (1 Cor 11:21-23)? And why did Paul expect the man's spirit to be "saved in the day of the Lord" (1 Cor 5:5)? Was the apostle revealing a dualistic view of humanity (only the spirit matters because it is eternal), which would have contributed to the Corinthians' confusion regarding the resurrection of the dead (1 Cor 15:12)? These questions deserve good answers, but for the purposes of this study I would like to center on what I believe is the major point of Paul's directive in 1 Corinthians 5: sexual sin affects the entire church.

Even pagans know this: sexual immorality does not belong in the church. Priests who molest children, television preachers who hire prostitutes, pastors who run off with the church secretary—these stories often make local and national headlines because everyone knows it's wrong. In fact outsiders judge the entire church as a collection of hypocrites whenever these scandals come to light. That's because unbelievers tend to think like Paul when it comes to sexual immorality and the church: sin pollutes the whole body. So what are we to do? Remove all of the sinners from among us? That would result in a very small church, or even worse, a group of self-righteous legalists. Instead, we should take Paul's advice and mourn over our sin, because it is *our* sin. When a wife breaks her wedding vows and leaves her husband for another man, then a sister in Christ has violated the sacred promise she made to her fellow members. Since marriage is a social contract (just as it was in Paul's day), their union affects many people. Indeed, when a man promises to be faithful to his bride, he is making a promise not only to her, her family and his family but also to the entire congregation—to every sister in Christ, to every brother in the Lord. That's why Paul saw infidelity as defrauding and exploiting "a brother or sister in this matter" (1 Thess 4:6). Sex outside of marriage defiles the whole church, so we must all mourn over our sin.

Paul assumes that corporate confession will lead to the removal of the man from the church (1 Cor 5:2). And it's easy to see why: in a culture that prized social approval (honor) as the ultimate success, to be openly shamed by one's honorable group would cast aspersion on the individual and the entire group. But the Corinthians were not ashamed of themselves. Therefore Paul ordered them to remove the man from the church—forcing them to recognize their dishonorable behavior (1 Cor 5:7, 13). The goal of shunning was to shame the dishonorable member so that he would seek restoration within the very community that gave him identity. The purpose was reclamation, and the shameful man knew it. If he refused, he would be saying to the church, "I don't need you anymore." And in a world where group identity defined significance, such isolation would be the same as committing social suicide: no friends, no family, no honor, no life. Even worse for the rebel Christian, shamelessness would mean no church, no salvation, no hope, no Christ. To be "cut off" from church was the same as being "cut off" from Christ. (See Gal 5:4-6.) This explains why, for Paul, spirituality was both personal and corporate. For him one couldn't be a Christian without church anymore than church could be the body without Christ.

But we don't relate to Paul in this matter, because we have privatized our spirituality. We think sin is a private matter. Faith is an individual response. Sex is personal. Marriages are not arranged. Church is an option—take it or leave it. And that's what some Christians do: if we don't like what's going on, we find another church. Or when we hear another report of sexual misconduct by church leaders, we're relieved to know it didn't happen in our church or denomination. (Baptist preachers take no responsibility for the behavior of Catholic priests.) But Paul didn't think there was "another church." The problems of one house church affected them all; the sexual immorality of the incestuous couple "leavened" the entire church (1 Cor 5:6). Paul would say today that we're the ones being naive, thinking that our individual sins have no effect on the body of Christ. And wouldn't he be right? When we hear of another church scandal, don't we all groan within ourselves knowing the church is going to take another bashing from outsiders because they are justifiably enraged by our sin? Or when rumors rumble throughout a congregation about another couple divorcing due to infidelity, don't we all want to stick our heads in the sand and act like nothing's wrong? Saying, "It's *their* problem," doesn't make it go away. Trying to keep the lid on the subject as if such things were a "private matter" between a husband and wife is hardhearted. To carry on with the attitude, "these things just happen," is to deny that our sexuality has anything to do with our spirituality. This is more than about marriage; it's about family. These are our brothers and sisters in Christ. This is about *our* relationship with the Lord—every single one of us. We're supposed to "bear one another's burdens" just as Christ did for us (Gal 6:2). Paul was right. Our sexuality is dependant on our devotion to Christ. We can't have marriage without the church. In the body of Christ there is no such thing as private sin—especially when it comes to sex.

In all the years that I have talked with married couples who came to me in crisis, I've never heard a husband say, "I'm growing spiritually. My heart is pure. I'm giving my life for the kingdom of God. My relationship with the Lord is very good right now—in fact it's the best it's ever been. I just can't stand to live with her anymore." Nor have I ever heard a wife say, "I love the Lord. I'm spending much quality time with him. He fills me up. He makes life worth living. So I want to leave my husband." In fact whenever I have tried to be their pastor—the undershepherd of their souls—and have inquired about their spirituality in the midst of marital counseling, they often act like I am oblivious to their suffering, ignoring their complaints. "If he would just listen to me, it would save our marriage," or, "If she would just give me some space, I might be a better husband." When I remind them of our faith, that Christians are known for sacrificing themselves, following the example of Christ, they think I have moved off topic. Bringing Paul into the conversation only makes things worse. Suggesting to a woman in a loveless marriage that she should continue to do thoughtful things for her husband because he is a brother in Christ often provokes dismissive smirks. Telling a man that he should love his wife because she is his sister in Christ is often received with blank expressions of disbelief. What they want instead is for their pastor to take their side in the argument, to make their spouse do the right thing. When I told one couple that not even God operates that way—God loves us when we're unlovable—the husband mistook my words as practice for Sunday: "Look, preacher. We didn't come here for a sermon. We came to you for help." And all the while, that's exactly what I thought I was doing.

Some time ago I spoke to a man who had left his family for another woman. At first he thought I was striking up a conversation with him in order to get the sordid details of his affair. But when he found out I was simply inquiring about his soul, how he was doing spiritually, he was shocked and said, "You're the first person to ask me about my relationship with the Lord." The assumption, of course, is that a Christian guilty of sexual immorality couldn't possibly be concerned about his relationship with God. But nothing could be further from the truth. He felt all alone. Not only had he lost his family because of his sin, but he also no longer wanted to be around other Christians. The last place he wanted to go was church. Even worse than that, his heart had grown hard toward God, and that was the loneliest feeling of all. At that moment I said something like, "We miss you. We need you. All of us. Your family, your church, your friends. And you need us. We can get through this together. Come, we will all confess our sin together. Some sins are higher profile than others. Some sins seem harder to confess. But we're all guilty of falling short of what God wants. You're not alone. We all need to forgive each other. We all need the forgiveness of God." He simply bowed his head and said, "Thanks, maybe one day."

We all live as if we have all the time in the world. Paul didn't. Even though he changed his mind about living long enough to witness the return of Christ (2 Cor 4:14), Paul believed the eschatological clock was winding down. It was the last hour. "You know what time it is, how it is now the moment for you to wake from sleep. For salvation is nearer to us now than when we became believers" (Rom 13:11). We often speak of a woman's biological clock ticking, reminding her she only has so much time to become a mother. Paul's eschatological clock was ticking even louder, reminding him he only had so much time to be a father to his converts. That's why he wrote letters to the churches. Paul didn't write for posterity, believing one day his advice would become our Scripture. No, he wrote because he believed the time was short. The church needed to act like the body of Christ. His converts needed his advice so that they would reveal to the world what the end of the world looks like—where Jews and Gentiles are one people, where husbands and wives are brothers and sisters, where slaves and free inherit the kingdom. All of this—our lives, our marriages, our work, our faith— was supposed to be for the salvation of the world because the end is near. And I can't help but think, if Paul were alive today, he would tell us the same thing.

> The night is far gone, the day is near. Let us then lay aside the works of darkness and put on the armor of light; let us live honorably as in the day, not in reveling and drunkenness, not in debauchery and licentiousness, not in quarreling and jealousy. Instead, put on the Lord Jesus Christ, and make no provision for the flesh, to gratify its desires.
> St. Paul, a few months after his near-death experience in Ephesus, to the Romans (Rom 13:12-14)

# 8

# Generous Fellowship

## *Work and Money*

✿

IT FELT LIKE THE END of the world. I stepped outside the back
door of our house to see the lights of our little town a few miles away.
But this evening there was no shining city on a hill—it was completely
dark. We had been without power for a week. A devastating ice storm
had robbed us of nearly every creaturely comfort. Most of us were in
"survival" mode, looking for water and batteries, and our family was
nearly out of both. So I decided to venture into town to see what I could
find. As I drove on roads thick with several inches of ice, I marveled at
the destruction. Trees stripped of their branches, looking like badly
carved totem poles. Telephone poles snapped in half, power lines strewn
all over the road. House after house in the dark, some abandoned cars
in ditches and the silence—the eerie, unnerving silence, except for the
sound of ice cracking under the weight of my car as I slowly headed for
town. The parking lot of the grocery store was chaos—no orderly ar-
rangement of cars, the few parked where they wanted. The automatic
front doors were left pried open despite the frigid temperatures. The
building looked like a cave with explorers making their way into the
deep with flashlights. All I could hear was the shuffling of feet, a gen-
erator supplying power to the cash register and the whooshing sound of
a few gas lanterns providing a little heat. There was no time for conversation; we all headed straight for the coveted items only to find the
shelves nearly stripped bare. I got a couple of AA batteries and one jug

of drinking water, paid for my treasure at the makeshift checkout line and then headed back home—all the while thinking to myself, "I wonder if this is what the end of the world looks like."

Electricity is our currency; it is power. The absence of this taken-for-granted commodity brings our common way of life to a screeching halt. All of our talk of independence and the power to do what we want is delusional without electricity. In fact that's what has happened. We have created the illusion that we are on our own because technology has empowered us to be self-sufficient. But take away the irreplaceable source of our power—the reliable delivery of watts and amps through wire—and we are brought to our knees, begging for help (or demanding service with hostile complaint). Indeed, we have become a very dependent people, but we act like we don't need anyone. Untouched by the world outside our doors, safely tucked away in our man-made castles, we pretend we have everything we need. Then the rug is pulled out from under our feet. The light switches don't work. We're no longer able to control climate. Family resources are depleted. Forced outside we soon discovered we needed a community after all.

At first we were all in the same predicament. Everyone needed help. But after several days, power was restored to the more vital parts of our town. Banks became operational. The grocery store again began doing business in the conventional way. Gas stations opened back up. As the lights came on around town, those of us who lived in the country kept waiting for our turn. All conversation centered on one subject; customary daily greetings were replaced with: "Got power yet?" Some folks had their electricity turned on within a few days. Some waited four weeks. We found the average: without power for almost two weeks. In the meantime friends from our church invited us to their homes for warm meals and hot showers. It seemed like things had returned to normal for those few hours, but then the drive home brought us back to reality. The closer we got to our house, the darker the night. Seeing our house in the pitch dark of a winter's evening was anything but inviting. Usually a hospitable destination, there's something very unsettling about coming home to a dark, cold house.

We live in southwest Missouri, an area we refer to affectionately as the buckle of the Bible belt. When we gather for worship on Sundays we hear reports of our missionary efforts—not only in North America but also in El Salvador, India, Russia and many other countries. Unpretentiously we see ourselves as benefactors of the world, charged to take the gospel to the ends of the earth. Like most churches, appeals are often made for us to give time and money to help others in need. And that's what we do. We've sent supplies and workers to the Gulf to help with hurricane relief. We've organized teams of doctors, therapists and nurses to bring health care to San Salvador. Teachers have traveled all the way to Tomsk, Siberia, to help with the ESL program at the university. So when churches from South Carolina sent relief workers to our little town to help us dig out of our mess, we were relieved, overjoyed and puzzled all at the same time. We weren't used to this. Missionaries came to our town believing that God had given them the same calling: to take the gospel to the ends of the earth. As I saw some of these missionaries in overalls with chain saws organizing work teams one day, I couldn't help but muse to myself, "Who would have thought that, for some people, Bolivar, Missouri, would be the end of the world?"

I can't help but wonder if the first-century church in Jerusalem thought the same thing. They were the first followers of Jesus Christ. They saw the Spirit baptize the nations on Pentecost. They were the first missionaries, bringing thousands to faith in Christ. They were the mother church, the historians of Jesus' words and deeds, the guardians of the faith. James was their pastor and Peter their evangelist. Through them God had blessed the whole world. So imagine their surprise when Paul brought a relief offering collected from all of his converts to help the church in Jerusalem. Missionaries coming *to* the holy city must have seemed very strange:

James:   Paul! What a nice surprise. What are you doing here? I heard you were somewhere in Achaia.

Paul:    I've come with good news.

James:   Of course you have—that's true of every disciple of Jesus Christ.

Paul:    Yes, well, I didn't mean it like that. Anyway, I have a gift for you and all the church of Jerusalem. Nearly two hundred sesterces.

James: That's a lot of money, Paul. Tent-making business must be picking up, huh? Where did you get all of this money?

Paul: From my converts. From all over. From the Galatians, Macedonians, even the Achaeans.

James: But why did you bring it here? We didn't ask for this.

Paul: You said, "Remember the poor." Remember, that time in Jerusalem? When we said I would take the gospel to Gentiles and we shook on it? Then you said, "Just one thing: remember the poor."

James: Yes, yes. But I didn't mean us. I was talking about our kingdom mission, the work of God. Like the prophets of old have said, we must always remember the widows and orphans in their distress.

Paul: Well, you're in distress. You have no money, no property—you gave it all away. And of course we heard about the terrible famine. We knew you needed help, and so we gave—some out of their poverty—because we knew if we didn't you would starve. So here it is. It's yours. All of it.

James: This doesn't seem right. Perhaps we should give it to the temple. Right? It's the temple tax.

Paul: No, no. That's not why I did this. Don't you see? We are the temple of God now. We are his sanctuary—all of us, whether Jews or Gentiles, male or female, slave or free. So, yes, in a certain way this is the temple tax. We've collected money to build up the temple of God, the new Jerusalem.

James: Sssh, don't say that. You know there are people here who think you're a lawbreaker. If they hear that you're trying to divert the temple money to us, we'll all be accused of stealing from God. Let's not talk about it now. Come, why don't we go to the temple and worship the Lord? That'll prove to the naysayers you're still a Jew dedicated to God.

We don't know if James ever accepted the relief offering from Paul and his companions.[1] It's one of the great mysteries of early church history. There is no mention of the relief offering in Acts, even though Paul wrote about it several times (Gal 2:10; 1 Cor 16:1-4; 2 Cor 8:1–9:15; Rom 15:25-32). However, we know from Acts that Paul's visit to the temple didn't go well (Acts 21:17–22:29). And we know from Paul's letters that he expected trouble when he brought the relief offering to Jerusalem (Rom 15:30-32). Therefore some scholars read between the lines and say that Jerusalem rejected the money, which explains why Luke didn't write about it and why Paul counted on it so much.[2] Paul was hoping it would represent the final stamp of approval on his ministry (Rom 15:15-17, 30-32). To refuse the money would be the same as rejecting Paul's converts—something Luke wouldn't want to include in his story. So there was much at stake when Paul brought the monetary gift to James. For that reason, then, it could be that James accepted the money to seal their alliance, to prove the church was unified. Since neither Acts nor Paul gives us the details, we'll never know for sure. But one thing is certain: gifts always came with expectations. For even in their day, nobody received money for nothing.

## Will Work for Food

Second Thessalonians 3:10 is one of the few places in his letters where Paul sounds like an American: "For even when we were with you, we gave you this command: Anyone unwilling to work should not eat." The problem in Thessalonica was "idleness." Paul was trying to get his converts to follow his example and get back to work (2 Thess 3:6-8). But the reason some of the Thessalonians quit working is puzzling to scholars. There was no social security program for the elderly, no worker's compensation for the injured. Nearly everyone relied on their families to make ends meet, and that would take every able-bodied man and woman to work. The only other way to get money without work was begging—the only recourse for the diseased outcasts. So when Paul laid down the rule, "if you don't work, you don't eat," he was simply stating the obvious. There seems to have been no reasonable motivation to quit work. Why would they do it?[3]

It could be that Paul's teaching about the second coming of Christ convinced some of his converts that work was no longer necessary. They certainly were confused about the details of Christ's return, for example, what happens if you die before he comes (1 Thess 4:13-18)? Could it happen without us knowing about it (1 Thess 5:1-11)? Hasn't it already happened (2 Thess 2:1-12)? Their theological misunderstandings could have created social problems. In other words Paul must have preached the imminent return of Christ with such passion it convinced some of his converts to quit work. Both issues show up in both letters. In the first letter, Paul encourages the Thessalonians to "work with your hands" so that they will "be dependent on no one" (1 Thess 4:11-12) right before he deals with their confused eschatology. Then the situation got worse; they were still unclear about Paul's teaching regarding the return of Christ, and some had quit working. Paul deals first with the wrong idea that "the day of the Lord is already here" (2 Thess 2:1-15), then turns to address more directly the problem of "idleness" (2 Thess 3:6-15). This gives the impression that these two issues are connected—that the Thessalonians' confused eschatology led to a poor work ethic. But in certain respects that doesn't make sense. If the Thessalonians had come to believe that the day of the Lord "is already here," why in the world would they quit work? If Jesus isn't coming back, then quitting work makes no sense at all.

Some argue that a recent famine in Macedonia had created poor economic conditions for the working class (2 Cor 8:2).[4] Under these circumstances the Roman Empire usually funded a program to dole out bread to the masses. Paul's converts were ashamed to beg and too poor to refuse the bread dole but decided to offer their services to wealthy patrons instead. In other words most of Paul's converts were tradespeople or day laborers who couldn't make a living, so they "quit working with their hands" and tried to get on the payroll of these powerful men, who often had multiple business operations that required hired hands to do their dirty work. By becoming their clients, Paul's converts would be in service to these pagans, who expected allegiance to their gods, their family and their ungodly ways. But Paul doesn't seem concerned that his converts may have fallen into idolatry or immorality. (In fact he often applauds the Thessalonians for their steadfast faith [1 Thess 1:6-10; 4:1-7].) Besides, it would sound rather heartless for Paul to say, "Get back to work," when there was no work to be found. Paul was concerned about the Thessalonians, but it had more to do with the persecution they were experiencing because of their faith (1 Thess 2:13–3:10; 2 Thess 1:5-12) than with hard times brought on by a famine.

The simplest answer may be the best one: some of the Thessalonians decided to take advantage of the hospitality of the church. Christians were known for taking in complete strangers regardless of their status. (Conventional wisdom said that hospitality should be extended only to the honorable; shameful people would abuse the gift as deadbeats.) And since Christian worship involved sharing table in someone's home, then it can be easily seen how some members might take advantage of the situation. Who needs to work when all you have to do is go to worship to eat bread? But the question remains: why did *some* of the members quit work, acting like they were privileged? Maybe the "idle" were joining the teachers whom Paul said should be respected as "those who labor among you, and have charge of you in the Lord and admonish you; esteem them very highly in love because of their work" (1 Thess 5:12-13). Even Paul acknowledges that those who minister the Word of God should be paid for their labor (1 Cor 9:13-14). And it could be that the Thessalonian leaders were using James and Peter as their models of ministry. Peter used to be a fisherman, and James was probably a carpenter just like his brother—but neither of them "worked for a living" because they were supported by the church. But Paul believed *his* converts—the leaders as well as the "idle"—should follow *his* example. After all, he personified the gospel for Gentile believers: "For you yourselves know how you ought to imitate us; we were not idle when we were with you, and we did not eat anyone's bread without paying for it; but with toil and labor we worked night and day, so that we might not burden any of you. *This was not because we do not have that right,* but in order to give you an example to imitate" (2 Thess 3:7-9, emphasis mine).

And that's when Paul stops sounding like an American. The idea of exercising our rights is deeply embedded in our national psyche. To give up something that is owed us seems counterintuitive, if not completely wrong. Our sense of entitlement is so strong that we don't know what it means to give up our rights as an example for others to imitate. (Who wants to act like a "wimp"?) No, our heroes are the ones who fight for their rights. Indeed, when Paul said he decided not to charge the Thessalonians for his gospel services, to our way of thinking Paul was asking for trouble. He was simply encouraging his converts to take advantage of him. Give people an inch, and they'll take a mile. Let one person walk all over you, and you'll soon become the doormat of the world. In fact some of us might be inclined to point out the obvious irony: "See what happened? Because you didn't have the Thessalonians support your ministry, you've encouraged freeloaders to quit work and take advantage of the ministry of the church. Anything worth having is worth paying for, especially food—spiritual and physical. But you've given the impression that the necessities of life are free. Now you and the church have to live with the foolishness of your generosity."

That's our major concern, how to extend hospitality without being taken advantage of. How do we help others without creating dependency? We've heard the stories: the guest who stays too long, the adult child who won't get a job, the indigent who approaches every church in town with a different hard-luck story. We want to do the right thing and help, but we don't want people to think they can count on us indefinitely. After all, we have bills to pay, and a family to feed, and responsibilities to bear. We've all seen how generosity can breed complacency, or even worse, contempt. It's amazing how quickly some of us believe we're entitled to receive what we get.

In the first few days of the ice storm, there were only a few places that could provide shelter from the bitter cold because they had emergency power, for example, the hospital and the nursing homes. As word spread, those who lived close to these facilities began to show up looking for warmth. One nursing home was overwhelmed by the visitors who decided they didn't want to go home at night. So the nursing home made arrangements to set up a makeshift dormitory in the dining hall. The facility was gracious to their new residents, offering one hot meal every day. At first the guests were grateful for the hot food and warm bed. But it didn't take long until they began to complain about the quality of the meals. Then they made themselves at home, using the offices as family rooms for playing cards and taking naps. At times the workers felt like they were running a hotel as much as a nursing home. How were they supposed to get their work done? The temporary residents were tired of living in a nursing home. Who wants to go there before they have to? Once electricity came back to the neighborhood, everyone was relieved. The unwanted guests went home, and the employees went back to the work for which they were hired. Power restored entitlement. And yet, what was especially curious to me was how this social experiment (which everyone hopes will never have to be repeated) took place at a *nursing home*.

Paul believed the church was home, where no one operated with a sense of entitlement and everyone knew they were needed. Paul believed his converts were family, where every member worked for the good of everyone and no one could afford to be selfish. That's why he chose to work with his own hands. Although he was entitled to receive pay for preaching the gospel, he set aside the privilege so he wouldn't be a *burden* to the Thessalonians (2 Thess 3:8-9). Even while Paul was in Thessalonica, he accepted financial support from the Philippians (Phil 4:15-16; evidently Paul didn't find enough work in Thessalonica to support himself, even though he worked "night and day" [2 Thess 3:8]). So the Philippians—Christians of some means—sent money while he was laboring in Thessalonica. Evidently the Thessalonian believers were poor and relied on each other for economic support. In fact Paul describes the Macedonians (the province that included Philippi and Thessalonica) as churches that had endured a "severe ordeal of affliction" and gave to the relief offering in spite of their "extreme poverty" (2 Cor 8:2). Obviously the Philippians were not the impoverished ones; when the Thessalonians were persecuted by their neighbors, it must have included economic reprisals (1 Thess 2:14; 3:3-7). Ostracized by their community the Thessalonians looked to each other for food, work, help and support—they were family. To refuse to work would mean that others would have to work harder to supply bread for the family. Therefore by refusing to exercise his rights Paul modeled what church family is supposed to look like: a group of selfless people who put everyone's interests above their own, just like Christ. It's no wonder hospitality thrived in an environment like that; and it's no wonder early Christians were so vulnerable in their generosity. They worked hard and gave much. It would be easy to take advantage of a group like that.

I wish the church today had the same reputation: a group so generous it would be easy to take advantage of us. But I don't see us relying on each other like the church in Paul's day, for several reasons. First, we're convinced what happened in the early church should never be repeated (Acts 4:32-37). The Acts experiment only created needy people; selling possessions to help others didn't last long. Isn't that why Paul had to collect a relief offering in the first place? Second, we believe in self-sufficiency. We've been taught the only person you can count on is yourself. To rely on others for personal resources is failure. Being needy is foolish. But Paul saw the church as a family of needy people, which is why he believed it would take every single one of us to make it through life *together*—something I learned in the middle of an ice storm. We've also lost the first gift of the church: hospitality. The earliest church was "forced" to discover the power of hospitality because they met for worship in homes. "Welcome to church" was the same as "welcome to our family." But in our day hospitality is something you pay for; those who own hotels are said to be in the "hospitality business."[5] Churches have limited hospitality to welcoming visitors to worship services with a smile and a handshake—anything more you have to pay for. Finally, our sense of entitlement steals away any chance for us to be foolishly generous. We are entitled to the money we earn. So only those who are entitled to our help receive it. How soon we forget that most jobs require able-bodied persons, that there are no guarantees to good health and that no one owns their daily bread—all are gifts from a very generous God—something we call "grace." Indeed, if the power to work is a gift from God, how much more the fruit of our labor?

## Grace Is Like Manna

"I have more than I can say grace over." That's the usual response I received from an elderly gentleman every time I greeted him with, "How are you?" And he always said it with a big smile. As a young man at the time, I didn't know what to make of it. It sounded like an old saying—the kind that confuses novices and makes them wonder whether they're too young to appreciate sage advice. I knew he was making a point. In fact his response sounded very "Christian" to me; images of a big table spread with an abundance of food came to mind. Plus we said "grace" at meal time. But I was fairly certain he meant something more than "I have more food than I can eat." So even though I had heard him say it many times, I didn't know how to respond. There we stood: a smiling geriatric and a confused twentysomething. Should I say "good" or "too bad"? Was he bragging or complaining? He eventually broke the silence with a report about his business. He was always very busy; he was also very successful. Working long hours had made him a wealthy man. And he was generous too. Whenever there was a special project or need at our church, he always helped. Perhaps having more than what you can say grace over is motivation to give. So I came to the short-sighted conclusion that it's easy to give more when you have more to give. Philanthropy is a term we reserve for the wealthy.

Paul didn't believe that at all. He was convinced the poor Thessalonians had as much to give to the relief offering as the more endowed Corinthians. To our way of thinking he should have given the Thessalonians a pass since they were in such dire straits. Instead, he boasted to the Corinthians about how "they voluntarily gave according to their means, and even beyond their means, begging us earnestly for the privilege of sharing in this ministry to the saints" (2 Cor 8:3-4). Paul used the Thessalonian example in order to goad the Corinthians to make good on their monetary pledge (2 Cor 8:10-12). Obviously he had doubts that the Corinthians would finish what they started—an offering they were supposed to have been collecting for over a year (2 Cor 9:2-5; cf. 1 Cor 16:1-4). So he put the pressure on, telling the Corinthians about how he had boasted to the Thessalonians, Philippians and the rest of the Macedonians: "Listen, this is a great gift. You've given sacrificially. But wait till you hear what the Corinthians have given. They believe in this project—been collecting money for over a year. I can't wait to see how much money they have set aside. What? No, you

don't need to give more. You've already done well. Really? You insist?
Okay. I'll take it. Why don't some of you travel ahead of me to Corinth?
Tell them what you've done. That will really inspire them. Then after I
arrive we'll all celebrate together the great bounty of God's grace" (my
paraphrase, piecing together the details drawn from 2 Cor 8:1–9:5).

Given the fact that Paul had reservations about the Corinthians'
participation in the relief offering, his tactics appear somewhat manipulative. In fact Paul's approach has inspired many television preachers to make very bold appeals for monetary support—what they call
"seed faith" (2 Cor 9:6-15; I can't help but wonder what the apostle
would think of that). Paul claimed, however, he was doing the Corinthians a favor, trying to give them a "heads up." Essentially he was
saying, "Imagine how embarrassed I would be (not to mention you) if
your Macedonian brothers arrive with me and find out you haven't
given like I said you would" (cf. 2 Cor 9:3-5). It may be too harsh a
judgment to say Paul was being manipulative. To be sure, he admitted
he was stoking the fires of competition, "testing the genuineness of
your love against the earnestness of others" (2 Cor 8:8). But what sets
Paul apart from modern-day televangelists is that the money wasn't for
him; it was for the church in Jerusalem. Furthermore, the presumption
behind his appeal wasn't the same. Television preachers building em-
pires promise their viewers that God works on a quid pro quo basis. If
you do something good for him (which means giving them money),
then he'll reward you with more (what could be called a "works righteousness" approach to giving).[6] Paul's advice, however, operated on the
presumption of grace.[7]

Grace gives us what we cannot earn, which sounds weird when we
apply the concept to money, which is usually acquired because we've
earned it. And yet, throughout his "encouragement" to the Corinthians
to give money, Paul kept using the terms "grace" and "gift." It easy to
see the correlation in Greek; *charisma* ("gift") derives from *charis*
("grace"). That which is given (*charisma*) comes ultimately from God
(*charis*). As far as Paul was concerned, then, money is the evidence of
God's grace. We don't "earn" money; God has given it to us. Why
would God give us money, this grace? God gives us grace so that we

can be the grace of God. Grace kept to ourselves ceases to be grace—for us and for others. But if we "freely give as we have freely received," then we become the grace of God as we share the grace of God. We become God's gift to one another as we give to each other. This principle of reciprocity is the foundation of Paul's advice regarding money because he saw it as evidence of God's grace. To anchor the point, Paul appeals to Jesus Christ and Israel. Jesus gave up the riches of heaven and became poor so that "*by his poverty* you might become rich" (2 Cor 8:9). Notice that Paul doesn't say Jesus shared his riches with us. Rather, because Jesus became poor like us, in his poverty he makes us rich. His sacrifice defines true wealth. Jesus is God's grace to the poor. The giver is the gift.

Paul also believed that God's grace is sufficient for everyone. Since grace cannot be earned God never shortchanges one group compared to another. No one in the church can claim more of God's grace because of who they are or what they've done. But what happens when some of God's people have more money than others? Isn't that evidence of partiality? Not the way Paul sees it. Once again he presumes his converts will think of themselves as God's grace to each other—that they will *always* need each other because they need God. As the church they all experience the grace of God in perpetually equal measure. When some members of the church have an abundance of something, then others must have a need: "It is a question of a fair balance between your present abundance and their need, so that their abundance may be for your need" (2 Cor 8:13-14). Grace is a gift that keeps on giving, never finding rest in the hands of one person. To prove the point, Paul takes a lesson from Exodus 16:18, where Israel collects the "bread from heaven" they call *manna* (which literally means in Hebrew, "what is it?"). God gives manna to all of Israel. Those who try to collect too much can't keep it, and those who have too little are well fed. Paul applies the same logic to the economy of grace. "The one who had much did not have too much, and the one who had little did not have too little" (2 Cor 8:15). Grace cannot be counted as if it were mere money. Either you have grace or you don't. Either you share grace or you don't. So since money is God's grace to the church, then it must be shared by the church *for its ultimate purpose:* we are God's grace to each other that we might be God's grace to the world.

We can see now why Paul didn't believe in tithing. There is no store-house of God's grace, no repository of sacrifice. Since Paul believed that we are the temple of God, then we become God's sacrifice, and money supports the entire church. In fact Paul broadened the idea of wealth to include spiritual riches whenever he talked about money (not only in 2 Cor 8:9 but also Phil 4:17-19; Gal 6:1-10; Rom 15:25-27). To his way of thinking, sharing wealth was the only way to build up the body of Christ. (He applies the same argument to spiritual gifts—all are exercised for the common good [1 Cor 12:4-31].) If one part of the church receives spiritual blessings, then they should reciprocate with material blessings. If another part of the church receives material bless-ings, then they should reciprocate with spiritual blessings (Rom 15:27; 1 Cor 9:11; 2 Cor 8:14). By sharing wealth the entire church realizes how much they need each other to experience the grace of God. To put it on a practical level, whenever I speak to churches they often give money to me. I receive it as God's grace. And I give money to those from whom I have received spiritual blessings. In this giving and re-ceiving, God's grace becomes evident when we "work for the good of all, especially for those of the family of faith" (Gal 6:10).

That's why Paul prefers the farming illustration of sowing and reap-ing when he writes about work, money, spiritual riches and the gospel ministry (2 Cor 9:6-15; cf. Gal 6:7-9; 1 Cor 3:6-10; 9:10-11; 2 Tim 2:6). He didn't see our giving as "Christian charity." In fact I would suggest that in Paul's mind there is no such thing. Instead, Paul presumed we all *work* for the same thing: sowing the gospel seed into the hearts of every single person so that a bountiful harvest will come to the glory of God. Sown seed produces more seed. The more we give what we have received (God's grace!), the more "seed" he supplies for the sowing. God is our source of endless supply so that we give *everything*—work, money, time, thanksgiving, prayers—"cheerfully" in celebration of God's abundant grace (2 Cor 9:6-15). One can only give what has been given—we all are needy people. So all of us give out of our poverty, just like Jesus. All of us need God's grace everyday, just like manna. This is why Paul kept saying not to grow weary in doing what is right (Gal 6:9; 2 Thess 3:13). God's grace shows up every day. We'll never run out of seed. Therefore we know the harvest will come because God's grace is the gift that keeps on giving, even to the end of the world. "Grace has brought me safe thus far, and grace will lead me home."

When the homeless show up at Cherith Brook (a Catholic Worker house in Kansas City), they know they will receive God's grace. That's because a group of Christians are there to share what they have received: food, clothing, warm showers, coffee, kindness, Communion, Bible study, music, good conversation, gentle souls. Free showers, warm food and clean clothing are available three times a week. Various jobs require workers: bike repair, gardening, collecting dry groceries for area businesses, taking care of chickens and stray cats, washing clothes, and general upkeep of the house and storefront. Those who live there (a man, his wife, and two children; a single mother and her daughter; and three single men) have special days of prayer. On Saturday mornings they serve a pancake breakfast and celebrate Communion. Several times during the year they organize special activities for the kids. A former student of mine, "Mike," had invited me to speak to the group as they gathered one evening for one of their "clarification meetings." My topic was "Worship as Warfare: A Study of the Revelation of John." That night four groups of people came: the workers who lived in community at the house, those who supported the ministry by helping and giving money, the people off the street who were regular attendees, and guests who came because of their connections with one of the three groups. During the talk I asked a rather innocuous question, "When you gather for worship in your church, do you see it as warfare against the powers of this fallen world?" I expected all kinds of answers because the residents and workers go to different churches on Sunday—Episcopalian, Disciples of Christ, Methodist and Baptist. A few offered their observations about their worship experience, but the comment that surprised everyone came from a man who lived on the street. "In my church we know it's war, because it's hard to do what is right when you're out there every day trying to live for Jesus." One of the residents asked,

"Really? What church are you talking about?" And the homeless man said confidently, "This one."

Afterward, one of the residents confessed, "It never dawned on me that they would think of this as their church. But it makes sense: they come here for Communion. We have Bible studies here. They come here to pray. We sing together. Those of us who live here think of ourselves as members of our respective congregations—wherever we worship on Sunday is our church. But these friends of ours who come here from the street—to them this is church." Then I said something like, "Yes, maybe what you're doing here is church more than any of you realize. I know that to most twentysomethings *church* is a word that carries a lot of baggage. Most of my students prefer to talk about living in 'community.' But from what I have seen—your hospitality and sharing of resources and working for the entire community and praying together and worshiping together—for lack of a better word is church. This is family. This is home." Later that night as I bedded down for the evening in the house, I thought, "It makes perfect sense: if there were ever a place where a homeless man should find a home, it's church." Then I fell asleep, thinking about Revelation, the end of the world and how a homeless man reminded us all of what church is.

I came to a house off Twelfth Street in Kansas City because I thought I was taking the gospel to the ends of the earth. To be sure, different persons show up there every day looking for help because they've lost power. No place to take a shower. No way to make a warm meal. It must feel like the end of the world. And so they come. They come because they have discovered—even those who choose to live on the street—that they can't live by themselves. They need a community. They need a church. They need a family. For the exact same reason, Paul came to Jerusalem. He knew his converts couldn't be the church by themselves. They needed a community. They had to be church together. They were family, which is why he brought money. The church in Jerusalem needed their Gentile brothers and sisters as much as Paul's converts needed them. Paul admitted that he needed the church in Jerusalem too—to accept Paul's ministry to the Gentiles (Rom 15:16, 31), thereby preserving the unity of the church that is neither Jew nor

Gentile, male nor female, slave nor free (Eph 3:1–4:6). In fact by going to the ends of the earth and back Paul may have believed he was witnessing the end of the world when he brought the relief offering to Jerusalem.[8]

Isaiah predicted the end of the world would be marked by Gentiles bringing gold and silver to Jerusalem (Is 60:1-14). He also believed it would take a man covered by the armor of God to pull it off, wearing "righteousness like a breastplate, and a helmet of salvation on his head" (Is 59:17). This servant of YHWH would have the Spirit of God in his soul and the words of God in his mouth (Is 59:21). Because of his work the nations will bring their wealth to Jerusalem, along with "good news of the praises of the LORD" (Is 60:6 NASB). Then they will be welcomed into the house of God (Is 60:7). Coming from the ends of the earth— the coastlands—their sacrifices will bring glory to God's temple (Is 60:7-9). When these things came to pass, it would signal the end of the world (Is 60:15-22).[9]

Perhaps Paul believed he was seeing all these things come true. He may have even believed he was the man, "wrapped in zeal" and taking the "good news" to the coastlands (Is 59:17-18).

> The least of them shall become a clan,
>     and the smallest one a mighty nation;
> I am the LORD;
>     in its time I will accomplish it quickly. (Is 60:22)

Paul, the least of the apostles, was looking for the day when he would present his converts to the Lord on the day of Christ's return (1 Thess 2:19-20; 3:12-13). Only then would he know that his work was not "in vain" (1 Thess 3:5). Until that day, he would hasten the end of the world by taking the gospel to the ends of the earth. And in the meantime Paul believed the end was near because a group of people he called "the called out ones" lived like the end of the world had already happened— where Jew and Gentile, male and female, slave and free live together as one because grace is their currency. Indeed, Paul believed the end of the world should be marked by generosity because God's grace is never in short supply.

Therefore, my beloved, be steadfast, immovable, always excelling in the work of the Lord, because you know that in the Lord your labor is not in vain.

St. Paul, from Ephesus, to the Corinthians, when they were confused about the last day (1 Cor 15:58)

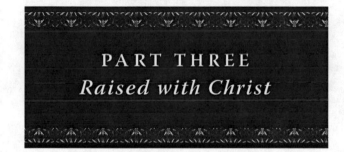

PART THREE
*Raised with Christ*

# 9

# Bold Confession

## *Wasting No Time*

"How's it going to end?" That's the unanswerable question hanging over the head of every viewer of the film *The Truman Show.* Both the fictitious fans of the reality-television show and the real-life people who watched the movie anxiously anticipated the end of Truman Burbank's world—a world created by the mysterious character Christof, a Hollywood director and producer. Orphaned at birth, Truman is adopted, named and cast by Christof to be the central character of a twenty-four-hour program that will chronicle Truman's entire life using hundreds of strategically placed cameras. The show becomes a smash hit, viewed by millions of people around the world. As Truman gets older, the television set gets bigger, eventually becoming the resort town Seahaven—a manmade key surrounded by water and encased in a massive dome where images of the sun, moon and stars appear on cue. More actors are hired to live and work on the elaborate movie set, creating the illusion of a real world for Truman, the only "actor" who doesn't know everything is fake. As time marches on, the entire world watches as Truman grows to be a man, graduates from college, falls into a career, finds a wife and finally grows discontented with his life. He often complains to his "best friend" that he feels like something is missing. His "arranged" marriage has grown wearisome. His job is boring. His everyday world has become meaningless. He wants more out of life than what has been given.

Peter Weir's film is a masterful exploration of the fundamental issues of life: Who am I? Where did I come from? Where am I going?
And the question that hangs over all of our heads: how's it going to
end? The open-ended eschatological dilemma is put in sharp relief
against the manipulated pseudoworld created by the godlike "man in
the moon" (Christof's production studio is located in the moon), who
seeks to control Truman's life by watching every move he makes. But
the viewers can't help but cheer for Truman as he tries to break free
from the prison that is supposed to be heaven on earth. ("Seahaven" is
an anagram for "As heaven.") Even though everything happens for
Truman's sake—he's the center of his world, the major player in the
drama of his life—the young man named after a major television city
(Burbank, California) unknowingly wants to discover the "real world."
Irony builds upon irony when Truman recalls a time when life was
good, when he pursued a college girl who, unbeknownst to him, was
not scripted to be his wife. During a chance encounter in the library,
Truman calls attention to a pin on the girl's sweater, a bit of popular
merchandise worn by television viewers all over the world. As Truman
flirts with the girl, he points to the pin (a round button that simply has
the words, "How's it going to end?") and says, "I like your pin. Was
wondering that myself."

*The Truman Show* is the Adam story turned upside down. He is the
true man, the second Adam, the American version of "the fall from
Eden." But in this story of paradise the hero does the *right* thing when
he rebels against his creator and leaves the world made for him. Compelled by a sense of vain labor, Truman has to discover for himself what
it means to live on his own terms. His self-discovery brings him to the
conclusion that his entire life has been a farce. His angst eventually
drives him to sail to the end of the earth, walk off the movie set (the
camera angle makes it appear as though he's walking on water) and
discover the real world in hopes of recovering the wasted years of his
life—a life that was chosen for him. Truman's "Damascus road" epiph-
any comes just before he walks out the door of the massive biodome
movie set. Christof's voice beckons him from the sky: "Truman." Truman looks to the heavens and asks, "Who are you?" Christof says ma-

jestically: "I am the creator [long pause] of a television show that gives hope and joy and inspiration to millions." Truman asks, "Who am I?" to which Christof declares, "You're the star!" Then Truman bows his head and muses, "Was nothing real?" Thus, in the end, Truman answers the eschatological question—how's it going to end?—for himself. Indeed, *The Truman Show* ends when Truman decides who he really is rather than what he was meant to be.

Paul's life looks like an upside-down version of *The Truman Show*. Paul expressed confidence in his pre-Christophany life, sure of who he was and what he was doing—what he called having "confidence in the flesh" (Phil 3:3-4). After his Damascus-road experience Paul seemed to lose that self assurance; several times he wonders "out loud" whether the work of his new calling is in vain (1 Cor 15:8-10, 14; 2 Cor 6:1-3; 9:3; Gal 2:2; 3:4; 4:11; Phil 2:16; 1 Thess 2:1; 3:5). The threat of a vain labor seemed to hang over his head throughout his apostleship, haunting him to the end. His doubts seemed to have been fueled by his pre-Christian campaign to persecute the "church of God" (1 Cor 15:9), by the shaky faith and occasional disobedience of his converts (Gal 3:4; 4:11) and by the current persecution of certain churches (1 Thess 3:3-5). What is surprising is that, unlike Truman, Paul already knew the answer to the question, how's it going to end? For as far as the apostle was concerned, the resurrection of Christ—the end of history—had already been played out in history.[1] The script had already been written. He would play the part till the end and therefore be raised from the dead just like Christ. But Paul believed he still had to overcome the curse of Adam's sin, where the ground of our labor threatens to yield thorns and thistles, even though he was convinced the resurrection of Christ had reversed the curse. Indeed, Paul believed he was already participating in the resurrection of Christ.

## Are We There Yet?

Like most good stories, when it comes to the Bible, the ending explains the beginning. Or, to put it in theological terms, eschatology is predicated on protology. What comes first anticipates what happens in the end. Last things complete first things. In our canon the Bible starts

with a garden and ends with a garden city. It begins with a son of God
and ends with the Son of God. It traces how all nations derive from one
man and then tells the story of how all nations will be drawn together
by one man. The timeline of all history begins and ends with God—
the Alpha and Omega. Indeed, except for the Persians the Bible presumes a philosophy of history that is unique to the Jewish people. Unlike their pagan neighbors who viewed time as a vicious cycle, always
repeating and never resolving, the Jews believed time moved on a
straight line—from start to finish. The question for them, of course,
was determining where they were on the line of the story of God and
his people. They knew the beginning: after God created a good world,
Adam sinned and brought the curse of sin and death on all his descendants. They also knew the part about how they were the descendants of
the one man whom God would use to draw all nations to worship the
one, true God. One day even Gentiles would call the progenitor of
Israel, "Father Abraham." Sure there were twists and turns in the drama
of how God would make things turn out in the end. Promises of land
and temple. Promises of a king and a kingdom. Promises of glory,
power and blessing—the day when everything was made right. The
problem was that day—what the prophets called, "the day of the
LORD"—never seemed to dawn on them.

When would God make good on all of his promises? Some prophets
said it depended on Israel. If God's elect could ever learn the lesson that
obedience is better than sacrifice, then God's blessing would return
and all promises would be fulfilled. Looking back on the past helped
them anticipate the future. What God had done was a clear indication
of what he would do. In this case history is the solution to the problem
because the story of Israel's disobedience and God's punishment kept
repeating itself. Who would break the cycle? It depended on the time.
After Moses they anticipated a great prophet. After Joshua they were
looking for a wise judge. After David they longed for a "son of David,"
a king, a Messiah. After Ezra, a teacher of righteousness. One prophet
even predicted that Elijah would come back from the dead to bring
about repentance before the great day of the Lord (Mal 4:5-6). But
heroes came and went, and nothing seemed to change; perhaps some

would say it even got worse: the righteous were persecuted, and the wicked were prospering. That scenario led some prophets to give up on history. What has always been is not determinative of what will be. History is not the solution but the problem. One day God will intervene and bring an end to history, re-creating a *new* world of peace and justice—where the righteous are rewarded and the wicked are punished. These "apocalyptic" prophets envisioned a new heaven and new earth. The old world passes away, and everything becomes new the day heaven crashes into earth, when God comes down and lives with his people forever—a day no one can predict.

Paul held onto both ideas[2] because he believed the resurrection of Christ is the day of the Lord—a day that started with Easter and ends at the second coming of Christ. This explains why sometimes Paul refers to the resurrection as a past event (1 Cor 15:14), and also speaks of the resurrection to come (1 Cor 15:50-55). Like the prophets of old, Paul believed looking back can help us determine what will be. Since Christ has been raised, then we will also be raised. And Paul also shared an apocalyptic view of the world: God will intervene when Christ descends from heaven and returns to earth. In other words Paul believed the day of the Lord had "already" dawned on all creation through Christ's resurrection. But the curse of Adam's sin—the risk of vain labor and the reality of imminent death—proved that the day of the Lord had "not yet" fully come. This "already/not yet" eschatology explains why Paul could think of salvation as past, present and future (Eph 2:8; 1 Cor 15:2; Rom 5:9). The resurrection meant that all things have passed away and everything has become new for those who are "in Christ" (2 Cor 5:17). Paul said his converts were already "seated in heaven," raised with Christ to reign over everything that opposes God (Eph 2:1-7). At the same time he admitted that the enemies of God— sin, death and evil powers—still rule outside of heaven: in the air, on the earth and under the earth. Therefore the law of sin and death would continue to have its way until believers receive their "crown of life," the imperishable body, on the last day (1 Cor 15:42-55).

This two-stage view of the resurrection reveals why scholars are quick to point out that Paul was no dualist.[3] He didn't operate with a sense that heaven is up there and we're down here and never the two shall meet. Nor did he believe that we must simply survive an evil world, gritting our teeth and holding on till it all hits the apocalyptic fan at the end of time. Instead, Paul was convinced that heaven and earth overlap, that the new age has already broken into history. This cosmic and temporal fusion has occurred because of the resurrection of Christ. The glorified body of Christ is what heaven looks like. The resurrection—the transforming power of Christ's victory over death— is already at work in the life of every believer. This is why he could speak of Christ's resurrection as something that has already happened and is not yet fully realized. Indeed, the resurrection is the evidence that Christ *must* reign until he defeats every enemy, especially the *last* enemy of all creation: death (1 Cor 15:25-26). In the end all die; but for those who are "in Christ" all are made alive in the end. *Then* Christ's reign will be *undeniably* present, when the body of Christ is raised on the last day: "We are expecting a Savior, the Lord Jesus Christ. He will transform the body of our humiliation so that it may be conformed to the body of his glory" (Phil 3:20-21). Until then the reign of Christ— the resurrection of Christ—is evident on earth. But it is hidden, a mystery to those who lack the wisdom of God (1 Cor 2:7-16).

So what does resurrection power look like on earth? On the outside it looks like death. It looks like weakness and groaning.[4] It looks like loss, foolishness and failure. It looks like a hopeless cause, a problem that never goes away, a wasted effort. Indeed, it looks like a man who labors in vain. But even as "our outer nature is wasting away," Paul believed "our inner nature is being renewed day by day" (2 Cor 4:16). "Because we look not at what can be seen but at what cannot be seen," believers operate with an abiding hope that God is at work in our lives in mysterious ways. Our transformation is incomplete. Resurrection growth is hard to track. It isn't quantifiable. You can't point to a measuring stick and say, "See how much I've grown this past year?" But that doesn't stop us from counting up our days, taking inventory of our lives and wondering "out loud" like Paul whether our life's work was in vain. It's the human condition; we all want to know if we've made a mark on things, left an indelible impression, found immortality. That's because we have no doubts about our mortality. We know we're going to die. What we don't know is whether we have truly lived. Thus the nagging speculation, how's it going to end? is eclipsed by the more troubling question, did my life matter at all?

At times Paul acted like that question wouldn't be answered until the parousia of Christ. He envisioned the day when he would be vindicated, when all doubts would be put to rest, when every question would be answered—the day he presented all of his converts to Christ as blameless children of Abraham. Then and only then would Paul's boast be legitimized: "For what is our hope or joy or crown of boasting before our Lord Jesus at his coming? Is it not you?" (1 Thess 2:19). Paul longed for the day when he would stand before Christ, with every Gentile convert standing behind him as an eternal witness to the truth of the gospel he preached. (By the way, I love Paul's vision—that one day I will stand with all the Gentiles who have believed in Jesus Christ. A vast multitude behind the apostle to the Gentiles, we will all celebrate that his work was not in vain.) At the same time, Paul also spoke of a confidence, a boldness of resurrection faith that gave him courage to face every trial with a sense of divine blessing (1 Thess 2:1-2). Regardless of how things looked on the outside—his body wasting away, his enemies hindering his mission, his converts ignoring his instructions— Paul was convinced he was experiencing the resurrection of Christ on the inside. A renewed mind. An encouraged heart. A satisfied soul. An undefeatable Spirit. Indeed, only the glorious resurrection of Christ could explain how a man could undergo such a radical transformation from the inside out (2 Cor 3:4–4:1).

"If it weren't for the resurrection of Christ, I wouldn't be a believer." My friend "Todd" and I were fishing and trying to sum up the essence of our faith. "I know what you mean," Todd said in an unusually somber tone. Then it hit me why the conversation had turned so serious; we weren't just talking theology anymore. To hope in the resurrection power of Christ—that God can turn death into life—is more than a declaration of faith for Todd. In fact it is the story of his life. When he was a little boy, he and his younger brother were orphaned when his father murdered his wife (their mother) and committed suicide, having

burned their house to the ground. Todd said he remembers very clearly
what happened that day. His father sent the two boys across the street
to play with the neighbors. Then after a few hours someone noticed the
house was on fire. Todd says he remembers the sirens, the sight of his
house burning down, neighbors gawking, people crying, policeman investigating, and then someone sitting him and his brother down in the
living room of their friend's house and telling them rather matter-of-
factly that both of their parents were dead. "I remember feeling very
empty, very lost—like I didn't know what I was supposed to do. Where
do I sleep tonight? Who will take care of me and my brother? Where
will we live? Will we still have Christmas? What do I do now? I just
remember being so confused."

Todd's story gets even worse. He and his brother were shuttled from
Southern California to Idaho to Missouri within a few years, as different family members tried to take care of the boys. The family that finally agreed to take them had meager resources to take care of their
own; now with the additional burden of two more mouths to feed, two
more bodies to clothe, frustrations mounted, tensions grew, and Todd
decided that living on his own was better than sleeping under the roof
provided for him. As soon as he finished high school, he left "home,"
eventually going to college and graduate school, married his college
girlfriend, found a successful career and became the father of four children. His brother didn't follow the same path; he was always getting in
and out of trouble. Being the "big brother," Todd felt responsible for the
only family member he had—a troubled brother who kept making self-
destructive choices that eventually led to his own death. Reflecting on
the tragedy, Todd told me: "My brother had a good heart. People tell
me they don't understand it when I say, 'I don't blame him for all the
trouble he got into.' In fact I think I'm the only one who truly understands."

But here's the amazing part of Todd's story. You would expect a man
like this to be jaded, cynical, always given to a melancholy mood of
perpetual self-pity. But that couldn't be further from the truth. Todd is
a happy-go-lucky kind of guy. Loves life. Enjoys the simple things.
Relishes the everyday moments of good conversation and friendly ban-

ter. In fact most people might draw the wrong inference and say, "That man must have had it easy. He always acts like life is good. Probably had everything handed to him." The truth is: he's had a very hard life. And yet he's not a hard man. He has a soft heart. He's a gentle soul. He has a bedrock confidence that God loves him. To me the only way to make sense of Todd's life is to utterly believe in the resurrection of Christ—then and now. So on the day we were fishing for some luck, when Todd said, "The resurrection of Jesus is my only hope," I knew he meant every word.

The resurrection of Christ is an unstoppable work of God in the life of every believer. In spite of life's disappointments—regardless of how things appear—Paul was convinced that God would finish what he started: "I am confident of this, that the one who began a good work among you will bring it to completion by the day of Jesus Christ" (Phil 1:6). For just as believers experience the death of Christ and are buried with him through baptism, we are also destined to share in his resurrection. But it isn't simply a matter of our body—suffering from the effects of sin—being restored, reclaimed, remade after death. As far as Paul was concerned God has already begun to raise the dead when any person turns to Christ in faith. It was God's design from the beginning not only to raise a worn-out body from the dead but also to raise a broken heart from the dead, to raise a contrite spirit from the dead, to raise a corrupt mind from the dead, to raise a troubled soul from the dead. When it comes to Christ's resurrection, nothing is left behind. When old things pass away, *everything* becomes new. On the last day the resurrection will be obvious. Until then we simply have to wait for time to catch up with the reality of what God has already done through Christ *in us*. Indeed, if the resurrection of Christ teaches us anything it's this: death's days are numbered—it's only a matter of time till *everyone* sees the resurrection reign of Christ.

## What Time Is It?

Paul used several metaphors to explain how the resurrection of Christ has already happened but is still yet to come. Paul refers to Jesus' resurrection as the first fruits of the harvest that will be fully gleaned one day (1 Cor 15:23). Jesus is the "firstborn within a large family" (Rom 8:29), the "firstborn from the dead" (Col 1:18). Paul describes the believer's participation in the resurrection as sharing in Christ's inheritance because we are adopted children of God. The papers have been signed; the adoption will be complete when our bodies have been redeemed on the last day (Rom 8:23). The surety of receiving the inheritance comes in the form of a down payment; God's promise of raising us from the dead is evidenced by the "first installment," that is, his Spirit (2 Cor 1:20-22). In fact Paul repeatedly pointed to the work of the Holy Spirit whenever he tried to assure his converts that they had already begun to experience the resurrection of Christ. The presence of Christ's Spirit in the life of every believer was proof that God would finish what he started. God's Spirit raised Christ from the dead; therefore he will do the same for us (Rom 8:11). Thus Paul refers to the Holy Spirit as the first fruits (Rom 8:23), the Spirit of adoption (Rom 8:15), the down payment of God's work in us (2 Cor 5:5; Eph 1:14). God's Spirit poured out on all flesh is the prophetic dream becoming reality (Joel 2:28-29). The gift of the Holy Spirit triggered the end of the age. The night is passing; the day is dawning (Rom 13:12). Christ's resurrection started the dominoes falling. This is why Paul could speak so confidently that he and his converts were witnessing the end of the world; they were the ones "upon whom the ends of the ages have come" (1 Cor 10:11).

Of course, we don't think Paul was right about that. Paul didn't know then what we know now. If the end-of-the-world dominoes started falling in A.D. 30, then (unbeknownst to Paul) God must have set up a very long line of them; and still there's no end in sight. But before we pronounce upon Paul a short-sightedness that compelled him to pronounce "prematurely" the end of time, perhaps we need to explore whether we're the ones with the vision problem. Or another way of putting it, perhaps we're the ones with the *timing* problem. We are more than willing to accept that the resurrection of Christ is already happening now as inward transformation. But believing just like Paul that the return of Christ and the resurrection of the dead are right around the corner would mean for us that the last days have been happening for two thousand years. To put it bluntly time is a problem for us. But it's more than the apparent "delay" of Christ's parousia that troubles us. We have a hard time accepting Paul's eschatological perspective because of how we see time. To us time is a constant, immovable force, a temporal concrete. Like a welder joining two pieces of metal, once heat is applied and the welding bead is formed, the past is fused into permanence. We also see time moving along a line that joins the events of our lives into history, a welding of moments that cannot be undone. But Paul didn't see time as one line of unbroken history that cannot be changed. Instead, he believed history is the work of God; therefore the past can be redeemed. And he believed that we can experience the future as a present reality (what scholars call "prolepsis").[5] According to Paul, Christ believers are not bound by time and space—not only are we seated in heaven while living on earth, but we are also raised with Christ, buried with Christ, co-crucified with him, even chosen "in him" before time began (Eph 1:3-4). In other words time wasn't a problem for Paul.[6] It can be redeemed, renewed, recreated, transformed, transposed and even transferred. Like everything that has been created, time does not exist on its own. Therefore, like all creation, time ultimately serves the purposes of God. God is the Lord of time.

Paul certainly experienced time like we do. He used stock terminology to describe time as a quantifiable, moment-by-moment experience (*hēmera*, "day"; *hōra*, "hour"), a definite period of time (*kairos* and *chronos*, "Now concerning the times [*chronon*] and seasons [*kairon*] . . ."), and an undefined duration of time (*aiōnes*, "ages"). But unlike us (and more like his contemporaries), Paul thought of time as a power created by God. There was a time when time was not (1 Cor 2:7), when wisdom existed *before* the ages (Prov 8:22-23). Then God created the heavens and the earth, and ordained time to *rule* as moon and stars by night and as the sun by day (Gen 1:14-18; Is 24:21-23). But God did more than set up daily rule of time; God marked boundaries of time— "the ages" (or "eons," *aiōnes*)—that would distinguish different periods of God's dealing with humanity (what Paul called "predestination").[7] Some scholars suggest Paul believed there were three eons of time (Adam, Israel, Christ); most are convinced Paul divided history into two ages (the old age and the age to come).[8] Whether two or three, this Jewish view of the temporal mechanics of the world probably provides the basis of Paul's remarks in 1 Corinthians 2:6-16 and Ephesians 2:1-7.

Paul worked with the presumption that there were different kinds of wisdom because there have been different ages of time. Indeed, wisdom resides in time; it is the knowledge drawn from the experience of creation. And yet Paul believed that there is a superior wisdom that existed before time, before creation. It is God's wisdom, not bound by time and space. In other words time cannot rule over this kind of wisdom. The way Paul puts it, "the rulers of this eon" were ignorant of it—they only know the "wisdom of this age [eon]" (1 Cor 2:6-8). The preexistent wisdom that God "decreed before the ages [eons]" is also the end-of-the-world work of Christ, in other words, the gospel Paul preached. That is to say, Paul believed the gospel is the timeless wisdom of God—it existed before time and it is a "sneak preview" of the end of time, a mystery revealed to those who have spiritual eyes. The "present evil age [eon]" (Gal 1:4) is ruled by the "course [eon] of this world," identified by Paul as the "ruler of the power of the air" and the "spirit that is now at work among those who are disobedient" (Eph 2:2). So for Paul there seems to be a spatial realm to the temporal rule of the eons. That's why scholars have a hard time sorting out what Paul meant by the expression "the rulers of this age." Was he talking about human governing authorities or some spiritual realm of unseen powers, what we would call the "power behind the throne"? We will take up the topic of how Paul understood "the powers" in chapter eleven. But for now, since Paul wrote about time (eons) as if it were a created power, and claimed that the gospel supersedes time (perhaps, even rules over time), what we want to know is this: what are the implications of Paul's view of time for his spirituality?

Paul believed that all creation is being redeemed from the curse of sin and death (Rom 8:19-23). Therefore, if time is a created power, then it shouldn't surprise us that Paul believed time is redeemable (Eph 5:16). But as far as Paul was concerned "redeeming the time" wasn't a matter of simply making sure the present is claimed for God's purposes. Paul believed the past can be redeemed too.[9] God can correct our mistakes. Take, for example, how Paul makes sense of the timing of the Christophany. The resurrected Christ appeared to several men, making them apostles of the gospel (1 Cor 15:3-7). When it came to Paul, however, it seems as though Christ appeared to the apostle of the Gentiles at the *wrong* time: "Last of all, as to one untimely born, he appeared to me also" (1 Cor 15:8). Why was it the wrong time? If Christ had appeared to Paul when he commissioned the others, then obviously Paul wouldn't have persecuted the church. That made Paul "the least of apostles, unfit to be called an apostle" (1 Cor 15:9). And yet Paul claimed his life had not been in vain: "By the grace of God I am what I am" (1 Cor 15:10). He was convinced God's predetermined plan/preexistent gospel—that God would have a people conformed to the image of his Son—was coming true in his life too (Rom 8:28-39). Paul was not a prisoner of his mistakes, because all time (past, present and future) is under the purview of God's redeeming work. God's grace can work backward as well as forward.

This rather "flexible" view of time explains why Paul believed he and his converts went "back in time" to participate in the death, burial and resurrection of Christ. It also provided Paul a handy tool to wedge the Gentiles into the history of God's people. Since Jews believed that every descendant of Abraham was seminally present in his loins when God spoke blessing upon Abraham and his seed (Heb 7:10), then Paul had to explain how Gentiles, who by definition are not children of Abraham, could realize that blessing *without* becoming Jews. One strategy was to claim that the "seed of Abraham" was Christ. All who are "in Christ" (they have faith like Father Abraham, believing the promise of God) are part of Abraham's seed and receive the blessing of God (Gal 3:13-14). Since God granted the promise of blessing to Abraham, then those who belong to Christ are Abraham's offspring too (Gal 3:18, 29). Paul takes a more "organic" approach in Romans, claiming his Gentile converts have been grafted into the olive tree of Israel (Rom 11:16-24). Even though the tree had grown for quite some time—a "holy" root system that produced "holy" branches—Paul argues that Gentile branches could "share the rich root of the olive tree" as if they had been a part of it all along (Rom 11:17). God grafted them into the tree because the "gifts and the calling of God are irrevocable" (Rom 11:29).

That is to say, even God (the Lord of time) would not start another tree; if the Gentiles were to receive the promises he made to Abraham, then they would have to be grafted into Israel, the olive tree of God's work. So the past work of God (blessing to Abraham/Israel) has been transformed by the present work of God (the salvation of Gentiles in Christ), which would even hasten the future work of God (the regrafting/salvation of Israel, Rom 11:14-15, 23-32). This is more than revisionist history; Paul is doing more than redacting a story. Paul believed God could bend time to his purposes.

In the history of time, God made time stand still (Josh 10:13), reversed time (Is 38:8) and will even cause time to speed up at the end (Mt 24:22). So when God raised Christ from the dead (an end-of-the-world event), the old way of reckoning time—the old age—was eclipsed by new-creation time. Every day in Christ old things pass away and everything becomes new. In every moment of the new age the past can be reformed and the future can be revealed. There are no irreversible mistakes; sins are forgiven. There is no such thing as a hopeless future; God has already shown us the plan. In other words, according to Paul, there can be no wasted time. All things are redeemed in Christ. "All things work together for good for those who love God, who are called according to his purpose" (Rom 8:28). Sometimes we act like time is our enemy, marking off days as if we were serving a prison sentence. At the same time, we often speak of time as if it were our friend: "Time heals all wounds." But for those of us who already share in the resurrection of Christ the truth of the matter is, time is neither friend nor foe. Time is simply a created power that has been redeemed by the work of Christ. Indeed, to those who think they've lost time due to foolish decisions or live in dread of what may happen because of short-sighted mistakes, believers should boldly confess: "His wounds heal all time." That's because, like Paul, we're convinced the resurrection (the *new* creation!) changes everything—even our past, our present and especially our future.

Every day I work with college students who are tortured by the decisions they have to make. It is an unusual time. During their brief college career they face many decisions that may affect them for the rest of their lives: marriage, career, beliefs, identity. We've put such a premium on the power of choice that it often misleads students into thinking they control their own destiny, they make their own future. In fact sociologists have said these "millennials" were brought up by well-meaning baby-boomer parents who thought they were building their children's self-esteem as they sent them into the world by repeating the mantra: "You can do whatever you choose to do." But I see them as they take that last step, before entering the rough-and-tumble "real" world, and they don't know what to do. They feel the pressure of making the *right* choice. Do I major in this or that? Do I give my heart to him or not? Do I still believe what I learned in church? Is this what I want to do for the rest of my life? They act as if one mistake, one false move, one poor choice will seal their fate forever. And yet time marches on. After two years, they have to decide their major. Another friend gets engaged, and it seems their opportunities for marriage are slipping away. They learn so much in such a short time that some are not sure what they believe anymore. Four years fly by. Now everyone's asking the dreaded question, "What are you going to do now?" The idea of settling on one career, doing the same job for the rest of their lives, sounds like a death wish. They want to truly live. But they know life's responsibilities are pressing in on them like never before. On the precipice of graduation, it's déjà vu all over again—they're reliving their childhood, when everyone wanted to know, "What are you going to be when you grow up?" Only this time a childlike answer detailing the pursuit of foolish dreams will no longer do.

When Truman Burbank sailed to the end of the world, he was fulfilling a childhood dream. He always wanted to be like Magellan, discovering the unknown by sailing around the world. Finally overcoming his fear of water (and of the future?), Truman's quest to discover the unknown world leads him to the end of his world—a world made for him by his "father," Christof. Whenever we watch this film for my Bible and American Culture class, students have a different take on the movie. They don't see it as a revision of the story of Adam and paradise lost. To them *The Truman Show* is a commentary on Christian subculture. Indeed, Truman is their hero—a man who breaks free from all

the expectations placed on him by a pseudoworld of Christian idealism
that is stifling to those who want to truly live. The script for the "ideal"
life is: Find friends who promote what you already believe. Live in a
community where everyone looks the same. Get married in your twenties. Choose a career, buy the picket-fenced house, take to safe hobbies
(like gardening), plan your 2.5 children and live the rest of your days
pretending like this world that has been created for you is heaven on
earth. So when Truman looks up to the sky and asks the heavenly voice,
"Who am I?" students despise it when Christof responds: "You're the
star!" They grew up with a camcorder pointed at them their whole lives.
They recognize the fear and uncertainty of wanting to break free from
the life that has been planned for them. They've had this nagging sus-
picion for quite some time that the "Christian world" is not the real
world. Therefore they feel Truman's pain when he bows his head and
says, "Was nothing real?" And when Truman leaves the sterile, man-
made heaven on earth to discover the real world they cheer for him as
if he were embarking on their quest, chasing down the fear of entering
the unknown: "How's it going to end?"

Paul believed the resurrection of Christ is the real world; heaven had
come to earth. Paul didn't live in fear of discovering the unanswerable
question; he already knew how it's going to end. And he believed that
the church—the body of Christ—is supposed to picture what the end
of the world looks like: resurrected lives. Indeed, according to Paul, we
can be in two places at one time (heaven and earth overlap), and we can
be in two times at one place (experiencing the end of the world now).
So regardless of the time or where we are in the course of this world—
whether college graduate or a middle-aged man with four children—
the question, what do you want to be when you grow up? is still relevant.
And the answer is timeless: a new creation.

> For it is God who is at work in you, enabling you both to will and to
> work for his good pleasure. Do all things without murmuring and argu-
> ing, so that you may be blameless and innocent, children of God with-
> out blemish in the midst of a crooked and perverse generation, in which
> you shine like stars in the world.
> St. Paul, from a Roman prison, to the Philippians (Phil 2:13-15)

# 10

# Blessed Hope

*The Wait/Weight of Glory*

✻

A FEW YEARS AGO our youngest daughter, Grace, was trying to explain how she negotiated the daily drama of her social world at middle school. One student was giving his female classmates fits, but Grace was able to dismiss the boy's antics; she claimed he never got to her because she was able to size him up. "He's a telepathic liar," she said confidently. Grinning from ear to ear, Grace's older brother and sister almost said simultaneously, "You mean 'pathological liar.'" But before Grace could agree, I wanted to enjoy her unintentional pun: "You know, I think she's right. Maybe he is a telepathic liar. He may look like he's telling the truth. But Grace knows different: *she's* reading *his* mind." Then, turning to my thirteen-year-old daughter I said, "Grace. I hope you're able to keep that ability. It will come in handy when you get older and have to deal with boys on a regular basis," at which point our son (who majored in philosophy) and our oldest daughter (who majored in biology) playfully began to debate the metaphysical question "what is real?" by correlating gender issues and the differences between pathology and telepathy. They bantered about comments like "men are pigs" and "women are trappers" as each combatant relied on science and reason to score points in the battle of the sexes.

Nature ("men are pigs") versus nurture ("women are trappers") is the common dialectic by which we make sense of human behavior. We rely on science to tell us why certain persons do certain things. Social scientists argue that context is key; individuals are conditioned to respond in certain ways due to the sum of their past experiences. Biological scientists maintain that we're all hardwired to behave a particular way; our genetic makeup predetermines how we will respond to different situations. In either case the presumption of our quest—explaining why "men are pigs" or why "women are trappers"—is that science holds all the answers. In fact it may be safe to say that science is the state religion in the West. Geneticists are prophets who predict our future; physicians are priests who serve in the temple of health. When they are unable to answer our questions, why did this happen? or, what is the prognosis? or, what is the remedy? we fall into despair, troubled by the uncertainty of life. We want—we crave—certainty. So a new "Calvinism" has been developed to make us feel better about our lot. Its theology is biology, where faith is the gift of reason, and the doctrine of predestination is sorted out in the lab. We believe because test results are determinative.

What I find most puzzling is how this new "religion" found fertile soil in the land of American individualism. The mapping of the human genome should cause great angst among the very people who prize personal freedom. "I am not a robot." We should resent the fact that some of us are predisposed to high cholesterol simply because we are the progeny of our parents. "I will eat what I want." When we look in the mirror and see our father's reflection staring back at us, we should bow our heads in resignation, knowing that our future has been predetermined by genetic code. "I am my own person." And yet, despite what the prognosticators say—"you're just like your father" or "you'll probably die of heart disease before you're sixty"—we persist in our personal faith, convinced we will defy the odds of our "family history" and make our own destiny. Perhaps the power of our choices will override the predestination of our genetics. We all want to believe we can create the future even though scientists tell us it's already been decided for us. Indeed, when I see a new doctor it seems she's more interested in my past than what ails me in the present.

We were working out in the wellness center at the university, commiserating over our similar family histories, when my colleague said, "My doctor says I have a lousy gene pool." Her father died of heart trouble when she was only fifteen years old. Her mother died recently of Alzheimer's disease—a long, wearisome battle that took the woman's mind, then her body. My colleague also has a long line of cancer that runs in her family. "They have tests now to determine whether I'm genetically predisposed to Alzheimer's." "Are you going to take them?" I wondered out loud. "No, why would I?" she said calmly. "It wouldn't change a thing." I asked: "But don't they have drugs to delay the process?" "Yes, they do. I saw what it did to my mother. And I wouldn't want to put my family through the same ordeal. There came a time when I had to decide 'enough is enough.' Her mind was gone. Her body was wasting away. A family member shouldn't have to be put in that position, having to decide the end." Empathizing with her plight, I said, "As a believer, makes you want to ask: 'Where is God?' doesn't it?" Without hesitating she replied, "Exactly. That's why, in certain respects, it can be very comforting to say, 'God, it's up to you. If I get Alzheimer's, so be it.'" Then, at that very moment, we recognized the irony of having such a conversation in the wellness center, where we both show up nearly every day trying to delay the inevitable.

Predestination versus free will. Because of the advances in medical science we're realizing this is not just a theological debate anymore. And yet, when we're adding up the evidence of our biological future, I'm surprised how often it feels like we've left God out of the equation. We've been taught the future belongs to God. We speak of providence, sovereignty and predestination as divine work. We quote familiar passages to each other (sometimes taken out of context) like, "For surely I know the plans I have for you, says the Lord, plans for your welfare and not for harm, to give you a future with hope" (Jer 29:11)—to find assurance in the midst of uncertain times. Nevertheless we act resigned to our fate when we rehearse our family history. Thinking back, I'm surprised how often I've said, "I know the day will come when a doctor brings me into his office and says, 'you have cancer.' It's just a matter of time." Admitting it makes me feel better about my future, as if I'm in control of what will happen to me. That's when, occasionally, a small voice within me tries to speak up, reminding me that I'm still a believer: "But what about God?"

## Christian Destiny

Paul maintained that all humanity shares the same fate. The law of sin and death will have its way with every single one of us because we come from Adam (Rom 5:12-14). Much to the chagrin of Augustine and Pelagius or Barth and Brunner, Paul never explained *why* it had to be this way; that is, even though Adam was made in the image of God, why did he sin against God? Rather, Paul simply described the human condition as a given based on the pervasive reality of sin and death. We all sin; we all die. That is our common destiny because we share a common ancestry. Adam's story is our story. According to Paul this explains why we needed another Adam to undo what the first Adam did to every one of us (Rom 5:15-21). The Lord Jesus Christ, the second Adam, died for sinners so that we might live to God. That is to say, the second Adam vanquished the power of sin and death (Adam's legacy) by dying for sinners (Adam's descendants). Where there used to be condemnation, there is justification. Where there used to be judgment, there is grace. Where there used to be the dominion of death, there is eternal life. So that those who belong to the second Adam have a new legacy, a new heritage, (dare I say?) a new fate. They no longer share the image of God reflected only in the first Adam—the fate of all humanity. Christ believers are destined to reflect the image of God of the second Adam—a resurrected life. In fact according to Paul this hope is blessed because God had planned for it from the beginning (Rom 8:29-30).

Paul's talk of predestination was nothing new to his converts. That's because nearly every religion of the first-century world was built on a doctrine of divine sovereignty. The gods designed the world to operate according to their plans. The divine order was clearly seen in the rhythms of life: the course of the stars, moon and sun; planting and harvesting; birthdays and funerals; marriage and children. Certain individuals were predestined by the gods to rule, to serve as priests, to manage wealth, to learn a particular trade. No boy could decide for himself what he was meant to be (of course, girls were destined for domestication). The gods had already established a boy's career path by making him the son of a king, or priest, or landowner. Even in Jewish life a young man couldn't claim a divine call to serve God in his temple. That privilege was reserved for Levites; predestination was revealed by one's genealogy. Beyond the destiny prescribed by family heritage it was quite apparent to most that the gods seemed to favor certain individuals. "Fate" and "fortune" were seen as divine powers that wielded some influence over daily affairs. Taboos marked off danger zones; religious habits increased the odds of favorable results. Appeasing the gods, then, was the daily ritual of those who believed everything happened for a reason.[1]

What made Paul's ideas about predestination unusual was that he believed human destinies could change. As Gentiles, his converts were destined to endure the wrath of God. They used to be "enslaved to beings that by nature are not gods" (Gal 4:8). Dead in their sins these one-time idolaters—fools who did not know God—"turned to God from idols, to serve a living and true God" (1 Thess 1:9). But it wasn't merely the power of human choice that made this possible; Paul believed his converts were "called" by God (notice how Paul self-corrects): "Now, however, that you have come to know God, or rather to be known by God . . ." (Gal 4:9). Even though God had formed these clay pots to be vessels of destruction, the potter seemed to change his mind. He decided to show them mercy as if they had been prepared "beforehand for glory" (Rom 9:22-23). And Paul found a sympathetic voice in the prophet Hosea. It's as if God had decided to call these who are not his people, "my people," that is, "children of the living God" (Hos 2:23; Rom 9:25-26). And how did this happen? How did the fortunes/ destinies of Gentiles change so drastically? Because the second Adam changed the destiny of the descendants of the first Adam—those set up for sin and death found righteousness and life in Christ Jesus. This changed forever the game of negotiating a fallen world: for if God is now for us, who could be against us (Rom 8:28-39)?

Everyone wants to believe God is on their side. When good things happen, most of us are inclined to thank God for our success. This is especially evident when athletes compete. After winning the Super Bowl, American football players who boasted of their superior abilities before the big game will often thank God for their victory. (By the way,

I find it a little amusing that the name of the Greek goddess of victory, Nike, is often plastered all over their jerseys.) The celebrants act like God favored them in the contest. Occasionally an athlete will give the *real* reason why his team won: they trained hard, they worked hard, they prepared all season for this contest. In other words they deserved to win. But what lingers in the mind of most is the knowledge that all athletes work hard. All teams play hard. That's when even the most boastful player will try to acknowledge the intangible, nearly unidentifiable reason why their team won: luck (what the ancients called "Fortune"). They say things like, "Yeah. We got several breaks," or, "This is a game of inches," or, "Football is an odd-shaped ball, and we were fortunate the ball bounced our way." Recognizing the intangibles of their game, baseball players are notorious for counting on pregame rituals to ensure the longevity of hitting streaks or team victories. Their superstitious behavior, even during the game, can be downright entertaining—the mechanical routine some batters re-create *every* time they come to the plate looks like a religious ritual. And yet who can blame them? The ability to take a round object (bat) and hit another round object (ball) traveling over ninety miles per hour—moving up, down, left or right, sometimes more than a foot—with the batter having only milliseconds to decide whether to take a swing at the spinning orb seems miraculous. No wonder sports fans worship athletes as if they were gods.

Ever since the Olympic games of ancient Greece, athletes have been admired for their superhuman strength. Superior eyesight, lightning-quick reflexes, amazing eye-hand coordination—it's as if God predestined them to play baseball or football, which is why all athletes believe they deserve to be in the big game. It's not enough for them that they've earned a king's salary playing a boy's game. They long for the highest level of competition to display their divine talent. Most athletes believe god/fate is on their side. God made them special. Indeed, when they win the championship, talk of "destiny" fills the postgame locker room. What must be confusing to these highly trained, well-paid professionals is when they *lose* the game. Does it mean that God doesn't like them, that he wasn't for them, that they weren't as special as they thought? Indeed, would any of them have the guts to admit they were *destined* to lose the big game?

I'm sure many have noticed that we never hear athletes during post-game interviews thank God for their loss. It seems the god of athletics only shows up when players win. But as we've already discovered Paul believed the God of Israel delights in showing up in the midst of loss—the resurrection of Christ proves it. God turns losing into gain, death into life, sorrow into joy, weakness into strength, futility into glory. Indeed, if God can turn a cross (the greatest injustice of the world) into resurrection (the greatest hope in the world), then he can work *all* things for good. But that's hard to see when you're battered and bruised after losing. Paul knew this better than most. Even though he was literally beaten and bruised by disappointing losses (what might be called "failed" attempts to take the gospel into Jewish synagogues and Roman courts), Paul tried to see these things from the vantage point of the resurrection. In fact he played down the beatings and the stoning and the imprisonments as "slight momentary afflictions" that produced in him "an eternal weight of glory" (2 Cor 4:17). I can't get over that. Really? He thought the times he was nearly beaten to death were little more than "slight momentary affliction"? I can hear Paul say, "Yes. No big deal. When I think about how one day I will have a resurrected body just like Christ, then I imagine looking back on these brief excursions and thinking, 'Those little tussles were nothing compared to what I enjoy now. Look at me! See what the sufferings of Christ did to me? I'm glorified.'" So I can imagine Paul throwing his arm around the athlete who's just lost the World Series and saying (without an ounce of cynicism), "Son of Adam, life is a game we're all destined to lose. Let's go celebrate the good news."

It's what one scholar calls "the conversion of the imagination."[2] Paul challenged his converts to see the resurrected life in their bodies that were "wasting away" (2 Cor 4:16). He emphasized over and over again how Christ's resurrection is evident when our minds are raised from the dead. We have to see ourselves as "living sacrifices"—that is, a death that produces life, a transformation that comes about by "the renewing of your minds" (Rom 12:1-2). This helps us to see God's will in our lives, when we realize we're sharing the destiny of the second Adam—a cross that is worn like a crown. It's as if we see the end in the middle of life, the resurrection in the midst of our dying, hope when many despair. Paul saw the glory of God—the presence of God—when others pronounce his absence. He refused to kowtow to the world's perspective, that harsh circumstances should make us doubt the love of God: hardship, distress, persecution, famine, nakedness, peril and sword (Rom 8:35-39). Paul readily admitted to unbelievers that we look like stupid sheep led by God to the slaughterhouse. But he claimed we cling to the preposterous notion that God loves us no matter what *because of the resurrection of Christ*. In fact he goes a step further and boasts that we are "more than conquerors [*hypernikōmen*, "hyper"-Nike!] through him." Indeed, no matter what his opponents did to him, Paul found victory in the love of God.

That's why Paul sounds to me like an athlete boasting during the contest of life as he taunts death and the grave in light of the resurrection: "'Death has been swallowed up in victory [Nike].' Where, O death, is your victory [Nike]? Where, O death, is your sting?" (1 Cor 15:54-55). To Paul's contemporaries it must have seemed extremely foolish to ridicule such a powerful opponent. Who mocks death and gets away with it? The fear of death reigns supreme—then and now. But Paul refused to quiver in the face of death's ugly pallor. The grave is no match for the resurrection victory we have in Christ. So here's the way I imagine the "athlete" Paul "talking trash" to our enemy, death:

> You think you're unstoppable, that you can't be beat. You act like you always win. That we're supposed to be scared of you. Well, here's the truth of the matter: we're not afraid of you. You should be afraid of us! We're going to swallow you whole, drink in all of your poison, fight you to the end. Want to know why? Because we know the only way to victory is through you. In fact we have a champion who already defeated you. Remember him? He's shown us the secret of your weakness—that your push is our pull, that our suffering is your defeat, that your fatal blow will result in our eternal bliss. Don't you see? You've already lost. It's over. When the clock runs down, we'll be the ones celebrating—and you'll be a faint memory, a whisper, a ghost of a menace. Poor death. You don't stand a chance in hell of winning.

It's not that Paul denied death will have its day. He knew the law of sin and death would have its way with every descendant of Adam. Sin is the necrotic stinger that has poisoned our mortal bodies (1 Cor 15:56). Indeed, death looks like it wins in the end—the grave seals the apparent victory. Death rules without saying a word; it is God who said: "You are dust, and to dust you shall return" (Gen 3:19). But Paul believed the sentence of death was not God's last word on the matter. Made in the image of God, we were destined for more than death—the second Adam made sure of that.

## Eat My Dust

The first time I read through Paul's letters in Greek, I was struck by the number of times he referred to his "boldness" or "confidence" in the gospel. One of the words, *parrēsia,* sounds almost like a homonym of *parousia,* the word he used to describe the second coming of Christ. What is especially interesting is how often Paul talks about his confidence in the gospel whenever he's distinguishing himself from sly, deceitful, cunning, smooth talkers (2 Cor 2:17-3:12; Phil 1:15-20; 1 Thess 2:1-8). It's not that Paul tried to make the gospel sound good to his listeners, talking like "a man pleaser" (1 Thess 2:4; Gal 1:10). He knew the message of Christ crucified, buried and raised from the dead was foolishness. In fact that was the problem. Paul talked a good game. He was bold with the gospel message. He claimed not only that he was crucified and buried with Christ; but Paul also boasted that he was living the resurrected life. The question was whether he could back it up, especially since it appeared as though his life were a complete mess. Indeed, Paul's good news always seemed to lead to bad situations. Acts records the repeating scenario; Paul admits the same. Nearly every time he preached the gospel, it got him and his converts into trouble: "But though we had already suffered and been shamefully mistreated at Philippi, as you know, we had courage in our God to declare to you the gospel of God in spite of great opposition" (1 Thess 2:2). It's hard to make the claim that "old things have passed away and everything is new" when the same old problems keep resurfacing time after time. "Really, it's okay. It's not that bad. Everything's going to be all right."

After a while some people may not believe your words anymore.

But Paul didn't rely on words alone to justify his confidence in the gospel. He kept pointing to his life, the message of the gospel seen *in him* contrasted with the hucksters who merely used words to flatter their listeners (1 Thess 2:5-7). Indeed, Paul believed he couldn't "share the gospel" without sharing his life (1 Thess 2:8). Paul's life looked like the gospel—not only the death of Christ (sacrificing for others) and the burial of Christ (needing the church) but also the resurrection of Christ (overcoming sorrow with hope). Paul claimed God had raised him from the dead several times, snatching his life from the depths of despair:

> We do not want you to be unaware, brothers and sisters, of the affliction we experienced in Asia; for we were so utterly, unbearably crushed that we despaired of life itself. Indeed, we felt that we had received the sentence of death so that we would rely not on ourselves but on God who raises the dead. He who rescued us from so deadly a peril will continue to rescue us; on him we have set our hope that he will rescue us again. (2 Cor 1:8-10)

> I know that through your prayers and the help of the Spirit of Jesus Christ this will result in my deliverance. It is my eager expectation and hope that I will not be put to shame in any way, but that by my speaking with all boldness, Christ will be exalted now as always in my body, whether by life or by death. For to me, living is Christ and dying is gain. If I am to live in the flesh, that means fruitful labor for me; and I do not know which I prefer. I am hard pressed between the two: my desire is to depart and be with Christ, for that is far better; but to remain in the flesh is more necessary for you. Since I am convinced of this, I know that I will remain and continue with all of you for your progress and joy in faith, so that I may share abundantly in your boasting in Christ Jesus when I come to you again. (Phil 1:19-26)

> For even when we came into Macedonia, our bodies had no rest, but we were afflicted in every way—disputes without and fears within. But God, who consoles the downcast, consoled us by the arrival of Titus, and not only by his coming, but also by the consolation with which he was consoled about you, as he told us of your longing, your mourning, your zeal for me, so that I rejoiced still more. (2 Cor 7:5-7)

Paul knew whereof he spoke. I take comfort knowing he knew what it feels like to be "utterly, unbearably crushed." That's why he believed in the resurrection, boasting in the salvation of God because he had been saved many times from the pit of despair. I think we can all relate. When you think you're going to die and God saves you, it feels like resurrection. You can't help but talk about it. "Look at me! I'm alive! Thank God I'm alive."

It's no wonder unbelievers think our faith consists of nothing more than words. We read words from the Bible. We hear words from pulpits. We sing words to one another. We pray words to God. Words, words, words. Even we believers might be inclined to think that our faith can be reduced to words. That's why when God does something undeniable—resurrection—it gets everyone's attention. We see shadows of resurrection when winter gives way to spring, or when the morning sun lights up the dewy grass, or when a branch shoots out of a tree stump. Even though God's reliable care of creation is predictable, it still inspires hope. Yet when we catch a glimpse of the resurrection of Christ in flesh and blood, it looks like hope of a different kind—a hope built on faith—what Paul called "hope against hope" (Rom 4:18) and the "blessed hope" (Tit 2:13). Indeed, when we see God raise someone from the dead, we're all comforted knowing that he has done something wonderful. It gives me a strange confidence to think God loves to make us wonder.

When a physician says, "This is the time for prayer," you know God is your only hope. We had waited several hours for word from the intensive care unit about the status of my colleague "Dan." At that point, all we knew was that he was suffering from some form of encephalitis. It started out as a migraine, but within a few days the debilitating headache was joined by horrific nausea, chronic vertigo and dangerous fever. Lab results were inconclusive. He kept getting sicker by the hour. When I saw him, he was incoherent, writhing in pain, eyes bulging from the relentless pressure building up in his head. His wife, parents, pastor and friends—we were all waiting for some news, some indication the experts would be able to diagnose Dan's disease. Then the specialist gave the bad news: they didn't know what was wrong. They didn't know what else they could do. "There's a good chance he won't make it through the night." I thought, "How can this be? He's a young man— only in his forties. He was the picture of health just a few days ago, teaching his classes, enjoying his wife and son." We all stood in stunned silence. The physician reassured the family they would do everything within their power to help Dan. Then he said, "This is the time for prayer."

When you hear a wife ask God to save her husband, a heaviness fills the room that can only be borne by prayer. When you hear a father thank God for his son, trusting his heavenly Father to take care of him, a sorrow builds up in your heart that drives you to your knees. When it feels like the experts have given up and your friend is going to die, you can't help but turn to the resurrection God and say, "You are our *only* hope. Please save Dan." It's one thing to ask God to bless medical procedures, or to help certain drugs to work, or to give healthcare professionals wisdom. But when you know God is the only one you can trust, hope takes on new meaning. I have found it much easier to pray for knowledge and wisdom, for negative test results and positive surgical outcomes, for new drugs to work and known diseases to fail, for strength to rise and fevers to fall. To pray to God when there is *nothing* to say— then the shortest prayer becomes the heaviest burden. Sometimes you run out of words, when sighs, tears, sadness and groans come closer to Paul's idea that we should "pray without ceasing" (1 Thess 5:17) than lengthy prayers based on the latest science.

Inexplicably Dan made it through the night. Not getting any better (but not getting any worse), the physicians shipped him to another hospital, then after several weeks to another hospital, then after several months to another hospital. The best hospitals in the country took their turn, trying to diagnose Dan's illness(es). I marveled over his wife's tenacity, her undying faith, as well as the resilience of Dan's parents, their constant vigilance, exhausting every resource to help their son. I don't see how they did it. Every new doctor acted like he found the problem, prescribing treatment but with limited results. Then another expert was on the case, convinced she would make Dan better; new drugs would be given and more therapy applied. Every time I got a call from

Dan's wife, she sounded so hopeful, "I'm sure this time it will work." This went on for months, getting our hopes up only to be dashed once again. I had no right to do so, but I got mad—angry with the whole process. I thought about how hard it must have been for Dan and his entire family. New hospital, new city, new temporary living arrangements for the family, new doctors, new tests, new diagnoses, new treatment, same result. Nothing new; he was still sick. It felt as if medical science were playing with our emotions, like a big cat toying with a frightened mouse. Even though I had grown impatient—"Lord, when are *you* going to do something? This can't go on forever"—his wife never gave up. His parents never lost hope. And even more astounding to me, Dan never complained. Never felt sorry for himself. Took every day as a gift from God. Whenever I had the chance to talk with him on the phone, after recounting the doctor's latest attempts to help him, he would often say, "We'll see."

"Yes," I thought to myself, "we'll see." We want to see. We must see. Oh that the day would come when we see. Sitting in my office, trying to digest the latest "bad news," I envisioned the day when Dan would return to the classroom. I found myself daydreaming every now and then about what that day would look like: Students celebrating his healing. Colleagues welcoming him with shouts of praise to God. Wife and son beaming as he comes home after a day's work. Dan well again. I thought that day would never come. But it did. Two years later, Dan is teaching again—a full load. He's back in his office. Students are asking their questions. Colleagues are sharing conversations in the hallway. Every time I walk by his office, I can't help but think about the dark days, how nobody knew what was wrong. (They still don't know what happened.) I remember the helplessness, the despair, the hope. And I remember what many of us said to God in our prayers, "Lord, if Dan is healed, we'll know for certain it was you." That's why we'll never take it for granted that Dan is back. In fact to many of us, he will always be a living memorial of the resurrection of Christ—a work only God can do. It makes you wonder.

The way Paul saw it, groaning was a sign of confidence in the irrepressible work of God's wonderful glory (Rom 8:22-25).[3] When "we do not know how to pray as we ought," Paul claims our inarticulate groaning is the Spirit's resurrection work in us, when he "intercedes with sighs too deep for words" (Rom 8:26). Creation is decaying. God's glorious work suffers from the fall. Creation is subjected to the futility of death. But according to Paul this present suffering, this subjection to death, was by divine design to inspire hope (Rom 8:18-25). We pray because things are not the way they are supposed to be. Even though death appears as a constant we know it has no eternal dwelling place here in God's glorious creation. That's why we groan along with all creation; we know God's regenerative work must be evident. The new creation is not a different creation—as if God plans to throw away the refuse and start over. God's glory must be revealed in what he has already made. He is renewing creation, reforming creation, redeeming creation, resurrecting creation. Therefore the fact that creation is suffering from decay, that all things die, is evidence of God's glorious work of making all things new. The reason we get older, that our "outer nature is wasting away," is to reveal that our "inner nature is being renewed day by day" (2 Cor 4:16). There can't be resurrection without death. There can be no decay without re-creation. This is why Paul spoke of the gospel with such confidence. The present gives evidence of the future; death points to the victory of Christ's resurrection. "I consider that the sufferings of this present time are not worth comparing with the glory about to be revealed to us" (Rom 8:18). That's why "we boast in our hope of sharing the glory of God" (Rom 5:2) when death is all around us. Indeed, a heavy hope is born in the midst of despairing for God's glory.

Paul keyed on the Hebrew word for glory, *kābôd* (which also means "heavy"), in order to explain why the resurrection of Christ was the undeniable presence of God in the life of every believer. In the stories of the old covenant, God's legendary glory was weighty; his appearance was a grave matter. God's *kābôd* was a *heavy* presence. Paul emphasizes these same themes—weight, gravity, death, glory—when he recounts the story of Moses and the law (2 Cor 3:3-11).[4] When God gave the law to Moses, the "people of Israel could not gaze at Moses' face because of the glory of his face" (2 Cor 3:7). The law was heavy—literally "chiseled in letters on stone tablets." It was ominous too; Paul called it a "ministry of death" (2 Cor 3:7). And yet the point he was trying to make was that if the law came with such divine bravado, such serious intent, such glorious weight, how much *weightier* is the glory of God carried in the resurrection of Christ (2 Cor 3:9-11)! The previous glory was heavy. The glory of Christ's resurrection, however, is heavier, more glorious, because it is permanent. The density of God's presence borne in the lives of those who bear the image of the resurrected Christ outweighs the glory of the past. For the old covenant was written on tablets of stone; but God has written the new covenant on "tablets of human hearts" (2 Cor 3:3)—the heaviest glory of all. Incarnation is the ultimate revelation of God's glory; we are the heaviest work of God, more glorious than all creation, for we bear the image of the second Adam. Knowing that we're "being transformed into the same image from one degree of glory to another" (2 Cor 3:18) helps Paul infer that all suffering is therefore "light" since it produces in us "the *eternal weight of glory* beyond all measure" (2 Cor 4:17).

To put on the resurrection of Christ is to wear the heavy armor of God (Eph 6:10-11), to groan under the weight of the unfinished work of Christ (2 Cor 5:4).[5] We are not making light of the serious matter of death and dying when we bear the image of the second Adam. No doubt the first covenant is weighty; the law of sin and death is a grave matter. When we bear the burdens of those who are staring death in the face, we sense the heaviness of our souls, our hearts falling into our chests, the gravity of the situation. But these things do not weigh us down, dragging our souls down to Sheol. Instead, we embrace the heaviness as God's glory. For when we feel the weight of these things, we know we are bearing the burden of Christ, the resurrection of our bodies. So we say gladly, "Let our bodies decay. Let the lines on our faces grow deeper. Let the hair of our head turn gray. Let the glory of our fading youth be evident to all. We refuse to hide the glory that is past. Rather, we shall wear gray hair as a crown of resurrection glory. We shall groan under the increasing weight of our burden—a body wasting away—as a prayer for the continuing resurrection work of God. We shall embrace every hardship, every burden, every distress as evidence of the resurrection of Christ in our lives. For we are confident that we grow old and die because we are being made alive in Christ Jesus our Lord. It is our destiny."

Christ believers should be offended by a youth-obsessed culture that tries to focus our attention on the wrong end of living. The mythical quest in the West for the fountain of youth implies that growing old is a curse that must be reversed. We're told we should be ashamed if we "let ourselves go," knowing that hard living adds years to our appearance. So we spend millions of dollars on products and procedures in our battle against biology, trying to preserve the glory of our past. Diet and fitness become less about healthy living and more about looking young. Some give up sooner than later, overcome by genes that make them look older than their age (whatever that means). Or some of us try to convince ourselves that things are not as bad as they seem, relying on useless sayings like "forty is the new thirty." Really? Once a few of us arrive at the century mark, will we feel better about ourselves by saying, "Hundred is the new ninety"? Yet we persist in hiding the inevitable, denying the destiny of our humanity, pretending like our only hope is cosmetic. Projecting a false image to everyone—this is the real me!— turns us all into telepathic liars. Our compulsion to look in the mirror every day, however, brings us back to the ugly truth. We can only lie to ourselves for so long.

Paul looked into the mirror of Christ's resurrection and saw the glorious image of a man who was dying, decaying, growing old, growing frail, yet very much alive (2 Cor 3:18; 4:11). When he saw his reflection in the death, burial and resurrection of Christ, Paul knew he was living the gospel. To be sure the image was pale; we see shadows of the resurrection in the darkest of times. But the prospect of simply catching a glimpse of that kind of glory encouraged Paul: "For now we see in a mirror, dimly, but then we will see face to face" (1 Cor 13:12). To look into the mirror and see the face of Christ staring back at us—the transformation from image to image, from glory to glory—that is resurrection. Indeed, until we see him face to face, we wait for the glory that is to be revealed in us. And every day the weight of that glory becomes more evident because we are destined to be like him. Our future is more than a biological certainty; it is our theological hope.

> We boast in our hope of sharing the glory of God. And not only that, but we also boast in our sufferings, knowing that suffering produces endurance, and endurance produces character, and character produces hope, and hope does not disappoint us.
>
> St. Paul, toward the end of a very difficult mission trip, to the Romans (Rom 5:2-5)

# 11

# Putting up a Fight

*Opposing the Powers*

❧

I THOUGHT I KNEW what worry was until I became a parent. Overcoming the typical fears of childhood—afraid of the dark, fear of abandonment, scared of death—seemed challenging enough. But when you act like your children have nothing to fear because you're there to protect them, that's a far more sophisticated form of anxiety. Isn't that the job of every parent, to convince your children they have nothing to worry about, that "everything is going to be all right"? At first it seemed like we could pull it off, creating a safe haven for our firstborn. Before we brought him home from the hospital, we had "childproofed" our house with all of the latest products: safety latches for doors, safety plugs for electrical outlets, safety highchair, safety swing, safety this and safety that. We had created a virtual safe house for our child, a sanctuary of security, a risk-free refuge, paradise before the fall. After surviving the first couple of nights without incident, I begin to think to myself, "I can do this." Then things changed, got more complicated. In the beginning a baby is one-dimensional; I would leave the room and return to find him exactly where I left him. Then he became a two-dimensional creature, moving to and fro, and the world became a riskier place. "What do you have in your mouth? Where did you find that?" But horror of all horrors, the little crawler decided to take on the world of the vertical, becoming a three-dimensional biped, a teetering toddler who persisted in testing the laws of gravity. Pretending like I was his divine protector, I tried to anticipate his every fall, covering the sharp corners of furniture with my hand as he aimlessly muddled through the living room.

The pretense that we control our world is built on occasional success. Made in the image of God, we know we're supposed to "get dominion" and act like we run the place. But a parent soon realizes we are unable to re-create paradise before the fall. We may have limited success against the perils of a world filled with weeds and chaos—sometimes there's order—where everything goes according to plan. But then the unexpected creeps in; the dangers of an unpredictable world invade sacred space and you soon realize you're not in control; you cannot deliver on the promise of keeping your child safe. There are no guarantees. You can't prevent bad things from happening. Control is an illusion. Fears feed on what could be. Nightmares become reality. Worry is a way of life.

We were trying to enjoy adult company for a change, sitting down for a meal with our neighbors, hoping for dinner conversation without interruption. Our one-year-old son was in his highchair, chewing on a teething biscuit, which usually kept him quiet for at least half an hour. We were so engaged in table conversation—peace and quiet!—we lost track of time and weren't paying attention to Andrew. By the time Sheri noticed something was wrong, Andrew had already begun to turn blue. "He's not breathing," she shouted, "he's not breathing." At that moment I did the very thing you're not supposed to do, sticking my finger in his mouth hoping to dislodge the teething biscuit. He still wasn't breathing, and his little body began to wilt. I tried again, this time removing some of the biscuit with my finger, but he still wasn't breathing. This is every parent's nightmare; your child is choking, nothing helps and panic sets in. "We've got to get him out of there," Sheri screamed as she pulled the tray table of the high chair out of the way. I instinctively grabbed his little arms to yank him out of the seat, forgetting that he was still strapped into the chair by the safety belt. By lifting him up so quickly, I unknowingly performed the Heimlich maneuver as the belt, cinched around his waist, forced air through his lungs and dislodged the pulverized biscuit, shooting it across the table. Andrew began to cry. Sheri began to cry. We dismissed ourselves from the table, retreated to our bedroom and all three of us had a cry. That night lying in bed, reflecting on the day's trauma and pondering what could have happened, I gave up. "God, I can't do this anymore. I can't be his protector. I can't be his provider. I can't be his god. I'm not even sure I can be his father. But you can; you are. From now on, you are his God. You are his protector. You are his father. I'll try to do my part. But, it's all up to you."

Worry is my besetting sin. At the end of the day, before I fall asleep, I can create imaginary, scary scenarios that *could have happened* if things had been different. Recounting the past, I relive narrow escapes, potential tragedies, near misses, knowing that sometimes things don't work out well. Bad things happen to all of us. But dwelling on the worrisome details of life can wear you out. Living in fear of what can happen sucks the joy of living out of you. Yet worry is a hard habit to break. When the phone rings in the middle of the night, when one of the kids has a high fever that can't be broken—these things set my mind racing, heart pounding, adrenaline pumping. I try to remind myself: I'm supposed to be a believer, someone who confesses, "God is great and God is good. If God is for us, who can be against us?" But then I see—like everyone else—a world filled with violence and fear, evil and hatred, tragedy and suffering, and impulsively say, "Who can be against us? *Everything.*"

## Reigning with Christ

That's the way they saw it in Paul's day: everything was against them because everything is animated by unseen powers. Paul's converts had no doubts about living in a fallen world. Evil forces were constantly out to get them. When a child suffered from fever, it was a malevolent power attacking them. When storms on the sea shipwrecked sailors, it was a malevolent power attacking them. Famines, earthquakes, disease, maladies, pestilence, illness, calamity—much of what we call "natural disasters"—all evil and suffering comes at the hands of unseen powers that can wreak havoc on anyone at anytime. That's why everyone needed a good god on their side to protect them from the ever-present evil in a broken-down world. Temples were everywhere, always open for business, ready to accept sacrifices from those hoping to placate powerful gods. In Ephesus the priests of the temple had perfected the art of persuading the masses to worship their deity. The larger the temple, the bigger the god/goddess, and Ephesus housed one of the seven wonders of the ancient world: the magnificent temple of Artemis (Diana was her Roman name). Every merchant traveling through Ephesus would pay respects in her temple. Every ship sailing into Ephesus would pay the harbor toll in hopes of securing divine protection from Artemis.

Trading in fear was big business in Ephesus. The priests of Artemis sold amulets—lucky charms—to protect devotees from malevolent powers. The Ephesians wore them around their necks, wrists, waists and ankles to cover the vital zones of the body: head, heart, hands, loins and feet. Of course the power of amulets would wear off after some time (apparent when a child became sick), requiring a return visit to the temple to buy more protection. But what really kept business hopping was the selling of curses. Priests sold curse tablets to men who wanted their enemies to suffer misfortune. These magical incantations called down evil powers on their targets, bringing misery on those who didn't have the right amulet to protect them from a certain malady. Imagine, then, what would happen when a man saw his enemy heading for the temple of Artemis. Convinced his opponent was going to buy a curse against his family, or his business, or his loins (the most dreaded and therefore most common curse against men), the man would have to visit the temple and buy an amulet that would protect him from the curse of the malevolent power. The vicious cycle of curse and protection fueled the fears of the Ephesians to rely on the power of Artemis. But what about Paul's converts in Ephesus? Should they look to Artemis for protection? Indeed, when Paul reminded his converts that "our struggle is not against enemies of blood and flesh, but against the rulers, against the authorities, against the cosmic powers of this present darkness, against the spiritual forces of evil in the heavenly places" (Eph 6:12), they knew exactly what he was referring to.[1]

One of the reasons Paul wrote to the Ephesians was to correct their "worldview." They didn't see the world with Christian eyes, so he wanted the "eyes of [their] heart" to be "enlightened," knowing the "immeasurable greatness of his power for us who believe," that is, the resurrection power of Christ (Eph 1:18-20). In other words he wanted his converts to view all things with resurrected eyes. Rather than see the world as a scary place where tragedy lurks around every corner because oppressive unseen powers are prepared to attack at any moment, Paul tried to get the Ephesians to see themselves as blessed "in Christ with every spiritual blessing in the heavenly places" (Eph 1:3). Since Christ has been raised from the dead and reigns with God above every power ("far above all rule and authority and power and dominion"), he has "put all things under his feet" (Eph 1:21-22). These malevolent powers appear to rule over humanity, bringing sickness and death to their unprotected victims. But Paul is convinced that Christ defeated all of these invisible powers through his resurrection. Sickness and death looked like they won in their death match with Christ, but he defeated them through his resurrection. So to Paul's way of thinking, these powers are no match for Christ's resurrection power. What can sickness and death do to the one who is raised from the dead?

A resurrected body is impervious to the effects of sickness and death. Once these enemies of humanity have unleashed every weapon, the resurrected body will be renewed, reclaimed, restored, remade in the image of Christ. Believers will pass through the grave and come out on the other side the same, but different. (This is the point Paul was making in 1 Cor 15:35-57.) We shall be embodied but eternal. Terrestrial and celestial. Scarred and glorified. Of Adam but in Christ. After death's final blow God won't start over, giving believers something completely different. He refuses to throw away what was made in his image. Indeed, the resurrection of Christ proves that sickness and death cannot spoil the glory of God; our bodies will be reclaimed from the grave. To use a common illustration, after yeast leavens a lump of dough, once the bread is baked, the loaf comes out of the oven the same, but different. If we sprinkle yeast on baked bread nothing happens. So also, once our bodies have taken in the yeast of sickness and passed through the oven of death, believers will come out of the grave resurrected, no longer vulnerable to the powers that ruled over us. The resurrection is the reign of Christ over sickness and death. But what do we do in the meantime, since these invisible powers rule like stars in the sky above us? In fact Paul used common terms *(rule, authority, power, dominion)* when describing the evil powers that ruled over humanity in the heavens.[2] The stars were gods according to pagans; or, as the Jews believed, these celestial beings were angelic powers (Mt 2:9; Rev 12:4, 9) that looked down on human affairs from their celestial thrones.

Paul admits that his converts were once held hostage to the powers that rule in the heavens (Eph 2:1-3). The "ruler of the power of the air" was above them, enticing them to live selfishly, for their own "desires of flesh and senses." But Paul claims the Ephesian believers are no longer under the dominion of these hostile super-powers because they are already "raised up with [Christ]" and seated "with him in the heavenly places" (Eph 2:6). In other words, because Christ has put all these enemies "under his feet" through the power of his resurrection (they are no threat to him anymore), these same powers are also put under the feet of Christ believers. Why? Because Christians are the body of Christ (Eph 1:20-23). If Christ reigns in heavenly places, then Christians reign in heavenly places too. Heaven and earth overlap. If evil powers have been vanquished by Christ's resurrection power, then Christ believers have overcome the same malevolent forces by the resurrection power of Christ. The end has already happened. That is to say, the "already" of Christ's resurrection is apparent when believers no longer live in fear of these powers that temporarily reign in the heavens. With resurrected eyes Christians should see these malevolent powers under our feet because Christ reigns *now*, and we reign with him by his resurrection power. This is a huge claim to make, especially in a fallen world: sickness and death do not scare us anymore because we've already seen the end of the world.

Have you ever wondered why end-time scenarios described by the prophets often include stars falling from the sky like figs? To us this is a cosmic cataclysm predicted even by physicists. We know this will happen one day—billions of years from now the sun will burn out, implode, turn into a black hole and drag everything "down" (planets, stars) with it. But that's not the way Paul and the prophets understood it. The stars were divine creatures, placed in the heavens by the Creator to rule. When God comes to rule on earth, no power can be above him. The powers/stars must fall at his feet, abdicating their thrones in the heavens. The gravity of God's presence pulls down all powers; there can be no creature above him. So too, when God-in-flesh came to earth, the malevolent powers (sickness and death) fell at his feet via the resurrection. When his resurrection is complete on the last day (what we call the "second coming of Christ," when the dead in Christ shall rise), then all stars will fall to earth. They will bow down before him. Indeed, Paul claimed the resurrection of Christ proved that he has "already" and "not yet" put all things under his feet, especially the last enemy: death (1 Cor 15:25-28). Therefore, if we are the body of Christ, then all things have already and not yet been put under our feet too. It may look like the stars reign above us—permanently fixed in the heavens—but it's just a matter of time till they all fall down.

Security is an important word in our country. We speak of financial security, social security, trading in securities, hiring security, security systems, internet security, job security, national security, security guards, security cameras, airport security and homeland security. Built into our vocabulary is the presumption that we can make our world secure, predictable, reliable because we are intelligent (technology) and strong (military). Therefore when the twin towers of the World Trade Center came crashing down on that infamous September morning, we immediately began to seek new ways to make sure this would never happen again—to "beef up" security. After all, American ingenuity not only made our country great but also the entire world a better place. That's why we still have a hard time making sense of what happened on 9/11. So many lives were lost because our technology failed us. Our own citizens were sacrificed as weapons to destroy us. Our common need to travel was used against us. Our enemies outsmarted us. And to think a few years ago there was much talk about a "star wars" defense system that would protect Americans from missiles falling from the sky. Instead, it took the unparalleled courage of a few passengers to bring a hijacked airplane down in rural Pennsylvania, short of the terrorists' intended target.

But what happened on September 11, 2001, was more than a breach of security. More than a failure of military intelligence. More than an attack on the economic center of the West. What happened on 9/11 was evil. This is why we are haunted by the tragedy. I think about the men and women who, after their usual morning routine of getting ready for work, never imagined that they would be hanging out of their office window, eighty-seven stories high, seeking relief from the hellish heat that eventually compelled them to leap to their deaths. I think about the excited family, a father, mother, son and daughter, gathering their suitcases, heading for the airport, anticipating their trip to the West Coast—perhaps on vacation?—never expecting the horrible end of a journey that started out so innocently. Every one of us knows we could have been on that plane; none of us are immune to evil. We may pretend like we can keep evil at bay, away from our pristine shores, from our spacious skies, from our purple mountain majesties, from sea to shining sea. We want to believe that evil spirits plague only foreign countries—especially the so-called third world. What we can't accept is that malevolent powers live in America too. I've often said sarcastically to my students that our churches don't hire ministers of exorcism because we don't believe demons make it through customs. How do we promise national security against the threat of invisible, evil powers? It's hard to control what you can't see. So we make the mistake of fighting the "war on terror" against flesh and blood, targeting people with olive skin and native dress.

The Ephesians also worked with the presumption that they could control evil powers. But Paul tried to convince his converts that they didn't need to worry about making their world safe and secure. They were already saved in Christ. They didn't need to buy into the notion that they could "beef up" security with additional protection. They had already trusted in Christ (Eph 2:8-9). They were already "strong in the Lord and in the strength of his power" (Eph 6:10). They had everything they needed in the resurrection of Christ.[3] To be sure living between the already and the not yet of the resurrection wasn't easy. In fact Paul was more than willing to admit it was a fight; he often used pugilistic terms to describe the struggle of believing. And part of the struggle was helping his converts identify the real opponent. Those who fight against evil powers mistake human adversaries as their enemy. Instead, Paul wanted his converts to remember that "our struggle is not against enemies of blood and flesh, but against the rulers, against the authorities, against the cosmic powers of this present darkness, against the spiritual forces of evil in the heavenly places" (Eph 6:12). War against evil powers requires spiritual weapons.

## The Armor of God

Acts tells the story of what happened in Ephesus after Paul preached the gospel (Acts 19:11-20). First, there were "extraordinary miracles." The Ephesians began to treat Paul like Artemis, using him as a source for magical amulets. The Ephesians discovered that whatever touched Paul's body—like handkerchiefs or aprons—had healing powers for the diseased and demonized (Acts 19:12). Who needs Artemis when God's magic is free? It comes as no surprise, then, that Paul's converts decided to have a public burning of all the magical paraphernalia they had collected over the years—amulets, incantations, curse tablets. Luke was impressed; as a physician he especially appreciated the sight of "fifty thousand silver coins" worth of magic going up in smoke that day (Acts 19:19). Paul's gospel was affecting current business too, especially those who made amulets and miniature statues of Artemis (idols). Evidently temple traffic decreased dramatically. Merchants got mad, and Paul's companions almost became victims of a lynch mob (Acts 19:23-41). Christ believers who acted like they had nothing to fear (who needs Artemis?) threatened the rest of the Ephesians. Indeed, they saw Paul's gospel as a direct attack on the Ephesian way of life—their business, their religion, their civic duty. By refusing to support the Ephesian economy and their department of homeland security, Christians in Ephesus were accused of being unpatriotic (Acts 19:26-27). Political operatives pumped up the crowd with "God and Country" slogans: "Great is Artemis of the Ephesians" (Acts 19:28, 34). But the rally lost steam when a government official intervened and calmed the angry mob (Acts 19:35-41). Paul and his companions were able to slip out of town unharmed.

When the euphoria of their new faith waned after Paul left town, evidently the Ephesian Christ believers began to doubt the wisdom of their impetuous actions. Imagine how difficult it must have been for a new Christian father when his young son or daughter was struck down with a high fever—especially if it happened a few days after he saw his enemy leave the temple of Artemis carrying a new curse tablet. "Did the power of Christ leave with Paul? Should I send a napkin to him so that he can rub it on his skin and send it back to me?" With Paul gone the urge to run to Artemis and buy a magical amulet was probably irresistible. This is why Paul opens his letter to the Ephesians with a lot of "power talk" (Eph 1:19-2:10). He was reminding his converts that they had already defeated evil powers through the resurrection of Christ. It also explains why Paul ends his letter with a description of the armor of God (Eph 6:10-17). Paul wanted his converts to see the world through resurrected eyes, that they wore the resurrected Christ like body armor. He was their magical amulet, covering them from head to toe. The resurrected Christ was their bulletproof vest, protecting them against "the flaming arrows of the evil one" (Eph 6:16). Christ believers shouldn't live in fear of the powers like they used to—like their pagan neighbors who live "in the futility of their minds" (Eph 4:17). According to Paul, the Ephesians were foolish to believe such nonsense, "darkened in their understanding, alienated from the life of God because of their ignorance and hardness of heart" (Eph 4:18). Such thinking leads to sinfulness, greediness and impurity. But "that is not the way you learned Christ" (Eph 4:20). Instead, Paul's converts learned how to "put on" Christ like new clothing, mentally dressing themselves in the "likeness of God" (Eph 4:23-24).

As far as Paul was concerned this was the fulfillment of what Isaiah predicted: God would show up one day dressed in the battle armor of righteousness and salvation and defeat his enemies (Is 59:15-19). When Christ believers, dressed in the body armor of Christ's resurrection, take a stand against evil and suffering, they represent the justice/righteousness of God on earth. Rather than cowering in fear, believers wage war against malevolent powers knowing every vital zone is protected: truth covering their loins, salvation protecting their heads, the good news covering their feet, righteousness protecting their heart (Eph 6:14-17). Faith is their shield. The Word of God is their sword. Prayer is their battle cry (Eph 6:18-19). These are the weapons of our warfare because we fight a spiritual battle against invisible forces of darkness that want to destroy us. It might be easy to think the person seeking to do harm is our enemy. But Paul trained the eyes of his converts on their real foe—the opponent of *all* humanity—the evil power behind sickness and death. That's also why Paul thought slaves were being short-sighted to think they were merely obeying their masters. Instead, they should see their obedience as offered to Christ (Eph 6:5-8). Whether serving Christ or fighting the devil, Paul saw the world animated by spiritual powers—the ultimate conflict of good versus evil was being played out for everyone to see. But only those who had resurrected eyes could see they had nothing to fear.

This is where we need to be very clear about how Paul saw the armor of Christ work as protection against evil powers. Paul never claimed that bad things would never happen to Christ believers as long as they remembered to dress themselves in the armor of God. In fact that would have made things worse, fueling the fires of fear in their fight against evil and suffering. "Oh no! My wife had a terrible accident; her leg is broken. She must not be proclaiming the gospel of peace like she should." Rather, Paul claimed that his converts would be able to face the difficulties of life by standing firm in their faith. The point is *not* that Christ believers never get sick or never get hurt or never die as long as they're wearing the armor of Christ. Instead, wearing the resurrection of Christ like body armor helps believers stand during hard times in the strength of the Lord's power (Eph 6:10). The picture Paul paints is of a warrior ready to face the assault of a horrific battle—a battle for the soul—defying the devil by refusing to give in. And what would it look like to give in to the devil? To no longer "stand firm" or to "stand against" or to be able to "withstand" the assault "on that evil day" (Eph 6:11-14). In essence Paul was saying, "Take a stand against evil and suffering by remaining strong in your resurrection faith. The enemy is trying to take you down. But we won't go down without a fight! No matter how bad it gets, till the day we die, we will declare, 'Our God reigns, for Christ is risen.' Fight through the night! Fight till the end! The victory is ours for we are the resurrection of Christ."

Lest we think Paul was being naive, seeing the world through rose-colored glasses, ignoring the horrible pain of injustice, we must remember that he was in prison when he wrote his letter to the Ephesians (Eph 6:20). As a matter of fact some believers might question whether Paul had put on the entire armor of God since evil powers got the better of him. How can a man claim he's protected by Christ's armor when he's in a Roman prison awaiting the death penalty? In what respect is that living a resurrected life? And yet that's the very place—in the darkness of prison—where we see resurrection in Paul. Rather than shy away from the battle, Paul saw his imprisonment as a chance to "dare to speak the word with greater boldness and *without fear*" (Phil 1:14). Paul refused to be intimidated by his opponents, knowing that they were not ultimately responsible for his predicament. How else do we explain the fact that he didn't fault the prison guards for his circumstances; instead, he tried to win them to Christ (Phil 1:13)! He didn't take it personally when Jewish or Roman authorities persecuted him; rather, he considered them enemies of the *cross* of Christ (Phil 3:18). Paul didn't even harbor hard feelings toward those who wanted to increase his suffering in prison (I love Paul's response): "What does it matter?" (Phil 1:18). Regardless of what his earthly adversaries did to him, he kept saying, "What's the difference? If I live, I'll live for Christ. If I die, I'll live again in Christ. You can't stop the resurrection work of God in me." Paul refused to live in fear of what would happen to him. Rather, he rejoiced in the fact that "Christ will be exalted now as always in my body, whether by life or by death" (Phil 1:20). One might be tempted to say the powers made a huge mistake by throwing Paul into prison, for it only made his faith stronger. All Paul needed while doing "hard time" in prison were the prayers of his converts and the resurrection power of the Spirit of Jesus Christ (Phil 1:19).

Paul counted on the prayers of his converts to sustain him during his imprisonment. But what did Paul want his converts to pray for? That he would not suffer in prison? No. That he would not get sick or die while he was in prison (a very common occurrence in his day)? No. Paul asked his converts to pray that he would be bold with the gospel (Eph 6:19-20; Phil 1:20). He asked his converts to pray that Christ would be exalted in his body whether he lived or died (Phil 1:20-26). To be sure Paul hoped he would be released from prison; and he asked his converts to pray for "his deliverance" (Phil 1:19). But "his deliverance" had as much to do with remaining strong in the Lord while he was in prison—facing death with confidence—as being delivered from the captivity of a prison cell. That's why recent "scientific" studies to determine whether prayer actually "works" are ridiculous. The presumption is that prayer is supposed to stop bad things from happening. And it's no wonder: we think bad things happen only when there's been a breach in security. So scientists supposedly study the effectiveness of prayer—the callous, cold, hard facts—by observing whether the health of certain patients improve as they battle illness. The scientists presume effective prayer is based on desirable outcomes. But what would they say about Paul? "Hmmm. This case study is inconclusive. It seems prayer worked sometimes. Paul was released from prison. But eventually prayer failed him because we know he died in a Roman prison, beheaded for his faith."

But I think I hear Paul protesting: "Oh, you think the prayers of my converts failed because I died in prison? Here's the truth of the matter: even though I was beheaded, the helmet of Christ's salvation protected me from the pits of hell. Even though they tried to destroy my will, the breastplate of Christ's righteousness protected my heart from despair. Even though I died without fathering any children, my immortality is not in my loins but in the truth of the gospel of Jesus Christ—I have millions of children, as many as the stars of the sky and the grains of sand on the seashore. Faith in Christ shielded me from every adversary—especially the devil and his minions—because the Word of God is my weapon against all evil and suffering. I died with my boots on. There is no chink in the armor of Christ. So let the refrain of our faith echo in hell throughout all eternity: Christ is risen. He is risen indeed!" (See 2 Tim 4:6-8, 16-18, for Paul's "deathbed" declaration of victory.)

Because Paul wore Christ's resurrection like body armor, the apostle knew he was in for a fight. He wasn't surprised when he encountered resistance to the gospel (2 Tim 3:10-12). In fact the armor of God explains why Paul kept returning to the same places where he was nearly killed. When you know you're going to be raised from the dead on the last day, then no one or nothing can stop the proclamation of the gospel. To march in the army of Christ's resurrection is an act of war against the devil. This is why Paul kept asking his converts to pray for him and for one another while he was in prison (Eph 6:18-20; Phil 1:3-11; 4:6; Col 4:2-4). It wasn't simply a matter of asking for divine protection in the face of suffering and death. Paul knew Satan wouldn't give up the battle. If the devil couldn't threaten Christ believers with fear of suffering and death, then he would use other "schemes" to try to subvert the work of Christ. If he couldn't win the fight using a frontal assault (worry, fear, suffering and death cannot penetrate the armor of Christ), then he would get Christ believers to fight one another, stabbing each other in the back. That's when the devil shows up in Paul's letters. Paul accused Satan of trying to sneak into the churches as an "angel of light" and create dissension (2 Cor 11:13-15). Paul warned the Corinthians that Satan would exploit the unforgiving spirit of the house churches when a repentant member was excommunicated (2 Cor 2:5-11). Paul told the Ephesians not to "make room for the devil" by lying, cheating and talking bad about one another (Eph 4:25-29). Embittered and angry, the Ephesians were grieving the Holy Spirit because they weren't being "kind to one another, tenderhearted, forgiving one another as God in Christ has forgiven you" (Eph 4:30-32).

This is why Paul kept reminding his converts to pray; Christ believers overcome Satan through prayer (1 Cor 7:5; 2 Thess 3:1-3). Prayer is confidence, an act of defiance against evil and suffering in a fallen world (Eph 3:8-21; 2 Thess 1:5-12). Prayer is a memorial, an act of remembering what God has done (Phil 1:3-5; 1 Thess 1:2-3). Prayer is perseverance, an act of thanksgiving, knowing God will always be on our side (Eph 6:18-20; Col 4:2-4). When we pray for one another, we're claiming God's power is supreme. When we pray for one another, we remember our battle is not against "flesh and blood" but against the powers of darkness. When we pray we remind each other that we're living between the already and not yet of Christ's resurrection.[4] When we pray we contend for justice. When we pray we are telling the world we have nothing to fear. When we pray we prove that we're still fighting. When we pray we find peace with God because he "is able to accomplish abundantly far more than all we can ask or imagine" (Eph 3:20). When we pray we are taking on the powers. The fact that we are able to fight proves that we have already won the battle.[5]

"Prayer Changes Things." The sign on my office wall once hung in the bedroom of my grandmother—a woman I never knew because she died before I was born. She was only forty-four, a wife to my grandfather and the mother of two children, my uncle and my mother. Mom was sixteen years old when her mother died of cancer. She has told me the horrible story of how my grandmother fought death to the ugly end. A woman of great faith, my grandmother believed that God would heal her of the dreaded disease. And at first it seemed like the prayers of her family and friends were answered. But then the cancer returned—this time with a vengeance. Mom said that the last days of her mother's life were horrible. She would writhe in pain for hours, crying out all hours of the day and night. There seemed to be no relief; the doctors could do very little to ease her agony. My mother remembers sitting in the hall outside her parent's bedroom, hearing her mother wail and moan, praying to God for help. She tried to see her mother, to comfort her, to help her before she died. But the relentless pain turned my grandmother into a madwoman; mom said she had never seen her mother like that—flashing wild eyes of anger, hateful words spewing from the mouth of this one-time dignified, kind-hearted woman. My grandmother died the next day. The house grew quiet—almost a welcome relief. Family and friends arrived quietly to bring comfort to the widow and his two children. Hushed tones filled the hallways that once bellowed with agonizing screams of a tortured woman. Death—our enemy!—seemed to come as a welcomed friend.

Every time I'm in my office I am faced with the message on the rectangular placard: "Prayer Changes Things." I think about how it represented the hopes of a dying woman, a sign she read every day till she died. When my grandmother cried out to God in her final days, did she see the sign and wonder if it was true? When she heard her daughter crying outside her bedroom door, did she see the sign and wonder if it was true? When she contemplated her own death, anticipating the moment she would cross over to the other side, did she see the sign and wonder if it was true? When she thought about her family going on without her, especially her sixteen-year-old daughter—if there were ever a time a girl needs her mother it's when she's sixteen—did she see the sign and wonder if it was true? She wouldn't be there for her daughter's wedding. She wouldn't be there to welcome her grandson home from the hospital. She wouldn't be there to celebrate every wonderful moment of her daughter's life, to walk beside her, covering the sharp corners of a broken down world, trying to protect a girl's heart with the hand of a mother's love. Or did she offer a prayer in defiance of the inevitable, trusting that God would be a Mother to her daughter, that his loving care would guide her every step of the way, that he would be her God, that she would see her daughter again one day? Did she believe to the end that "Prayer Changes Things"?

One day I will meet the faithful grandmother I never knew, and I will tell her about the sign. That God spoke to her grandson through the sign, that I remembered to pray because of the sign, that I learned to trust God that he will take care of my children because I believe the sign is true: "Prayer Changes Things." The resurrection of Christ proves it. Sickness and death will not reign forever. Every power will fall before him on the last day—all creation will tell of his glory. And I will be there too, along with my grandmother, her children, her grandchildren, her great-grandchildren—all who share in the resurrection of Christ—the day every knee bows to the glory of God the Father, Jesus Christ his Son and the Holy Spirit.

Oh, how we long for the day.

> For this reason, I bow my knees before the Father, from whom every family in heaven and on earth takes its name. I pray that, according to the riches of his glory, he may grant that you may be strengthened in your inner being with power through his Spirit, and that Christ may dwell in your hearts through faith.
>
> St. Paul, awaiting the verdict of a capital charge in a Roman prison, to the Ephesians (Eph 3:14-17)

# 12

# Seeing Things

*Mystical Journeys*

❧

I SAW AN ANGEL. She was sitting on the end of my hospital bed the night after I had knee surgery. I was twenty years old, long past the age when children want to believe they see things adults are unable to see. As a matter of fact, when I first saw her, I didn't recognize her as an angel. Instead, I thought she was the "good nurse"—the nickname I gave one of the day-shift nurses who was particularly kind to me. It had been a very rough day. Before the surgery a friend had told me the horror story of a guy who lost his leg to gangrene after knee surgery because his cast was too tight, which cut off circulation to his toes, eventually forcing the doctors to amputate his leg. That thought kept me up most of the night before the operation. I tried to find comfort in the promise: "He who began a good work in you will complete it until the day of Christ Jesus" (Phil 1:6, my translation). After surgery, lying in bed with a cast from my hip to my toes, my leg began to swell, my toes turned a bloodless white and my friend's prophetic warning seemed to be coming true. At first no one was alarmed; the nurses said this was typical, that my leg would eventually quit swelling. But it didn't. Excruciating pain began to shoot down my leg. Losing all inhibition I screamed out loudly for help. The good nurse checked on me several times, eventually getting the surgeon to agree to have the cast cut open to relieve the pressure. The pain subsided, my fears were relieved, and the night brought medicated rest.

The next day I told my parents about my night visitor. When the good nurse came into the room, my mother wanted to thank the woman for going beyond the call of duty: "Rodney said you came to see him in the middle of the night last night." The nurse was confused. "No, it wasn't me. I only work the day shift. It was probably the night-shift nurse." But I knew that wasn't the case. (The night nurse was a rather large woman.) "She came to my room—long past midnight. She had long brown hair, big dark eyes. She was wearing white. She sat on the end of my bed, head turned toward me. I sat up and asked, 'What's wrong?' She said, 'Shh. Be quiet. Lie back. Go to sleep. Everything's going to be all right.' I remember saying to myself, 'She's right,' letting out a big sigh and falling back to sleep." My mother said, "Rodney, this girl you call the good nurse has short hair. Where was she sitting?" "There, at the end of my bed." Then mom pointed out the obvious: "But there's no room; your long legs take up the whole mattress. She would have to have been sitting on your legs." After a few moments, talk of dreams and drugs between my parents and the good nurse convinced everyone but me that I had been hallucinating.

As far as I know I haven't seen an angel since then (Heb 13:2). And that's surprising given the fact that I've faced far more significant challenges in my life. You wouldn't think an angel would show up simply because there were minor postoperative complications after knee surgery. In fact it seems far more reasonable to conclude this divine visitation was a drug-induced hallucination. Even if it could be proved that it was all in my head, I wouldn't be disappointed. I've never derived any sense of being "special" in the eyes of God because I saw an angel. (Many people claim similar stories.) Besides, in the overall scheme of things it doesn't seem to be that important. It would be easy to rationalize, to explain away the experience. And yet to this day I believe it's true. I can't shake the feeling; I can't get out of my head the image of her sitting on my bed, looking at me with those big, dark eyes and reassuring me with comforting words. In fact I've often wondered whether this experience has opened my mind to the possibility of other divine encounters that rational human beings easily dismiss. Indeed, I find it much harder to hang on to these irrational possibilities in a disenchanted world.

Paul, however, found it easy to believe the "irrational" because he knew he lived in an enchanted world. Paul didn't suffer from a God-of-the-gaps supernaturalism—God only shows up when we can't explain what happened. Rather, to Paul *everything* was "supernatural" because everything was created by God—the seen and the unseen, the reasonable and the mysterious, heaven and earth. Just because something could be explained didn't mean it was not divine. In fact Paul believed the life of the mind—making sense of the world—was a spiritual reality. The knowledge of God instructs every person. The voice of God speaks to all creation. The revelation of God enlightens every mind (Rom 1:18-32). But not everyone knows God, hears God, understands God, sees God. That only comes through the gospel of Jesus Christ. And according to Paul the gospel of Jesus Christ must be seen, heard and understood by divine revelation (Rom 10:1-21). One doesn't go looking for a god who is everywhere; God must *be seen*. One doesn't merely follow the teachings of the Nazarene; Jesus Christ must *be believed*. At the heart of the gospel is the revelation of God, and Paul believed this "revealing" could be seen in what is heard (the message) and heard in what is seen (Christophany)—all by the resurrection work of the Spirit.

## Reflecting on the Scriptures

Paul saw the gospel of Jesus Christ in the Hebrew Scriptures, what we call the Old Testament. His letters are filled with allusions to and quotations of the Torah (Genesis through Deuteronomy), the Psalms and the Prophets (especially Isaiah, his favorite prophet). Whenever Paul heard the Scriptures read in the synagogues of the Diaspora (Jews living outside of Palestine), he heard the gospel. And that's what we forget sometimes: the average Jewish man or woman didn't read the Scriptures for themselves; only the wealthy owned copies of the Scriptures. Jews heard the Word of God read to them. The readings in the synagogue were probably patterned after the temple services, so most worshipers would hear only the Torah, the Psalms and Isaiah on a regular basis. The rest of the Hebrew Scriptures—like parts of the Song of Solomon, the "Minor" Prophets or Esther—would be read during the festivals. Every time Paul worshiped in the synagogue, hearing the story of Abraham or the prophecies of Isaiah, Paul believed the gospel was being preached to the attendants. What he couldn't understand was why his Jewish brothers and sisters didn't hear the same message—they didn't see Jesus on nearly every page of the Scriptures like Paul did.

As a former Pharisee, Paul's mind was saturated with the Scriptures. The average Jewish man memorized small portions of the Torah, in particular those parts that were commonly recited during worship, like the Shema (Deut 6:4-9). The Pharisees, however, were known for mastering much of the Torah, the Psalms and the Prophets, able to recite extended passages along with the teachings of the rabbis. This may have given Paul special privilege when he visited the synagogues during his mission trips, because guest teachers were often called on to read the Scriptures and offer instruction (Acts 13:15-41). Luke records what usually happened: Paul would get into arguments over the meaning of the Scriptures (which was typical of *all* Jewish teachers—among the rabbis there were different schools of thought on nearly every verse); sometimes leaders and members of the synagogue would dispute Paul's teaching; and at times some would believe Paul's gospel interpretation. But trouble almost always followed Paul's visit, sometimes requiring Roman leaders to intervene and keep the peace.

One of the favorite pastimes of the rabbis was to find prophecies in the Torah, the Psalms and the Prophets that they believed were being fulfilled in their time. (The approach is called pesher, a Hebrew word meaning "interpretation.")[1] They constantly looked for the promises of God that were coming true for their generation (both the warnings and the blessings). Of course Paul found dozens of promises coming true in the gospel of Jesus Christ. The promises God made to Abraham were fulfilled in Christ (Rom. 4:1-25; Gal 3:6-18). The promises God made to David were coming true for Paul's converts (Rom 4:7-8; 11:9-10). And *many* promises God made to Israel through Isaiah were fulfilled in the gospel according to Paul (e.g., Rom 9:27-33; 11:25-36; 1 Cor 2:14-16; 14:21-22; 15:50-57; 2 Cor 6:2-3; 9:8-12; Gal 4:21–5:1). The promises of God in Isaiah are especially intriguing because Paul believed he saw the prophecies coming true in his life too. That is to say, Paul not only saw Jesus in the pages of Isaiah, but he also saw himself. Therefore when Paul was arguing for the verity of the gospel message— "Jesus is the Messiah"—he was also defending his gospel ministry—"I am the apostle to the Gentiles."[2] Paul believed his reasoned arguments were spiritual weapons in the war against mental blocks to the gospel (2 Cor 10:3-5). His opponents relied on counterarguments that Paul considered "strongholds" and "proud obstacles" to the "knowledge of God." But Paul was convinced he had the advantage in these debates, because his arguments were divinely empowered to tear down their defenses. In this war of ideas Paul believed he could "take every thought captive to obey Christ"—especially since the Scriptures point to Christ. Indeed, when we read passages like this, it becomes quite apparent that Paul was defending himself as much as the gospel he preached. (See the verses surrounding 2 Cor 10:3-5; 2 Cor 10:1-2, 6-16.)

This is where we differ from Paul and, ironically, where Paul becomes an example of how Christians often read Scripture. When the Jewish people heard the Scriptures, they knew they were listening to stories about themselves. This was their family history. This was their story. But more than that, this was their life experience. For example, when they heard the story of Jacob (who was called Israel), the descendants of Jacob saw the narrative as a "script" for their world. In other words the experiences of the man called Israel were read as prophetic stories about Israel. Indeed, Jews in Paul's day knew what it felt like to live in fear of Edom (the descendants of Esau) because Herod was an Idumaean (Edomite). The lessons drawn for every generation were palpable: "Be careful, nations, how you treat descendants of Jacob! You will find the covenant blessings of God are irrevocable. Israel will be blessed, perhaps even at your expense!" So also Paul, when he looked into the Scriptures like a mirror, saw the story of Israel being played out in his generation. What made Paul's pesher approach unique, however, was that he tried to get his gentile converts to read Israel's Scripture the same way, as if these stories were their stories too (1 Cor 10:1-14).[3]

This was crucial to Paul's ministry because he believed, like all Jews, that hearing the stories of Scripture were the same as hearing God's voice. When Jews attended synagogue and heard the Hebrew Scriptures, they were listening to the very words of God. This was more than a faith statement about the divine inspiration of sacred texts. When the Scriptures were read the Jews were actually hearing the voice of God because everyone knew God spoke in Hebrew. When Moses talked to God like a man speaks to someone "face to face," they conversed in Hebrew (God's secret name, YHWH, is the Hebrew word for "I AM"). But in Paul's day the average synagogue attendant didn't know Hebrew, so the Scriptures were translated into the local vernacular (both Aramaic and Greek)—the Scriptures must be heard *and* understood. So when Paul read the Scriptures in Greek to his converts, he wanted them to hear God's voice—as if he were speaking to them too—because they were children of Abraham by the promises of God fulfilled in Christ Jesus.

When we hear the Scriptures read during Christian worship services, we certainly don't act like we're hearing God's voice, nor do we believe we're reading our life's story. Instead, to most of us the Bible is an ancient book of old stories that must be renovated and updated to have any relevance for today. There may be lessons to learn deep within the pages of this antiquated collection of lore, but the stories must be mined for the rare gold layered in the boring bedrock of history. Preachers cultivate "truths" from the Scriptures, finding precious pearls of wisdom that must be illustrated with modern anecdotes that are sensible and practical. We find in the Bible "Seven Steps to Success" or "Ten Principles of Happiness" to assure Christians that the Scriptures still speak to our everyday lives. And to make sure we don't lose the audience, a movie clip from the most recent Hollywood blockbuster film is used to flesh out the moral of the story. In other words we don't hear the voice of God in his Word—it only comes through "relevant application." That's why reading Scripture as an act of worship—trying to hear the voice of God *in his Word*—has nearly faded completely from the liturgy of most evangelical churches. God has something to say only when we can make sense of it. We certainly don't take the stories of the Bible at face value, as if we're hearing a prophetic word for our generation (Ananias and Sapphira; Acts 5:1-11).

And yet many Christians believe God speaks to them personally when they read the Bible by themselves. They hear God's voice during their morning "quiet time" reading Scripture. Ignoring historical context, they will read First Corinthians as if it were First Americans, acting like Paul wrote the letter just for them. Or when individuals read a text like, "The one who began a good work among *you* . . . ," they don't care that the pronoun is plural in Greek. (Paul was talking to the church as a whole not to an individual reader.) The young man anxiously awaiting surgery hears God's voice—a word of comfort precisely for that moment—believing the Creator of all things is talking to him personally. It is indicative of our culture; when we read the Scriptures together, we're simply looking for a life lesson that we either accept or reject. (Obviously we're not hearing the voice of God, for who would want to be accused of rejecting his Word?) And yet when I read the verse, "'I know the plans I have for you,' says the LORD," I believe God is talking to me. In fact some verses become so clearly identified with God's voice that Christ believers recite them as their "life verse," a promise for them to claim, God's personal Word suited just for them. Even though scholars despise such an egocentric approach to reading the Scriptures (always ready to disabuse laypeople of their individualistic interpretations), Paul did the same thing. He heard God's voice speaking personally to him when he read portions of Isaiah. Indeed, Paul claimed that Isaiah was not only talking about Jesus when he prophesied the arrival of the servant of the Lord, he was talking about Paul too. Paul believed he was the fulfillment of Isaiah 52:7–53:1 (Rom 10:14-11:1, 13-14; 15:20-21).

I think Paul's "life verse" was:

> How beautiful upon the mountains
> are the feet of the messenger [Paul!] who announces peace,
> who brings good news [gospel!],
>> who announces salvation [Jesus!],
>> who says to Zion, "Your God reigns." (Is 52:7)

It is quite evident that Paul identified with the prophet as Paul struggled with the fact that his kinsmen refused to believe the message God gave him to deliver "to the Jew first and also to the Greek" (Rom 1:16). Here is Paul's lament:

> But how are they [the Jews] to call on one in whom they have not believed? And how are they to believe in one of whom they have never heard? And how are they to hear without someone to proclaim him? And how are they to proclaim him unless they are sent? As it is written, "How beautiful are the feet of those who bring good news!" But not all have obeyed the good news; for Isaiah says, "Lord, who has believed our message?" (Rom 10:14-16)

I hear Paul resonating with Isaiah when he said, "Lord, who has believed *our* message?" Isaiah's message of good news was Paul's gospel message too. Thus, like Isaiah, Paul claims his kinsmen have heard the message (but rejected it) because he preached it to them (Rom 10:18–11:1). Therefore Paul sees for himself a major role in the *eschaton* (the last days); his ministry to the Gentiles will make Israel jealous, and Isaiah's prophecies will come true (Rom 11:7-27). "All Israel will be saved" because God called Paul to preach the gospel to the Gentiles. Paul believed he was the herald of the Suffering Servant predicted by Isaiah the prophet (Is 53:1-12).

I imagine Paul gathering with the synagogue in Ephesus or Corinth, hearing portions of Scripture read to the congregation, grinning to himself when the lector gets to the reading from Isaiah:

> Listen to me, O coastlands,
>     pay attention, you peoples from far away!
> The LORD called me before I was born,
>     while I was in my mother's womb he named me.
> He made my mouth like a sharp sword,
>     in the shadow of his hand he hid me;
> he made me a polished arrow,
>     in his quiver he hid me away.
> And he said to me, "You are my servant,
>     Israel, in whom I will be glorified."
> But I said, "I have labored in vain,
>     I have spent my strength for nothing and vanity;

yet surely my cause is with the Lᴏʀᴅ,
and my reward with my God." (Is 49:1-4)

After the reading I see the synagogue ruler asking the visitor for his comment. Paul takes the seat of Moses, looks into the eyes of his kinsmen and explains how this Scripture has been fulfilled in their hearing. "I am the mouth that is a sharp sword. I am the polished arrow. I am God's slave, sent to you who live on the coastlands, to tell you the good news predicted long ago by Isaiah the prophet. Hear, O Israel, the voice of the Lord! It's time to bring the light of God to the nations—that his salvation (Jesus!) may reach to the ends of the earth."

Why didn't they believe him? According to Paul their eyes were blinded by "the god of this world" (2 Cor 4:4). Even though Paul could see very clearly the gospel of Jesus Christ in the Scriptures, his kinsmen could not—it's as if the veil on their head had fallen over the eyes of their mind (2 Cor 3:15). Indeed, Paul knew it would take resurrected eyes—the work of the Spirit—to see the gospel in the Scriptures (2 Cor 3:16-17). And even though it took a glorious Christophany for Paul to see the truth of the gospel, he didn't expect everyone to have the same experience. Rather, Paul was convinced that *he* was the divine messenger, the embodied gospel, a prophetic fulfillment of Scripture, enough for anyone to see the glory of Christ through him (2 Cor 4:1-12).[4] In other words Paul believed his life reflected the glorious gospel of Jesus Christ; and whenever he preached, he was convinced it was "Christ . . . speaking in me" (2 Cor 13:3). It may have sounded like he was talking about himself whenever he preached about Jesus (2 Cor 4:2, 5), but for him the gospel was more than a prophetic word; it was the very revelation of God. Claiming Isaiah's prophecy was coming true in Jesus Christ was the same as affirming the apostleship of Paul. To deny the arguments he marshaled for the gospel (and his ministry) was to deny the power of the Spirit. Jesus was the Messiah, and Paul was his messenger. There was no convincing him otherwise—even if they beat him with rods in the synagogue and ran him out of town. For Paul knew what he saw, not only on the Damascus road but also in the Word of God.

Many Christians hear God speak to them through the Scriptures. It's a comforting voice in times of sorrow, an encouraging word when facing difficult decisions. We may have a familiar life verse that rings true for us, a touchstone that reminds us God is still there. The rock-solid truth of the passage is as reliable as the God we believe. At the same time, God's voice comes in unexpected ways. It may be a verse we've read dozens of times, but somehow God speaks to our heart like never before. It's almost as if we've never seen the passage; it leaps off the page and sinks straight into our soul. This transforming power of God's Word in the life of every believer Paul called having "the same spirit of faith that is in accordance with scripture" (2 Cor 4:13). And he expected his converts to have the same experience, allowing the "word of Christ [to] dwell in you richly" so that "the peace of Christ [would] rule in your hearts" (Col 3:15-16). Not everyone encounters a resurrected Christ on the road to Damascus. But Paul maintained, when referring to the reading of Scripture, that "all of us, with unveiled faces, seeing the glory of the Lord as though reflected in a mirror, are being transformed into the same image" (2 Cor 3:18). Peering into the mirror of God's Word, believers see Christ and ourselves—all at the same time—"from one degree of glory to another" (2 Cor 3:18). It should come as no surprise, then, that Christ believers (like Paul) contend for the faith as if we are defending ourselves. When we present reasoned arguments for what we believe, we're also justifying that we are the glorious work of God. It's hard to deny what we see in God's Word.

## Listening to Visions

Christians readily accept Paul's idea that we hear the voice of God in his written Word. To us this is normal, acceptable, conventional. But when we consider the other side of Paul's revelatory experience—visions and auditions—most Christians get a little nervous. Those of the Pentecostal tradition welcome such "unusual" revelations of God, primarily because Acts is filled with stories of apostles receiving visions and auditions, performing miracles and speaking in tongues. And yet Paul doesn't fit the apostolic mold in Acts. For example, Paul performs miracles, but he never speaks in tongues in Acts—the baptism of the Holy Spirit is not accompanied by the phenomena of Pentecost. (Rather, the evidence of Paul's Spirit baptism is that he is healed of blindness [Acts 9:17-18].) After the ascension the resurrected Christ appears to Paul on several occasions but never to Peter (Acts 9:3-9; 18:9-10; 22:17-21). Both Paul and Peter receive visions to direct their missionary efforts (Acts 10:9-35; 16:9-10; 22:6-11), but Paul has to rely on a prophet to make sense of the experience (Acts 22:12-16). Even though Paul depends on visions and auditions in Acts, he seems reticent to acknowledge them in his letters (2 Cor 12:2-4), often describing his decision-making process without mentioning the Spirit (1 Cor 16:5-9; 2 Cor 1:15-17; 1:23–2:1; 1 Thess 2:17-18). And yet throughout his letters he kept pointing to the Christophany (vision and audition) as the proof of his ministry (1 Cor 9:1), the undeniable demonstration of the Spirit's power legitimating the gospel he proclaimed (Gal 1:11-24). After all, if his gospel was an end-of-the-world message, then it must be accompanied by end-of-the-world happenings—not only dreams and visions but also prophecies, tongues and miracles (1 Cor 14:18; 2 Cor 12:12; 13:3).

Paul acknowledged that he performed miracles, that he prophesied by the power of the Spirit, that he spoke in tongues and that he received "revelation" from God. Paul referred to these mystical experiences as if they were a "normal" part of his spirituality. That's because dreams and visions were commonly accepted within Judaism as a means of divine communication. The Jewish people were used to hearing about angels showing up in dreams and visions, delivering timely messages. The Hebrew Scriptures are filled with stories of miracles, divine visitors and Spirit-endowed prophets declaring God's Word to the people. Sometimes God's presence is described as smoke and fire; other times he is not seen but heard—his voice is audible. Scholars refer to these unusual events as "theophany," Godlike appearances on earth. Add it all up and Israel knew God could be seen and heard in a variety of ways and through different agents, whether earthly or heavenly. So when Paul says he didn't go to Jerusalem until he received a "revelation" (Gal 2:1-2), he isn't trying to be coy, cloaking his travel plans in mystery. Rather, Paul is simply relating what happened to him. What Acts describes in terms of a vision/audition (e.g., Acts 22:17-21), Paul calls a "revelation" (apocalypse). Theophany was a regular part of Paul's spirituality.

At the same time, theophanic experiences didn't happen every day, and they didn't happen to everyone. There was a sense that when these things happened God was about to do something significant, that the time was ripe for the promises of God to come true (Acts 2:14-36; Gal 4:4-6). Those who received these revelations were chosen by God as special agents to make known the "mystery" of this divine work (Eph 3:1-11). That's why Paul put much stock in the Christophany—it was the foundational experience of his apostleship (1 Cor 9:1-2; 15:7-10)— and why he claimed that the miracles he performed and the Spirit he passed on to his converts were divine proof of his ministry (2 Cor 12:12; Gal 3:2-5). And yet Paul didn't feature these mystical experiences as much as we would expect, especially since he constantly had to defend his apostleship, not only to his opponents but also his converts. In fact even the few times Paul brings it up in his letters, he's reticent to talk about his mysticism. We never get a detailed description of what happened (like we do in Acts). Rather, Paul uses generic terms like "revelation" and "mystery" or sometimes speaks in veiled terms of seeing the "glory of God" or "image of Christ," trying to downplay the event. When he wrote about his out-of-body journey to heaven, he talked about it in the third person: "I know a man . . ." (2 Cor 12:2). How could something be so important to Paul and yet appear only marginally in his writings?

Scholars have only recently begun to explore Paul's mystical experiences in light of the Christophany. Before, we lumped all of Paul's mysticism into the category of his "conversion experience." And yet we know that Paul explored the transformational power of these mystical experiences throughout his life, indicating these visions continued to inform his spirituality (2 Cor 3:18-4:6; Phil 3:10-21; Col 1:15-29). Paul used the technical language of the mystics, the common vocabulary of those who dabbled in ecstatic experiences as found in apocalyptic literature and later strains of Jewish mysticism.[5] Some have suggested Paul's silence is a function of apocalypses—the seer is often told to seal up the vision, not to tell anyone about it (2 Cor 12:4). Or such visions were of the highest order, reserved only for those who could make sense of them, so they couldn't be shared with commoners.[6] Still others have suggested it is merely a function of Paul's rhetoric. In other words Paul minimized his ecstatic experiences because his converts had unnecessarily inflated the importance of them. That put Paul in a tricky spot. Either Paul didn't believe these mystical experiences were crucial to his authority as an apostle (but he still had them),[7] or they were important, but he didn't want to rely on them because his converts (in this case, the Corinthians) were claiming the same experiences for themselves, thereby disregarding the uniqueness of Paul's credibility. Which is why, much to their chagrin, Paul highlighted the *ultimate* proof of his apostleship: strength through weakness, what the Corinthians needed to imitate.[8]

Nevertheless, Paul saw Christ several times. Christ spoke to Paul more than once. Paul even saw heaven and heard things "no mortal is permitted to repeat" (2 Cor 12:4). From his Damascus-road experience to his journey to heaven, Paul had visions of spiritual realities. To see heaven before death was ecstasy. To hear the tongues of angels worship God was paradise. These glimpses of resurrection glory carried Paul forward with the momentum of "straining forward to what lies ahead" (Phil 3:13). What's fascinating to me is that Paul never expected his converts to "imitate him" in receiving these revelations. He didn't give them advice on how to pursue visions of Christ, how to replicate ecstatic experiences. Instead, he acted like it was up to him as God's messenger to reveal these mysteries to his converts (1 Cor 15:51). And yet Paul didn't deny the possibility that his converts could receive a revelation of the Lord (1 Cor 14:26). At the same time, he was quick to remind them that such experiences were not for personal gain but were supposed to benefit the entire body: "Let all things be done for building up" (1 Cor 14:26). Therefore it shouldn't surprise us that Paul was circumspect about sharing these experiences—when he did, he knew it sounded like he was boasting (2 Cor 12:1). Indeed, when believers talk about such unusual experiences, they often come across like they think they're special.

A few years ago a man came to our campus and, during chapel services, claimed he had been to heaven. He was the author of a recent bestseller recounting the story of his postmortem trip. He had been in a horrible automobile accident and was pronounced dead by emergency personnel. He remembered looking down on the entire scene as his spirit left his body. Then he talked about how he went to heaven, recounting the typical scenario of seeing a bright light and being greeted by deceased loved ones. He described the glory of heaven, the sights and sounds that still inspire him. Without a whisper of doubt in his voice, he spoke about his death. He knew he died. He knew he saw heaven. He knew God sent him back to earth to tell his story. He wanted everyone to find comfort in his words, whether they believed him or not. After his talk the campus was buzzing about the veracity of his experience. Some self-appointed skeptics claimed his out-of-body experience was nothing more than the biological effects of the human body shutting down—when the brain is deprived of oxygen, subjects see strange things. A few wondered out loud whether Satan was using him to deceive the masses. Didn't Jesus warn his disciples about false prophets who claimed they had come back from the dead? Most, however, were willing to give him the benefit of the doubt. They believed what they heard. The man died, went to heaven and came back again (almost sounds christological). Between classes, several students asked me for a "theological" response to the man's testimony.

"First of all, speaking theologically, the man didn't die. Death is not something you come back from without the resurrection—and that won't happen completely until the last day." The alarmists were vindicated: "See? We told you his experience wasn't legitimate." Then the true believers asked, "So you don't think he saw heaven?" "On the contrary," I assured them. "I believe he saw heaven, but he didn't go there." Now they were confused. "In other words, I believe the man didn't die, but he had a vision of heaven. He had a genuine, spiritual experience— like Paul talks about in 2 Corinthians and John describes in the Revelation." Then the skeptics spoke up, "Wait a minute. This whole thing can be explained by medical science. The reason all of these near-death experiences sound the same—bright light, long tunnel—is because their minds respond the same way when there's a shortage of blood to the brain." "Let me ask you this," I said, directing my question to the student scientists. "What if he claimed to have had the same experience without dying? In other words, what if there were no head trauma, no automobile accident, no bleeding out. What if there was no accident at all? Would you believe him?" One of the skeptics replied sarcastically, "Then I'd probably wonder what drugs he was taking," which prompted nods from the rest. After a few moments, I looked at the entire posse and said, "That's sad."

We are a disillusioned and disenchanted people. We are disillusioned by religious fanatics who manipulate their followers into believing their leader has received some special revelation from God. We shake our heads in disbelief, wondering how reasonable people could be suckered into following men like David Koresh, the Branch Davidian "messiah" who led his people to a fiery death in Waco, Texas. America seems to be the premiere breeding ground for all the cults; how often do we hear about the latest scandal involving another egomaniacal leader's bizarre behavior that has been embraced by devout followers? So we refuse to be taken in by any charismatic huckster who claims spiritual visions and supernatural powers. At the same time, we are disenchanted by science because it operates with the unquestionable assumption that all things can be explained through the powers of observation. But should we rely so heavily on what we see to know everything? Just because we can look through telescopes at distant stars, taking the appropriate measurements, we presume to know what they're made of. We study the microscopic world of human cells, figuring out their pathology, so that we can determine what ails us. But the truth of the matter is, we are more than matter. Biology cannot answer every question regarding the human condition. What ails the human soul? Where is the human spirit located in the body? And what about celestial bodies? When we gaze into the heavens, can astronomers tell us for certain that the stars are not angels?

I long for the mystery of God. I've grown weary of reasoned arguments that pretend to strip all things of their divine quality. Where did we get the idea that just because we might know how something works—how human bodies, for example, have been engineered—we've discovered the knowledge of God? We may be able to duplicate what has been created, plagiarizing God's work. But have we conveniently ignored the sheer genius of the one who came up with all of this? Shouldn't scientists be the first ones to admit we don't own the intellectual property of our "latest discovery"? Our knowledge keeps growing, developing, evolving. Even with our sophisticated telescopes, we still can't see the end of eternity. Which is why I still look up at the night sky with childlike wonder and ask: "Are angels watching over me?" And it's also why I still need to hear a prophet say: "Yes they are, because I've seen them."

I long for the justice of God. But we have grown weary of the prophetic voice because of the endless parade of false prophets who lead foolish followers down paths of self-destruction. Skepticism is our mechanism of self-defense as we shout down anyone who claims to have a word from God. We have no illusions. There are no heroes. We rely on no one. We will make sense of our faith without divine revelation; we will decide what is right and wrong. So sermons become life lessons, Christianity turns into a self-help religion, and the Word of God is marginalized because we're convinced we no longer need a prophet to tell us, "Thus saith the Lord." And yet justice requires a prophetic voice because none of us are immune to deception. Paul knew that very well, which is why he warned his converts not to "despise the words of prophets" while at the same time encouraging them to "test everything; hold fast to what is good; abstain from every form of evil" (1 Thess 5:20-22). And how were they to do that? By imitating Paul they would keep the traditions Paul taught them (1 Cor 11:1-2). But more than that, by imitating Paul they would be imitating Christ by observing the "pattern" they saw in Paul and other Christ believers (Phil 3:17). We still need to see the prophetic pattern, especially in our jaded, skeptical world.

Paul reminded his converts of the resurrected life. When they worshiped God, angels were watching over them (1 Cor 11:10). When they spoke with the tongues of angels they were delving into the mysteries of the Spirit (1 Cor 14:2). When miracles were performed among them

it was the sign of the Spirit (Gal 3:5). When Paul prophesied, it was
Christ speaking to them (2 Cor 13:3). When a man was saved from a
sickness that nearly killed him, it was the work of God (Phil 2:27, 30).
And when Paul went through difficult times the apostle heard the word
of the Lord (2 Cor 12:9). He didn't need to emphasize these mystical
experiences because Paul and his converts knew they lived in an enchanted world. Paul never felt obliged to explain his mysticism because
one needn't lose control of his or her mind to believe these things.
Rather, according to Paul intellectuals understand spiritual things.
Whether preaching or speaking in tongues, Spirit-filled people relied
on their minds to pray and prophesy (1 Cor 14:15-19). Meditating on
spiritual things brought the peaceful presence of Christ in ways that
defy human understanding (Phil 4:6-9). Faith and understanding were
never pitted against each other in an adversarial battle for truth. Rather,
because of our faith, Paul recognized that believers have much to
learn—our understanding is not complete until we see Christ (1 Cor
13:9-12). God's ways are unfathomable (Rom 11:33-34). And because
our minds are being renewed day by day, Paul knew our faith to be incomplete—we need revelations of Christ every day (Phil 3:12-16). A
maturing faith strives for the mind of Christ (Eph 4:13-16). Indeed, to
see the mysteries of God is to experience the resurrection of Christ:
"For now we see in a mirror, dimly, but then we will see face to face" (1
Cor 13:12).

I think I saw an angel when I was twenty years old. I also believe
God has spoken to me many times in his Word. I think I've even experienced what Paul called a "revelation"—prophetic visions that helped
me discern God's will. But I don't talk much about these things. I can't
tell if I'm reticent to share some of these mystical experiences because
I don't come from a Pentecostal tradition or because I live in a scholarly
world of intellectuals who relegate this kind of spirituality to the
simple-minded. (After all, we are enlightened people.) The few times
I've disclosed some of the details, I've felt silly, as if I were making
special claims of divine favor. I've kept most of the visions to myself; it's
hard for me to believe I saw what I saw. But then again, every now and
then it occurs to me: if I believe in the resurrection of Christ—a sneak

preview of what is to come—then it seems reasonable to conclude that God gives visions and auditions to help us see spiritual things and hear heavenly words until we see him face to face. Oh, how we need a vision of Christ! And even though Paul didn't intend it, I think many of us are imitating him when we experience these things. For when we read in his letters about how the resurrection of Christ compelled him to "press on toward the goal for the prize of the heavenly call of God in Christ Jesus" (Phil 3:14), our hearts are strangely warmed, and we can't help but say, "We know what you mean, Paul. We know what you mean."

> Let those of us then who are mature be of the same mind; and if you think differently about anything, this too God will reveal to you. Only let us hold fast to what we have attained
> St. Paul, after Christ appeared to him before he was thrown into a Roman prison, to the Philippians (Phil 3:15)

# Conclusion

*The Imitable Life*

❧

IF SOMEONE WERE TO IMITATE Paul today, what would it look like?

The marquee issues of our time are different from Paul's world. So we can't help but wonder what Paul would say and do given the questions that dominate social discourse today. For example, would Paul "go green"? Would he join efforts to advance social justice, such as trying to stop those who traffic in sex slavery? Would he promote fair trade? Would Paul support gay marriage? Would the apostle to the Gentiles encourage tolerance by respecting the religious beliefs of others, not trying to convert them to Christianity? Would Paul side with big government or big business? Would Paul support any current war securing a nation's interests? Would Paul be a member of the Association for the Prevention of Cruelty to Animals? What would Paul do?

Whenever Christians discuss these issues, we often drag Jesus into the debate, wanting to believe that he would be on our side. We must have a Jesus who thinks like us. Consequently Jesus ends up siding with all kinds of people. (It's amazing to me that even unbelievers want to claim Jesus as their advocate.) But I've never heard anyone claim Paul as an advocate for their "Christian" position (except in the case of opposing homosexuality). And yet even when we're arguing against the homosexual lifestyle—that the gay life is unbiblical—we are not imitating Paul. To be sure, like any other Jew of his time, Paul was opposed to homoerotic behavior (Rom 1:18-32). But the reason Paul highlighted the Roman way of life in Romans 1—with all of its ungodliness and immorality—was to expose the hypocrisy of the self-righteous judges in Romans 2:1-24. To act like the sin of others is worse than our own cuts against the grain of Paul's argument. Rather, he would have us recognize that "all have sinned and fall short of the glory of God" (Rom 3:23). Imitating Paul requires humility.

Is that it? Is that all Paul would have to say regarding explosive issues like gay marriage: "Be humble"? No. Paul would expect us to show what the gospel looks like in the midst of every situation. He would remind us of "his ways" in Christ Jesus, that the gospel is imitating Christ in his death, burial and resurrection, walking in the power of his Holy Spirit. He would encourage us to find a way to sacrifice ourselves for the sake of others, even for those with whom we disagree. Paul would remind us that we can't be Christians by ourselves, that together we are buried with Christ, that we need each other to be the body of Christ—every sinner!—even those who struggle with same-sex attraction. Paul would say we are empowered by the resurrection of Christ to stand against *all* evil and suffering (wherever we find it), that we have nothing to fear because Christ has conquered the enemies of all humanity (sin, death and the devil) and that our fight is not against "flesh and blood," even those who promote gay marriage. To live the crucified life, to share life together as the body of Christ, to walk in the resurrection power of Christ would be good news for his time and for our time. Paul wouldn't prescribe a to-do list, giving us detailed instructions for every scenario. Rather, Paul would tell us to count on the Spirit, who would guide us in all these things.

So Paul would probably be concerned about the environment. He certainly believed that human sin spoiled creation and that all creatures (including animals!) reveal the glory of God (Rom 1:18-31; 8:20-23). But Paul would be opposed to legalistic standards that are used to judge the holiness of others when protecting the environment. Since grace cannot be earned, Paul would probably support fair trade, but refuse to kowtow to manmade rules requiring economic boycotts. Even though Paul rarely addressed social justice issues in his letters, he would work to rid the world of child trafficking because he believed *all* sexual immorality is ungodly. Paul wanted his converts to live in peace with all people, tolerating the differences between Jews and Gentiles. But the only place where such diversity could be celebrated (not merely tolerated) as the work of God would be seen in the church. Therefore Paul would preach without embarrassment that all people need to turn from the darkness of their dead religion into the marvelous light of faith in Christ. Paul wouldn't be for big business or big government, because he was convinced weakness was the place where God's grace is most evident. Paul knew that God ordained human governments to protect their citizenry, but he would encourage us to live like citizens of heaven and overcome the evil of war with the good news of our lives.

In other words Paul would expect us to walk in the Spirit by living the crucified life (not according to the law), by promoting the welfare of all people by edifying the church (we are the hope of the world in Christ Jesus) and by caring for all creation because the glory of Christ's resurrection invades every corner of the earth (the ultimate act of God's justice is resurrection). This is the timeless gospel of Jesus Christ according to Paul. Whatever the circumstances, no matter the event, regardless of our social location, Paul believed we could participate in the death, burial and resurrection of Christ so that all might see the good news of God's reclamation of all things. Through Christ God reconciled Paul, his Gentile converts, his Jewish kinsmen and all creation. The gospel is good news for everyone, whether Jew or Gentile, male or female, slave or free. Therefore I think Paul would be convinced that he could show us how to live the gospel right now because the work of Christ is eternal. In fact, now that we've studied Paul's spirituality, I'm convinced the apostle to the Gentiles would say the same thing to us that he did two thousand years ago: "Be imitators of me, as I am of Christ" (1 Cor 11:1). After all, he is our apostle too.

How are Christ believers supposed to follow a man we've never met? Imitate Paul.

# Notes

### Introduction
[1]Roy A. Harrisville, *Fracture: The Cross as Irreconcilable in the Language and Thought of the Biblical Writers* (Grand Rapids: Eerdmans, 2006), p. 120.
[2]For example, this appears to be what Mormon spirituality emphasizes: living by the teachings of Christ.

### Chapter 1: Foolish Death
[1]See Johannes Munck, *Paul and the Salvation of Mankind* (Richmond: John Knox Press, 1959), pp. 24-31; and Seyoon Kim, *The Origins of Paul's Gospel* (Grand Rapids: Eerdmans, 1981), pp. 56-66.
[2]Oscar Cullmann, *Christ and Time: The Primitive Christian Conception of Time and History*, rev. ed., trans. Floyd V. Filson (London: SCM Press, 1962), pp. 163-67.
[3]See Rainer Riesner, *Paul's Early Period: Chronology, Mission Strategy, Theology*, trans. Doug Stott (Grand Rapids: Eerdmans, 1998), pp. 245-53.
[4]See Alan F. Segal, *Paul the Convert: The Apostolate and Apostasy of Saul the Pharisee* (New Haven: Yale University Press, 1990), pp. 58-71, and Kim, *Origin*, pp. 193-268.
[5]See J. Louis Martyn, *Galatians*, Anchor Bible (New York: Doubleday, 1997), pp. 97-105, 151-68.
[6]The word Paul used, *proegraphē*, can be translated "publicly portrayed," but it more literally means something written for public view, i.e., a public notice—a placard.
[7]See Michael J. Gorman, *Cruciformity: Paul's Narrative Spirituality of the Cross* (Grand Rapids: Eerdmans, 2001), pp. 88-94.
[8]Alexandra R. Brown, *The Cross and Human Transformation: Paul's Apocalyptic Word in 1 Corinthians* (Philadelphia: Fortress, 1995), p. 151.

### Chapter 2: Living Sacrifice
[1]Scott J. Hafemann, *Suffering and Ministry in the Spirit: Paul's Defense of His Ministry in II Corinthians 2:14–3:3* (Grand Rapids: Eerdmans, 1990).
[2]See Bruce W. Winter, *Philo and Paul among the Sophists: Alexandrian and Corinthian Responses to a Julian-Claudian Movement*, 2nd ed. (Grand Rapids: Eerdmans, 2002), pp. 113-202.
[3]Karl Barth, *The Epistle to the Romans*, trans. Edwyn C. Hoskyns from the 6th ed. (London: Oxford University Press, 1933), p. 35.
[4]Ralph P. Martin, *2 Corinthians*, Word Biblical Commentary 40 (Waco: Word, 1986), pp. 357-62.
[5]The "western" text of Acts is far more descriptive, relating details of how Paul's companions left him for dead, one keeping watch until the rest returned to bury him at sundown, only to find out he was still alive but very confused, stumbling around, needing guidance.
[6]See Alan F. Segal, *Paul the Convert: The Apostolate and Apostasy of Saul the Pharisee* (New Haven:

Yale University Press, 1990), pp. 58-62; Seyoon Kim, *The Origins of Paul's Gospel* (Grand Rapids: Eerdmans, 1981), pp. 229-39.

[7]"Disability is the condition of blessing," Frances M. Young, *Brokenness and Blessing: Towards a Biblical Spirituality* (Grand Rapids: Baker Academic, 2007), p. 121.

## Chapter 3: Holy Temples

[1]G. K. Beale, *We Become What We Worship: A Biblical Theology of Idolatry* (Downers Grove, Ill.: IVP Academic, 2008), pp. 216-20.

[2]For example, Douglas J. Moo, *The Epistle to the Romans*, New International Commentary on the New Testament (Grand Rapids: Eerdmans, 1996), pp. 113-22.

[3]Aleksandr I. Solzhenitsyn, *The Gulag Archipelago 1918-1956: An Experiment in Literary Investigation*, parts 3 and 4, trans. Thomas P. Whitney (New York: Harper & Row, 1975), p. 615.

[4]"Sexual immorality . . . and cruciform love cannot coexist, for *porneia* is at best a form of self-love, of self-indulgence that harms others and diminishes the holiness of both the individual and the community," Michael J. Gorman, *Inhabiting the Cruciform God: Kenosis, Justification, and Theosis in Paul's Narrative Soteriology* (Grand Rapids: Eerdmans, 2009), p. 127.

## Chapter 4: Free Slaves

[1]Thomas H. Tobin, *The Spirituality of Paul*, Message of Biblical Spirituality 12 (Wilmington, Del.: Michael Glazier, 1987), pp. 87-88.

[2]See the classic analysis by E. P. Sanders, *Paul and Palestinian Judaism: A Comparison of Patterns of Religion* (Philadelphia: Fortress, 1977), pp. 474-511.

[3]See Robert Jewett, *Romans*, Hermeneia (Minneapolis: Fortress, 2007), pp. 440-46.

[4]See Frank Thielman, *Paul and the Law: A Contextual Approach* (Downers Grove, Ill.: InterVarsity Press, 1994), p. 200.

[5]Even scholars who interpret Romans 7 as biographical rather than autobiographical still find existential implications, even for Paul, e.g., James D. G. Dunn, *Romans 1–8*, Word Biblical Commentary 38a (Waco: Word, 1988), p. 382.

[6]"Flesh" was a loaded term for Paul, referring more generally to the frailty of humanity/creation (finite, temporary) and bodily appetites (food and sex), or more specifically to ethnicity (identity and heritage) and deeds of the body (obedience to the law). Paul doesn't seem obliged to explain what he means by "the flesh," often moving freely from one intended meaning to another, e.g., in Rom 8:3-4.

[7]See Colin G. Kruse, "Paul, the Law and the Spirit," in *Paul and His Theology*, ed. Stanley E. Porter (Boston: Brill, 2006), pp. 115-29.

[8]Dietrich Bonhoeffer, *Letters and Papers from Prison*, ed. Eberhard Bethge, trans. Reginald H. Fuller (New York: Macmillan, 1953), p. 228.

[9]Ibid., pp. 239-40 (emphasis mine).

[10]Ibid., p. 14.

## Chapter 5: Whole Body

[1]James D. G. Dunn, *Baptism in the Holy Spirit: A Re-examination of the New Testament Teaching on the Gift of the Spirit in relation to Pentecostalism Today* (Philadelphia: Westminster Press, 1970), pp. 139-46.

[2]G. R. Beasley-Murray, *Baptism in the New Testament* (Grand Rapids: Eerdmans, 1962), pp. 130-46.

[3]See the discussion in James D. G. Dunn, *The Theology of Paul the Apostle* (Grand Rapids: Eerdmans, 1998), pp. 442-59.

[4]According to Jewish custom, the deceased would remain in the tombs until their bones could be relocated to the family shrine.

[5]Tertullian described the church as a burial society, *Apology* 39. See Wayne A. Meeks, *The First Urban Christians: The Social World of the Apostle Paul* (New Haven: Yale University Press, 1983), pp. 150-57.

[6]See A. J. M. Wedderburn, *Baptism and Resurrection: Studies in Pauline Theology Against Its Graeco-Roman Background* (Tübingen: J. C. B. Mohr [Paul Siebeck], 1987), pp. 287-95, 363-71.

[7]Andrew T. Lincoln, *Ephesians,* Word Biblical Commentary 42 (Waco: Word, 1990), pp. 318-20, 331-33.

## Chapter 6: Common Bonds

[1]Pliny the Younger *Epistle* 10.96.

[2]N. T. Wright, "Paul's Gospel and Caesar's Empire," in *Paul and Politics: Ekklesia, Israel, Imperium, Interpretation,* ed. Richard A. Horsley (Harrisburg, Penn.: Trinity Press International, 2000), pp. 177-83.

[3]The list of names in the different house churches reveals the ethnic and social segregation of the Roman church: Jewish names appear together (Rom 16:3-7), then slave names (Rom 16:8-9), followed by high status Greek names (Rom 16:10-11).

[4]See Bruce W. Winter, *After Paul Left Corinth: The Influence of Secular Ethics and Social Change* (Grand Rapids: Eerdmans, 2001), pp. 121-83.

[5]Dale Martin, *The Corinthian Body* (New Haven: Yale University Press, 1995), pp. 74-75.

[6]See Richard B. Hays, *First Corinthians,* Interpretation (Louisville: Westminster John Knox Press, 1997), pp. 200-203.

## Chapter 7: Sacred Community

[1]For an excellent treatment, see Ken M. Campbell, ed., *Marriage and Family in the Biblical World* (Downers Grove, Ill.: InterVarsity Press, 2003).

[2]Pheme Perkins, "Marriage in the New Testament and Its World," in *Commitment to Partnership,* ed. W. Roberts (Mahwah, N.J.: Paulist, 1987), pp. 23-26.

[3]Some scholars think Paul was a married man (like other rabbis) and that his wife had died or abandoned him before he wrote 1 Corinthians; see Jerome Murphy-O'Connor, *Paul: A Critical Life* (Oxford: Oxford University Press, 1996), pp. 62-65. But it's hard to believe that Paul would wish either situation on anyone (1 Cor 7:7-8).

[4]Richard B. Hays doesn't think so, *First Corinthians,* Interpretation (Louisville: Westminster John Knox Press, 1997), pp. 133-34.

[5]"The interesting questions now are what skills do we as Christians need to learn to survive when surrounded by a culture we helped create but which now threatens to destroy us," Stanley Hauerwas, *Dispatches from the Front: Theological Engagements with the Secular* (Durham: Duke University Press, 1994), p. 18.

[6]Richard B. Hays, *The Moral Vision of the New Testament: A Contemporary Introduction to New Testament Ethics* (San Francisco: HarperCollins, 1996), pp. 361-76.

[7]Gordon D. Fee, *The First Epistle to the Corinthians,* New International Commentary on the New Testament (Grand Rapids: Eerdmans, 1987), pp. 267-70.

[8]Bruce W. Winter, *After Paul Left Corinth: The Influence of Secular Ethics and Social Change*

(Grand Rapids: Eerdmans, 2001), pp. 90-93, 228-32.
[9]Gordon D. Fee, *God's Empowering Presence: The Holy Spirit in the Letters of Paul* (Peabody, Mass.: Hendrickson, 1994), pp. 871-76.

## Chapter 8: Generous Fellowship

[1]See Dieter Georgi, *Remembering the Poor: The History of Paul's Collection for Jerusalem* (Nashville: Abingdon, 1992); also Bruce W. Longenecker, *Remember the Poor: Paul, Poverty and the Greco-Roman World* (Grand Rapids: Eerdmans, 2010), esp. pp. 157-219.
[2]Philip F. Esler, *Conflict and Identity in Romans: The Social Setting of Paul's Letter* (Minneapolis: Fortress, 2003), pp. 129-31.
[3]See the discussion in Robert Jewett, *The Thessalonian Correspondence: Pauline Rhetoric and Millenarian Piety* (Philadelphia: Fortress, 1986), pp. 91-105.
[4]Bruce W. Winter, *Seek the Welfare of the City: Christians as Benefactors and Citizens* (Grand Rapids: Eerdmans, 1994), pp. 42-60.
[5]I owe this insight to Jan Peterson, whom I heard speak on the Christian grace of hospitality, along with her husband, Eugene.
[6]By the way, I've always wondered (somewhat cynically) why television preachers never take their own advice. If they truly believed that God rewarded givers with more money, then why shouldn't they give money to others so that God would take care of the financial needs of "their ministry"?
[7]John M. G. Barclay, "Manna and the Circulation of Grace: A Study of 2 Corinthians 8:1-15," in *The Word Leaps the Gap: Essays on Scripture and Theology in Honor of Richard B. Hays*, ed. J. Ross Wagner, C. Kavin Rowe and A. Katherine Grieb (Grand Rapids: Eerdmans, 2008), pp. 409-26.
[8]Scot McKnight, *A Light Among the Gentiles: Jewish Missionary Activity in the Second Temple Period* (Minneapolis: Fortress, 1991), pp. 47-48.
[9]Rainer Riesner, *Paul's Early Period: Chronology, Mission Strategy, Theology*, trans. Doug Stott (Grand Rapids: Eerdmans, 1998), pp. 245-53.

## Chapter 9: Bold Confession

[1]Wolfhart Pannenberg, *Jesus—God and Man*, 2nd ed., trans. Lewis L. Wilkins and Duane A. Priebe (Philadelphia: Westminster Press, 1977), pp. 66-73.
[2]Richard B. Hays, *Conversion of the Imagination: Paul as Interpreter of Israel's Scripture* (Grand Rapids: Eerdmans, 2005), pp. xi, 4-21.
[3]N. T. Wright, *Surprised by Hope: Rethinking Heaven, the Resurrection, and the Mission of the Church* (San Francisco: HarperOne, 2008), pp. 93-108.
[4]Marva J. Dawn, *Powers, Weakness, and the Tabernacling of God* (Grand Rapids: Eerdmans, 2001), pp. 35-71.
[5]What Keck called an "embodied future"; see Leander E. Keck, *Who Is Jesus? History in Perfect Sense* (Minneapolis: Fortress, 2001), pp. 65-112.
[6]"The church is called to embody a different posture toward time. For Christians the past is not a deterministic series of cause and effect relationships whose trajectories inevitably lead to the present. Rather the past—like the present and the future—is the arena of God's creative activity," Philip D. Kenneson, *Life on the Vine: Cultivating the Fruit of the Spirit in Christian Community* (Downers Grove, Ill.: InterVarsity Press, 1999), p. 124.
[7]Ps 74:12-17; 1QS 3:13-16; 4:13-20; *1 Enoch* 2:1–5:9.
[8]See the discussion in Oscar Cullmann, *Christ and Time: The Primitive Conception of Time and*

*History,* trans. Floyd V. Filson (Philadelphia: Westminster Press, 1964), pp. 121-38.

[9]What Gaventa called "reimagining of [the] past"; see Beverly Roberts Gaventa, *Our Mother Saint Paul* (Louisville: Westminster John Knox, 2007), p. 88.

### Chapter 10: Blessed Hope

[1]See David B. Capes, Rodney Reeves and E. Randolph Richards, *Rediscovering Paul: An Introduction to His World, Letters and Theology* (Downers Grove, Ill.: IVP Academic, 2007), pp. 23-53, 185-87.

[2]Richard B. Hays, *Conversion of the Imagination: Paul as Interpreter of Israel's Scripture* (Grand Rapids: Eerdmans, 2005), p. 5; Hays uses the expression more broadly, i.e., how Paul "reconfigured" Israel's story to include his Gentile converts because of the cross and resurrection of Christ.

[3]C. S. Lewis, "The Weight of Glory," in *The Weight of Glory and Other Essays,* ed. Walter Hooper, rev. ed. (New York: Macmillan, 1980), pp. 6-10.

[4]Paul also highlights the other quality of glory, "light," exploring the implications of light/darkness in 2 Cor 3:12-4:6.

[5]Marva J. Dawn, *Powers, Weakness, and the Tabernacling of God* (Grand Rapids: Eerdmans, 2001), pp. 123-64.

### Chapter 11: Putting Up a Fight

[1]See Clinton Arnold, *Ephesians: Power and Magic* (New York: Cambridge University Press, 1989), pp. 51-69.

[2]Walter Wink, *Naming the Powers: The Language of Power in the New Testament* (Philadelphia: Fortress, 1984), pp. 13-35.

[3]C. E. Arnold, *Powers of Darkness: Principalities and Powers in Paul's Letters* (Downers Grove, Ill.: InterVarsity Press, 1992).

[4]Oscar Cullmann, *Prayer in the New Testament,* Overtures to Biblical Theology (Minneapolis: Fortress, 1995), pp. 75-76.

[5]L. Ann Jervis, *At the Heart of the Gospel: Suffering in the Earliest Christian Message* (Grand Rapids: Eerdmans, 2007), pp. 108-10.

### Chapter 12: Seeing Things

[1]See E. Earle Ellis, *Paul's Use of the Old Testament* (Grand Rapids: Baker, 1981).

[2]Richard B. Hays, *Conversion of the Imagination: Paul as Interpreter of Israel's Scripture* (Grand Rapids: Eerdmans, 2005), p. 4.

[3]Richard B. Hays, *Echoes of Scripture in the Letters of Paul* (New Haven: Yale University Press, 1989), pp. 84-121.

[4]J. Christiaan Beker, *Paul the Apostle: The Triumph of God in Life and Thought* (Philadelphia: Fortress, 1980), pp. 3-10.

[5]Alan F. Segal, *Paul the Convert: The Apostolate and Apostasy of Saul the Pharisee* (New Haven: Yale University Press, 1990), pp. 34-71.

[6]See the discussion in Edith M. Humphrey, *And I Turned to See the Voice: The Rhetoric of Vision in the New Testament,* Studies in Theological Interpretation (Grand Rapids: Baker Academic, 2007), pp. 37-48.

[7]Gordon Fee, *God's Empowering Presence: The Holy Spirit in the Letters of Paul* (Peabody, Mass.: Hendrickson, 1994), pp. 348-49.

[8]Humphrey, *And I Turned,* pp. 46-48.

# Subject Index

# Scripture Index

CPSIA information can be obtained at www.ICGtesting.com
Printed in the USA
LVOW12s2348090114

368781LV00004B/77/P